425 - B+T - 5-66 (Swearingen)

BRITAIN IN THE WORLD TODAY

BRITAIN AND AFRICA

BRITAIN AND AFRICA

❀

Kenneth Kirkwood

Rhodes Professor of Race Relations
at the University of Oxford

THE JOHNS HOPKINS PRESS: BALTIMORE

Published in Great Britain by
Chatto & Windus Ltd.
42 William IV Street
London, W.C.2

Library of Congress Catalog Card Number: 65-17073

16576

CONTENTS

To Deborah

PREFACE

SINCE the invitation was accepted to attempt this essay on Britain and Africa the United Kingdom has sought to make or has made several important changes in external policy, each of which has taken substantial time to formulate and to negotiate. The decision to apply for membership of the European Economic Community (the Common Market) under the Treaty of Rome was followed by protracted and fruitless negotiations. The Monckton Commission's detailed review of the constitution of the Federation of Rhodesia and Nyasaland culminated in disagreement and eventual dissolution. There is never finality in international relations but the unsuccessful outcome of both these major ventures has necessitated the rearrangement of a book which has its focus upon the contemporary world. Thus a chapter on British Central Africa, on which the author is writing a separate study, has now been divided and absorbed into the chapters on Southern and Eastern Africa.

It is unnecessary to emphasize to the readers for whom this series is intended that of all parts of the world with which Britain is concerned, Africa has undergone the most profound upheaval during the past decade. But there may be point in saying that the overall form of the book has been designed to try to meet the challenge of dealing with an uncomfortably contemporary topic. There are now several new and up-to-date political and economic handbooks on Africa which obviate the need to overload the text with facts and figures, details of political parties and the like. Attention has been given rather to more fundamental general issues and to a consideration of British–African relationships over time. Recollection of the depth and nature of the historical relationship between Britain and each zone of Africa is essential if the problems of the urgent present are to be seen in proper perspective.

There is scarcely any problem which is new in Africa, certainly not in the area of special professional concern to the author—the achievement of unity, in the sense of political, social and economic co-operation, between peoples of different ethnic, cultural or racial origin. Realistic optimism as well as deeper understanding require that this fact be kept in mind. Human nature in Africa is the same as elsewhere and some recent romantic generalizations suggesting the contrary have hindered rather than helped national and international policy. Intractable problems of national, regional or continental unity will not be wished away by superficial assumptions that Africans are less prone to identify themselves in ethnic terms, still less by assertions that ethnic divisions between Africans are less important or of a different kind than those elsewhere in the world. Few if any of the better-known inter-African tensions—Somali–Ethiopian, or Hutu–Tutsi in Rwanda, for example—are solely ethnic in character but group identifications are nevertheless regrettably potent and frequently lethal. The same observations apply to the more widely known relations between Africans and Europeans, Africans and Arabs, and Africans and Asians.

My approach to Africa's problems and to the overall relationship between Britain and Africa nevertheless remains one of underlying confidence. There have been many acute tensions and difficulties during the years of rapid political change since 1948. Several are not only unresolved but are very probably going to be accentuated in the decades immediately ahead. Breaking-point was reached over South Africa's membership of the Commonwealth in 1961. It might be reached again in other cases, possibly over Southern Rhodesia, Zanzibar or even Ghana. But damage can be repaired by constructive action and more rewarding courses can be adopted within and between countries. Leaders of the African states and of Britain, commanding the support of substantial majorities in their countries, have repeatedly emphasized their confidence in the future. While such faith continues the remotest goals are attainable.

Thanks

I acknowledge with gratitude the generous help of Sir Miles Clifford, Mr Ehioze Ediae, Dr Ellen Hellmann, Mrs Beatrice Hooke, Miss Elizabeth Monroe, Dr Saul Rose, Miss Alison Smith and my wife Deborah.

St. Antony's College
Oxford

INTRODUCTION

AFRICA is a continent, Britain a single state. This obvious point must be made at the outset if only to offer a reminder of the many criss-crossing ties which characterize the overall relationship with which this essay is concerned and extend it far beyond any simple duality. But in the case of Africa there is another reason for this emphasis: the recent "discovery" of the continent by most people throughout the world, and also the peculiarly regional character of many past outside associations with the different parts—West, South, North, East—have tended to give Africa a vaguely diffused and a wholly imaginary unity.

The continent is large, its climates and terrain vary from extreme to extreme, its resources are scattered and its 270–300 million people are very diverse. To the racial, cultural and linguistic diversities of the many indigenous groups, such as the Bushmen, Hottentot, Negro, Hamite, Nilote and Bantu,* there have been added through the centuries substantial Asian, Arab and European elements. Christianity, Hinduism and Islam are present in various forms and interact with traditional religions and philosophies. They also compete in many ways. Secular conceptions of politics are no less significant and numerous conflicting ideas and institutions have been imported to supersede or to fuse with those of Africa. To the myriad local and regional languages which have long separated African nations or tribes, languages of Europe, Arabia and South and South-East Asia have been added; their effect at times has been to lower certain linguistic barriers but they have also erected new ones, backed frequently by the powerful pressures of external nationalisms.

If the unity of Great Britain is less imaginary than that of Africa it is nevertheless necessary in a study of this kind to remember the social and political structure and variety of the United Kingdom. There are significant senses in which Scotland, Wales, Ireland— north and south—and Cornwall, as well as England, have had distinctive relationships with Africa though, for the more immediately

* See for example Seligman, C. G. *Races of Africa* (3rd revised ed., London, 1957).

relevant past the party-political divisions of Great Britain have been more important than the ethnic or national. Britain possesses a high degree of linguistic and cultural homogeneity when compared with, say, Belgium, where domestic divisions between Flemings and Walloons have sometimes directly affected Belgian policy in Africa.

But Britain's political parties—Conservative, Liberal and Labour —have disagreed sharply over overseas policy and such differences have had their marked effect. Smuts, for example, at the turn of the century yearned openly for "that other Britain" of John Bright when he returned from Cambridge to Kruger's Transvaal to find himself confronted by the might of Imperial Britain. He and Botha felt no comfort until Campbell-Bannerman won the day. On numerous other occasions Africa has experienced effects of changes of government in Britain. Changes of this kind are perhaps an inevitable, some would argue a desirable, concomitant of democratic external policy, whether colonial, Commonwealth or foreign. Certainly several African leaders have expressed preference for this kind of democratic inconsistency rather than for the supposed coherence and consistency of more dictatorial governments. It is none the less essential to keep in mind the fact that Britain's internal differences have affected overseas and African policies, sometimes to the point of abrupt reversals which have led to local confusion and disruption of life.

For any ultimate analysis of Britain's relations with Africa scholars will require detailed information on every African people and locality of a kind which today scarcely exists for any. There is also a great deal to be done to collect, to catalogue and to examine sources on Africa which exist in Britain today in scattered and inaccessible form. But for an interim or tentative study there are fortunately certain major signposts which can serve as a guide. For present purposes the principal signposts will be supplied by British official policy so far as this can be understood from sources normally available to the inquiring citizen and student. Whether there are serious differences between such information and that contained in the secret or confidential materials which will become available only when official archives are opened cannot be known. Experience, however, suggests that the differences are unlikely to be so great as to alter broad preliminary interpretations. To official policy and practice will be added an indication of the views and actions of influential leaders of commerce, industry, the church and other important sectors of British life. The principal areas of

British activity in Africa, official and unofficial, have been the British possessions—dominions, colonies, protectorates, mandates, trust territories. Regional discussion will therefore be centred upon the British or ex-British territories, and the neighbouring territories of recent French, Belgian, Portuguese or Italian administration will be drawn in to complete the picture of each zone.

West Africa, South-Central or Southern Africa, East-Central or Eastern Africa supply the main divisions for separate regional consideration together with an outline of certain more relevant North and North-East African developments. The inclusion of any references to North and North-East Africa may require explanation because another volume in this series has dealt with Britain and the Middle East. There will be little repetition, however, and the inclusion of North and North-East Africa is deliberately intended to try to overcome an understandable yet arbitrary and sometimes very misleading division of the African continent between the larger part "south of the Sahara" and the desert regions and the littoral of the Mediterranean to the north. The Sahara has never been an impenetrable barrier and the Nile valleys in particular have supplied highways for men throughout history. From the Maghreb south by caravan, around the Horn of Africa, and down the west coast others have passed. Increasingly in the twentieth century men and materials from the richer southern lands of the continent have come to play an increasingly significant part in the affairs of the north.

The extent of significant inter-communication in Africa has been underestimated by many outside authorities. Western ethnocentrism explains much of the tendency to think of exploration and travel primarily in terms of European or American pioneers. The character of colonial rule, with its emphases on direct communications with the metropolis, and internal communications radiating from a colonial capital, also explains part. But Africa is a continent in which there are few physical barriers to be compared with the Himalayas and Alps or the English Channel and wider seas. Through the centuries influences have passed, albeit slowly, by word of mouth and the written word, on parchment and wood, along track and stream. Books and newsprint have widened the scope of influence and in more recent years radio and television, together with modern rail, road and air communications, have greatly accelerated the exchange of news and the discussion of ideas. Since 1948, in particular, inter-African exchanges have proved potent in their political and social effects.

Largely because of the importance of the web and pattern of relationships, notably the metropolitan-colonial and the inter-African, and their modifications over time, the first three chapters are devoted to a broadly chronological review of developments. The British entry into Africa, and the Indian Ocean, and the establishment of the principal foci of power before 1914 are outlined in brief in order to provide a convenient reminder of the early historical background and the time-depth of the overall association between Britain and Africa. The quarter-century spanning the First World War until the outbreak of the Second occupies the next chapter. The last of the development chapters is given over to the recent period embracing the crucial Second World War, its aftermath, and present times. The author's personal experiences and observations shortly before and during the war in different parts of Africa, in company with Africans from every zone, convinced him at the time that the years 1939–45 marked a decisive watershed. Retrospective analysis from the standpoint of the 1960's confirms his view, as also the contemporary opinion that 1948 was a year of peculiar significance in the total British–African relationship.

After the developmental chapters in which an endeavour is made to bring out something of the inter-relationship of the various parts, and the international context of certain important social, political and economic forces, the three major zones of contemporary sub-Saharan Africa are examined in turn. South-Central or Southern Africa, embracing nine constituent units, including Southern Rhodesia, is followed by West Africa with seven units, allowing four regions to Nigeria and one each to Ghana, Sierra Leone and Gambia. Eastern or East-Central Africa with a total of six territories, when Zambia (Northern Rhodesia) and Malawi (Nyasaland) are added to Tanganyika, Uganda, Kenya and Zanzibar, is then reviewed.

Historical, economic, financial and other criteria have determined the choice of the order in which the zones are taken because it would be misleadingly quixotic in an essay such as this to ignore the facts of the past centuries, and indeed of the present, in an effort to impose one's own view of how the scales of Imperial interest or concern ought to be, or ought to have been, weighted. In matters of investment, trade and defence Southern Africa is of longest-standing first importance to Britain, West Africa second, and Eastern Africa third. The decision to dispense with a separate chapter on Central Africa has been explained in the Preface but one might repeat here the point made in the body of the book that this rearrangement in no way minimizes the importance of the established bonds across the Zambesi. The hope is rather that such co-operation will increase.

The final chapter is directed to a consideration of the major international associations of which Britain is a member and with which she operates increasingly in African affairs in the aftermath of colonialism. An author in close touch with contemporary Africa is naturally tempted to enlarge on the subject of Pan-Africanism but this is a subject which must be left for separate discussion. Our focus is upon Britain and the British–African relationship. Not only is the "Pan-Africanism" of independent Africa in a state of rapid growth and frequent change, but its principal advocates seek consciously and determinedly to promote alliances which are exclusively based in Africa. Clearly "Pan-Africanism" must be kept always in mind and appropriate texts consulted.* In Africa Britain works in direct partnership with Commonwealth countries, with her North Atlantic associates, with fellow-European states, and with the United Nations. These four associations are therefore given priority.

Finally, I consider myself fortunate that my views and findings are in no sense out of accord with the values which inspired the sponsors of this series of studies. My own contribution to the total assessment of the position of Britain in the modern world is limited, and I am very conscious of the many deficiencies of this book, for which I accept sole responsibility, but I am pleased that the continuous appraisal of relations between Britain and Africa which this commission has entailed, and of which only part can be presented in these pages, should have led me to a confident view of the future. The case for pessimism is appallingly easy to make at this period of turbulent change, but alarm and despondency are as much out of place in regard to Africa at this time as they have ever been in the past. Facile optimism is always offensive and dangerous. Many contemporary political and other practices in Africa are unmistakably evil, abhorrent and scientifically unwarrantable—not least colour bars and other forms of ethnic discrimination. But the precipitate, even hysterical, severing of links, including those which allow most hope for the future, or the

* See for example Legum, C. *Pan-Africanism*. A Short Political Guide (London 1962) and "The American Society of African Culture": *Pan-Africanism Reconsidered* (University of California Press 1962).

fomenting of negative action such as destructive revolution by pen, speech, or sword are equally to be condemned. There is much on the debit side of the several British–Africa accounts but the total balance sheet is plainly one of credit, and of further opportunity, for both Africans and Britons after their three and more centuries of increasingly close contact.

BRITAIN AND AFRICA BEFORE 1914: ESTABLISHMENT OF THE FOCI OF POWER

(i) EARLIEST TIMES–1876: FOUNDATIONS

CELTS in Cornwall may have been the first Britons to hear of Phoenician navigations down Africa, though their awareness of the mass of the continent would have been shadowy in comparison with their knowledge of Mediterranean Africa. Imperial Rome supplied more knowledge to Britain of the northern littoral of Africa, which, centuries later, was brought sharply into British thought by the advance of Islam through Christian Egypt, Cyrenaica, Tripolitania, Carthaginia and across the straits of Gibraltar into Spain. During the Crusades there was a recurrent consciousness of embattled Christians in "Ethiopia" and endeavours were made to reach them by land from the West. It was, however, the Portuguese circumnavigations of the late fifteenth and sixteenth centuries which linked Western Christendom more firmly to the ancient Ethiopian Coptic Church and gave full shape to Africa's outline.

In the wake of the pioneer Portuguese there followed Spaniards, Frenchmen, Dutchmen, Englishmen and Danes. In 1562 Sir John Hawkins transported a cargo of slaves to the Americas and in 1588 the first English chartered company was established to trade with West Africa. By 1662 England was in full possession of a West African base on the river Gambia. Between 1680 and 1786 over two million African men and women, according to one estimate, were taken as slaves to British colonies in the West Indies and North America. In 1787 British opponents of slavery selected Sierra Leone as a site for the resettlement of liberated Africans. In 1807 Sierra Leone became a Crown colony, and Freetown, the capital, a principal base for suppressing the slave trade. From Freetown British evangelical, educational and commercial influence was to extend throughout West Africa to provide the "West African" nexus which has since been a distinctive part of Britain's overall relationship with the continent.

Despite the growing concern for West Africa on the part of many philanthropists, and the genuine interest of traders anxious to promote "legitimate commerce" in tropical produce, Britain's primary attention had been directed hitherto to the plantations and colonies of North America and the Caribbean and to the factories of the East India Company. Africa had long supplied important labour to the trans-Atlantic possessions but was otherwise of subsidiary interest.

So far as Eastern trade was concerned Africa was also of small importance, save as a geographical obstacle. In the circumnavigation of the continent islands such as St. Helena, Zanzibar and Mauritius were often more convenient ports of call than mainland harbours, though the latter were normally available to the confident seapower whose mastery had been acknowledged by France in 1763.

The success of the American revolution in 1783 and the renewed challenge of France prompted a stronger British concern for empire in the east. To forestall the threat of Napoleon the Cape of Good Hope was taken, first in 1795 from the bankrupt Dutch East India Company and, once more, in 1806, from the Batavian Republic to whom it had been briefly restored. Henceforth it was a separate British colony until it became merged into the Union of South Africa in 1910.

It would be an exaggeration to claim that Britain attached any great intrinsic significance to the Cape Colony until the discovery of diamonds in the 1860's, and of gold in the 1880's, wholly altered the economic image of Southern Africa. The secure possession of the Cape peninsula, notably the harbours of Table Bay and Simon's Bay, was nevertheless always important to the Asian and Australasian empire which was expanded in the nineteenth century by a powerful industrial Britain. Simonstown, like Freetown, was to continue to be a major imperial base until after the Second World War. During the one and a half centuries of its existence as the South Atlantic station of the Royal Navy it fulfilled a Gibraltar-like function in guarding the gateway between the Indian and Atlantic Oceans and protecting the passage of merchantmen and transports to Australasia as well as to Hong Kong, Singapore, Colombo, Calcutta and Bombay. To strengthen both the new colony and the imperial seaways the South African coast was explored by the Royal Navy, and ports and anchorages were progressively established at Port Elizabeth and East London in the Eastern Cape, and at Port Natal, Durban.

The temperate climate which had assisted the planting of a colony of European farmers by the Dutch East India Company in 1652 led Britain also to encourage permanent settlers to come from their homeland to build a bulwark of farms and towns on the eastern frontier, as well as to strengthen the British population of the Western Cape, where the Dutch, including the rapidly assimilated French Huguenots, were well entrenched. In 1820 a substantial party of British families was disembarked at Algoa Bay where the town of Port Elizabeth, together with the inland centre of Grahamstown, soon came into being. Numerous hardships were suffered by the 1820 settlers but their hazards of health were not to be compared with those of the British settlers in sub-tropical Natal, still less with Britons in West Africa where settlement was out of the question and where the Royal Navy, for example, experienced heavy casualties from disease.

The emphasis of imperial policy in the South, as elsewhere in Africa, remained upon the coastlands until the last quarter of the nineteenth century. Substantial groups of British settlers were encouraged to migrate from time to time, as to Natal in 1849, but the newcomers were largely confined to the environs of towns like Durban and Pietermaritzburg. United Kingdom emigrants to British South Africa were never so numerous as those to Canada, Australia or New Zealand, and there was little readiness on the part of Governors or High Commissioners to support large-scale ventures into the interior.

When the Dutch frontier farmers, who came increasingly to resent British authority, chose in 1836 to trek beyond the reach of the Cape administration, little effort was made to restrain them. They were prevented from seizing Port Natal but for the rest they were allowed to create, across the Orange and Vaal rivers, the landlocked republics which were formally recognized as independent by Britain in 1852 and 1854. During the next two decades there were disputes and skirmishes between Boer and Briton, as over Basutoland, which became a separate British colony in 1868, and over the diamond field of Kimberley in Griqualand West, which was annexed to the Crown in 1871. But, though High Commissioners like Sir George Grey urged closer association and the application of common policies towards the native African tribes throughout Southern Africa in the 1850's, the republics were left largely intact until Shepstone's short-lived annexation of the Transvaal in 1877.

Well before the year 1876 Britain was firmly established in both

West Africa and South Africa. In the seventy years since the annexation of the Cape a "South African" nexus, at least as strong and distinctive as that of West Africa, was forged with Britain. Both Freetown and Capetown were to serve as powerful springboards for further imperial advance when the hinterland of Africa was partitioned after 1876.

India and Egypt provided the major bases and supplied manpower for the British advances in East and North Africa. Both countries possessed long-standing links with Britain and these ties played their part in assisting the nineteenth-century expansion of British interests down the Nile and inland to the great lakes from the East African coast. Nelson's triumphs strengthened British command of the Mediterranean passages and of the bridgeheads required for the caravan routes east across Syria to Basra and over the Egyptian desert to Suez. Before the middle of the nineteenth century British steamship services were operating between England and Alexandria, and Suez and Bombay, and in 1857 a British railway was built to speed the desert transit. By such means mail and passenger services between the homeland and India enjoyed a substantial advantage over the time-consuming voyages around the Cape. The British presence in Africa was greatly strengthened by the Crown's assumption of control of the Government of India in 1858 and by Disraeli's purchase in 1875 of the shares in the Suez Canal held by the Khedive Ismail.

The new Indian empire which emerged from the mutiny was of fundamental importance to British influence throughout the world. The Indian army, as reconstituted, became an example of the integrated strength which can result from a skilful blending of diverse elements and traditions. Scots, Welsh, Irish and English were fused with Sikhs, Punjabis, Mahrattas and Bengalis. Alongside soldiers from elsewhere in the Empire, the Indian army played a foremost role in imperial and Commonwealth history until 1945. In several colonial conflicts they were the principal troops. In Africa their employment was often decisive. Lugard relied upon Indian soldiers for the pacification of Nyasaland. In the First World War Indian regiments were prominent in both East and West Africa. In 1941 they bore the brunt at Keren in the assault on Mussolini's East African stronghold and in the Western Desert and Mediterranean Indian divisions earned good reputations.

Indian workers as well as soldiers were the willing and efficient auxiliaries of empire. In 1858, barely a quarter of a century after

Emancipation, cheap labour, especially for agriculture, was in demand in many parts of the colonial empire where the indigenous peoples were averse to employment on sugar and other plantations. In 1859 the Governor and colonists of Natal were able to induce both the British metropolitan and Indian governments to permit the transportation of the indentured workers who first arrived at Durban in 1860. Canefields in the Caribbean and Pacific likewise drew upon Indian agriculturalists in the nineteenth century and others of different craft or calling accompanied them. Railway construction in East Africa, as from Mombasa to Lake Victoria, depended upon Indian skilled and unskilled labour and the subsequent operation and maintenance of communications owed much to Asians filling important intermediary offices: in the clerical ranks of administration and audit they were predominant. The use by British authorities of Indian soldiers, clerks and workers stimulated a concomitant flow of merchants and petty traders who reinforced the more ancient Indian merchant houses at Zanzibar and on the mainland.

India and Arabia meet at Zanzibar. Slaves and spices, gold, ivory, wood and hides have been carried for centuries by dhows coasting up past the Horn of Africa to Aden and Oman, or riding with the rhythm of the monsoon across the wider seas to Bombay. Into this world in 1497 had sailed Vasco da Gama and subsequently, from the vice-regal base at Goa, Portuguese rulers had sought to impose a new order upon the East African coast. In the neighbourhood of Mogadishu, at Mombasa, Mozambique and Sofala ancient monuments of Portugal still exist in the shape of coastal towers, fortresses and the like. It was not, however, until well into the nineteenth century that the old society was widely threatened. Modern industrial nations, equipped with all the resources of Western science and technology, effected changes beyond the scope of the Portuguese.

The United States, Germany, Italy, France and Britain were the principal rivals, though Britain's supremacy in India assured her priority throughout East, North-East and North Africa and into Arabia beyond. Of the many bonds contracted by Britain one of the more enduring was that initiated through Seyyid Said, Sultan of Muscat, who in 1840 moved the seat of his government from the Persian Gulf to Zanzibar. A British–Arab wedge was inserted between Egypt and India to diversify still further the overall pattern of Britain's relations with Africa and to provide an important alternative, if subsidiary, source of power. It was from territory ruled by the Sultans of Zanzibar that successive British explorers, missionaries and merchants penetrated to the Great Lakes and beyond.

Egypt was the last of the four principal bases of power to be secured by Britain. Not until 1904 was France ready to concede priority in the Nile Valley to her rival in return for British recognition of her pre-eminence in the Maghreb. French reluctance rested on France's numerous technical, cultural and commercial contributions which included de Lesseps' Suez Canal, completed in 1869. The British presence in Egypt and southward along the Nile was also a major obstacle to the fulfilment of French imperial ambitions in Africa, after defeat by Prussia in 1870 compelled metropolitan France to seek territorial gains, prestige and manpower beyond the continent of Europe. But already by 1876 Britain's position in Egypt was virtually assured through the acquisition of Ismail's shares in the Suez Canal. Four-fifths of the shipping which passed through the Canal was British and this vital "cross-roads of empire" was now scarcely likely to be abandoned by any government in Britain, as Gladstone's action against Arabi Pasha in 1882 confirmed.

In the southern dominions of Egypt also the foundations of subsequent British power were established through men like Baker and Gordon, servants of the Khedive. As governors of the Equatorial Nile Basin they initiated modern administration, including measures to control the slave trade over one of the world's most ancient slave routes.* These pioneer administrators paved the way for the Anglo-Egyptian condominium which followed the defeat of the Mahdi, after the latter had overthrown Egyptian rule in the heart of the immense and vaguely-defined "Sudan"—land of the Blacks. Khedival rule elsewhere was also to be taken over by British successors, as on the Somali coast, the southern shore of the Gulf of Aden.

(ii) 1876–1904: EXPANSION

British expansion in Africa between 1876 and 1904 was rapid in every zone. Vast new territories were acquired in both West and East Africa. Britain's major investment of men, money and material, however, took place in Egypt and South Africa. In Egypt after 1882 the "Dual Control" established with France in 1877 rapidly gave way to virtual sole control by Britain. The victors of Tel-el-Kebir soon became British troops in Egypt and were hence-

* For details see Gray, R. *A History of the Southern Sudan,* (O.U.P.) London, 1961.

forth a key element in imperial strategy. British soldiers and administrators with Egyptian experience were influential in South Africa. After 1956 the full extent and depth of British investment in Egypt over three generations and more was tragically revealed by expulsion and sequestration. Yet, of the two major zones, South Africa must be given priority. British investment in South Africa both before and after 1904 was of an order greatly in excess of that in Egypt and elsewhere. The investment before 1904 includes the lives of the twenty thousand who fell in the South African War, and the eighty thousand other casualties. That particular investment has played and still plays its part in the powerful bonds of emotion from which neither Britain nor South Africa have yet struggled free.

The gold of the Transvaal was revealed in its full richness in 1886 when the Witwatersrand deposits were added to those of Barberton. The year marks a turning point in British policy. Whereas Gladstone in 1881, harassed by Irish troubles, and mindful of Isandhlwana, had been content to accept defeat by the Boers at Majuba, and the retrocession to them of the Province of the Transvaal—the key territory in British plans for confederation—the new gold discoveries drew English-speaking immigrants in their thousands from North America and Australasia as well as from the British Isles. They entered through the Cape Colony and Natal and it was to British "Colonials", like Rhodes at the Cape, that they looked for protection and leadership during their residence as aliens or *uitlanders* in the lands over which Britain claimed the authority of suzerain. For his part Rhodes, as the confident spearhead of a powerful Britain, was able to take up the confederation ideas inherited from Carnarvon, Frere, Froude and others in the 70's and to re-fashion plans for a greater South Africa under the Crown. Imperialism was in the ascendant and Rhodes had little difficulty in securing support at the highest level in Britain including, in 1889, a Royal Charter for his British South Africa Company. His emissaries had previously outwitted Kruger's in treating with Lobengula to the north of the Limpopo; now, with his charter, he was able to employ agents of unusual distinction such as Earl Grey and Rochfort Maguire, Fellow of All Souls, in the occupation of Mashonaland and the conquest of Matabeleland.

The encirclement of the Transvaal and Orange Free State was completed in 1894. Save for the outlet to Lourenço Marques through Portuguese territory, Kruger's and Steyn's republics were flanked by British colonies and protectorates. German endeavours to secure Pondoland were frustrated, and the vast if thinly peopled Bechuanaland protectorate was firmly interposed between the republics and German South-West Africa. To the north of the Zambesi the British South Africa Company, and others directly associated with it, laid the foundation of extensive British interests. The Katanga as well as Northern Rhodesia and Nyasaland were brought within the compass of British financial influence, though the rich copper deposits of Central Africa were divided by the political frontier drawn between the Belgian Congo and Northern Rhodesia. To the north-east of Katanga British expansion was blocked by German East Africa. Both Northern Rhodesia and the Protectorate of Nyasaland, established in 1891 under Johnston, acquired long frontiers with Bismarck's *Mittelafrika*.

Jameson's easy overthrow of Lobengula's rule in Matabeleland in 1893 was not paralleled in 1896 when his troopers ran into disaster at the hands of Transvaal burghers near Krugersdorp. The troublesome Mashona and Matabele uprisings, facilitated by the removal of men for the Jameson raid, had not been complemented by the *uitlander* uprising in Johannesburg which had been confidently predicted. Rhodes was fully extended to pacify the Matabele, to consolidate his widespread company holdings and to defend his reputation. Three years later, in October 1899, and against a very different background of public opinion in Britain—as well as continental Europe and North America—the die was cast by Milner. Only then were steps taken to mobilize forces sufficient to secure the overthrow of Kruger's régime, and the government of his faithful and altruistic ally, President Steyn.

The South African War was prolonged, bitter and bloody. By the time that a majority of the commando leaders at Vereeniging in May 1902 were persuaded to sign terms of peace with Kitchener and Milner, an event comparable with the American Civil War in its local significance had taken place. This war between the states henceforth dominated relations between Boer and Briton in the Transvaal, Orange Free State, Cape and Natal. On the wider Empire or Commonwealth also the war made its deep impression. Britain bore the heaviest casualties and cost but Australia, Canada and New Zealand sent substantial contingents and were intimately involved in the painful birth of the fifth of Kipling's *Five Nations*.

Whether Germany and Holland might have done more to aid the burgher forces, who included a quota of nationalist Irish as well as German and Dutch soldiers, is a matter for speculation. So also is the question of the possible effect of French and American aid. It is probable, nevertheless, that the strength of the British Navy would have ensured military victory even if the Boers had received considerably greater physical support from outside. Less open to speculation is the fact that the South African War led in Britain to a crisis of confidence among many as to the moral justification of empire, especially when it involved the subjection of a small, independent people of European origin and occasioned the death and suffering of women and children of the kind and on the scale described by Emily Hobhouse. Such misgiving, reinforced at an intellectual level by the critical analyses of writers like J. A. Hobson,* had its slow effect during the decades which followed.

In 1902, however, a sense of jubilant relief was dominant and British people looked hopefully to the development of the rich lands newly won in Southern Africa. Milner was preoccupied with tasks of reconstruction and was seeking through immigration to achieve British majorities over the Afrikaners in both rural and urban areas. Joseph Chamberlain concurred fully and did not spare himself during his vigorous personal tour of South Africa and his subsequent campaigns in Britain on behalf of stronger bonds of empire. In the Transvaal and Orange Free State, Milner and his talented "kindergarten" rapidly prepared the framework of efficient local administrations, and by 1904 they had initiated several measures designed to bring about the unification of the two new Crown colonies with the older responsible government colonies, Cape Colony and Natal, which had enjoyed substantial autonomy since 1872 and 1893.

Though Milner's immediate focus was restricted, he included within his purview the several other territories of British Southern Africa—the Rhodesias, Nyasaland, Basutoland, Bechuanaland and the newly acquired Swaziland. Together with the four South African colonies they composed a vast contiguous land-mass. Between 1876 and 1904 British administration was extended from the Orange River to the southern shore of Lake Tanganyika. The Cape Colony, Britain's century-old possession, provided the main base for this great advance and the principal outlet for the landlocked northern territories flanked by Portuguese, German and Belgian territory.

North and North-Eastern Africa neither exacted from Britain

---

* See for example Hobson, J. A. *Imperialism: A Study* (3rd edition, London 1954), first published in 1902.

the toll nor conferred upon her the riches of Southern Africa. British expansion in the north between 1876–1904 was none the less both impressive and significant. Apart from achieving physical command of the Suez Canal, control of the Nile Valley was secured throughout its length from the delta to Lake Victoria. By 1904, with the addition of the East African Protectorate of Kenya to Uganda, a broad swathe of British-administered territory extended from the Mediterranean to the Indian Ocean encircling ancient, independent Ethiopia and the new Italian colonies of Eritrea and Somalia.

Egypt was the key to this expansion in the same way that the Cape Colony had provided the key to British advance in Southern Africa. We cannot re-tell the remarkable achievements of Cromer and his officers but by 1887 the Consul-General's fiscal and administrative reforms had done much to regenerate Egypt. During the next few years, hydrological, irrigation and land-tenure surveys of far-reaching significance were completed. The re-organization of the Egyptian police and army also permitted attention to be directed to the lands south of Wadi Halfa where the Khalifa Abdallahi ruled over the followers of the late Mahdi, Muhammed Ahmad, who had overthrown Egyptian rule after Tel-el-Kebir, and killed Gordon in 1885.

Opinions differ as to the state of the Sudan under the Mahdia and Khalifa.* Famine and epidemics struck cruel blows which would have taxed the resources of any administration. But present-day views on Abdallahi's Sudan, like those on Kruger's Transvaal, are irrelevant so far as past action is concerned. In contemporary eyes there were in the Sudan, threats and malpractices of a kind sufficiently disturbing and out of keeping with the new régime in Egypt to justify intervention, especially when the Khalifa's forces threatened to overwhelm Kassala in the year of Italy's disaster at Adowa. Kitchener pushed his Nubian railway to Abu Hamed in 1897 and won the battle of Omdurman in September 1898. Britain's determination to ensure the security of the Nile Valley was also manifest in Kitchener's confrontation of Marchand at Fashoda in 1898. In 1899 Britain proclaimed an Anglo-Egyptian condominium over the Sudan. Between 1898 and 1904 Britain and France engaged in intensive diplomatic skirmishes in all sectors of Africa to the north of the equator. The Nile Valley was, after 1898, effectively conceded to British rule, but it was not until the Anglo-French Agreement of 1904 that France fully accepted this position.

* A new contribution is made in Hill, R. *Slatin Pasha* (O.U.P., 1965)

The work of Cromer and Kitchener in consolidating Egypt and the Sudan, Britain's most extensive holding in Africa, was complemented by those who created British East Africa in competition with the new, nascent German empire. In the decades after the Berlin Conference of 1884–5 there were many encounters between Britain and Germany throughout Africa but by 1894 Lugard* had won his battle to persuade the home Government to take over Uganda from MacKinnon's insecure Imperial British East Africa Company. Though Lake Victoria was divided between British and German East Africa the source of the Nile was in British hands. In 1901 Britain's power of control was strengthened when the Uganda railway, a major strategic undertaking, was carried to Kisumu from Kilindini, the deep-water harbour at Mombasa.

Reference was made earlier to the Indian contribution to the construction of the Uganda railway and to the substantial immigration from the Indian sub-continent. Equally significant during this period were the plans to encourage European immigration into the British East African Protectorate. Lugard in 1892 envisaged both large-scale Indian and European immigration. The more temperate highland areas, including the area transferred from Uganda to Kenya in 1902, were the parts considered suitable for Europeans. This view was confirmed by Lord Delamere, Kenya's foremost pioneer settler, who, before the turn of the century, journeyed south from Hargeisa, in the dry Somaliland Protectorate, to the well-watered lands around Mount Kenya. But, although Kenya's first settlers' association was established in 1902, it was not until after 1904 that a sufficient nucleus of immigrant British farmers arrived to give to colonial Kenya its distinctive personality as one of the "White Man's Countries" of British Africa.

In West Africa, where there was never any question of Britain establishing "colonies of settlement", the era of rapid expansion saw the considerable extension inland of Nigeria and the Gold Coast. This was especially true after 1890 when the second Brussels Conference required effective occupation of the interior as well as the coastlands of Africa. Unlike the lands in southern, eastern and northern Africa, however, British territory was never contiguous. It comprised rather the isolated lands of Gambia and Sierra Leone in addition to the Gold Coast and Nigeria. France became the principal territorial power of the zone, with Portugal, Spain and

* See Perham, M. *Lugard*, two vols. *The Years of Adventure 1858–1898* (London 1956) and *The Years of Authority 1898–1945* (London 1960).

Germany the possessors of smaller colonies along with America's Liberia.

Isolated or not, the acquisition of Nigeria alone would have been achievement enough for Britain. Largest and most populous of all British territories in Africa, Nigeria was won by the courage and determination of traders like Sir George Goldie whose Royal Niger Company Lugard was proud to serve. Granted its royal charter in 1886, the Niger Company exercised governmental and military functions until 1900, when responsibility for the Colony and Protectorate of Lagos, the Protectorate of Southern Nigeria, and the vast new Protectorate of Northern Nigeria was assumed by the Crown, together with the command of the West African Frontier Force which had been raised by the Company in 1897 to hold off the French.

Though smaller than Nigeria, the Gold Coast, through Ashanti, presented Britain with a major obstacle in West Africa. A warrior people, confident of their own ability to rule their neighbours as well as themselves, the Ashanti resisted British penetration until 1901, when their territory was annexed as a Crown colony. By contrast with Asantehenes like Prempeh, whom Britain exiled in 1896, the chiefs of the Northern Territories welcomed British overrule. Sierra Leone also was doubled in area by 1895. Small in comparison with its two eastern neighbours of British West Africa, Sierra Leone, and notably the capital Freetown, retained much of its traditional importance. In particular it was called upon continually to supply men to all British Territories. The primary object in launching Fourah Bay College early in the nineteenth century was to train African clergy but over the years many associated with the local College made their important contribution to commerce, administration and other professions in Nigeria, the Gold Coast and the Gambia.

(iii) 1904–14: Consolidation

At the beginning of the twentieth century leaders of the Western world attempted to take stock of the new overseas holdings which had been acquired so breathlessly during the past few decades. Western expansion had taken place in every continent though Africa was the site of major partition. Social-Darwinist thought was prevalent everywhere, among socialists, liberals and conservatives, and there was little questioning of the legitimacy of the new

Western régimes which had been set up throughout the world: concepts such as the "right of conquest" aroused little moral misgiving and the greater beneficence of European government over traditional Asian and African government was accepted almost without question. The world of power was the world of the West and the politics of Europe commanded the first attention of statesmen. The strength of rival armies and navies was the pre-eminent concern of Prime Ministers, Chancellors and Emperors and the map of the world was the board on which they sought to move their pieces. Schemes were devised for the closer organization of the imperial economies and defence systems, and overseas territories were encouraged to impose levies upon themselves for the strengthening of metropolitan forces. Imperial arms would see to the safety of all within the law.

In the British imperial system the pre-eminence of the United Kingdom was beyond question. Only after the 1914–18 War was Lloyd George to be sharply reminded by the Chanak crisis of the feeling of national adulthood and independence on the part of the dominions of Canada, Australia and South Africa. Only then would the political aspirations of India be given serious attention. In the decade before the Great War* there were disputes over imperial protection and the degree to which the foreign policy of "Great Britain and the Dominions" might be made uniform. These disputes were aired freely at imperial conferences and at hustings within the separate self-governing countries. There was nevertheless a confident expectation on the part of many in the Empire that a high degree of co-ordination was possible. There was also a general view that all overseas territories, dominions as well as colonies, were automatically committed by a declaration of war on the part of the mother country. Colonial nationalism among Britons and other Europeans overseas was recognized as a definite phenomenon but it normally involved claims for greater political and cultural self-expression. Independence might be demanded but it was conceived as independence in partnership with the metropolis.

National feelings among Asian and African peoples within the Empire received scant acknowledgement. The social-evolutionist thought of the day ranked Asians and Arabs well above Africans but even the fact, for example, that the Indian National Congress had been in existence since 1881 was not taken seriously. Congress

* "Great War" is used interchangably with "1914–18 War" and "First World War".

was viewed as the child of altruistic British administrators and Western forms of political organization were considered alien to the Asian world. The Indian army was clearly of the greatest importance, and there was in prospect a possible African army, but such instruments of imperial power would be commanded by British officers.

In Africa itself the Indian Congress movement had taken root already through the presence in Natal of the young Gandhi. At his Phoenix settlement a few miles out of Durban the newspaper *Indian Opinion* was published. Educated African leaders in the eastern Cape and Natal also had initiated the modern organization of their people in the 1880's and 1890's. Men like Tengo Jabavu, editor of *Imvo Zabandtsundu*, owed their position largely to the teaching of British missionaries in the Cape; others in Natal, like Dr. John L. Dube, founder of the independent Ohlange Institute, drew inspiration from Negro endeavour at the Hampton Institute, Virginia, and elsewhere in the United States. The non-violence of Gandhi and the gradualism of Booker T. Washington were important intellectual influences of the day in South Africa. Among the Cape Coloured people there was a similar lack of militancy.

From the British imperial standpoint the nationalisms in Africa which most demanded attention were those of the Afrikaners and the Egyptians. Of these, Afrikaner nationalism was first given its head, only some twenty years later were effective avenues opened to its Egyptian counterpart. For the rest British Africa was a sphere of administration, not politics, and in many of the newly acquired territories the administration was perforce of the most rudimentary kind. Modern communications were required. Police posts and *bomas* had to be sited in districts where few if any Europeans had ventured or been seen by the local chiefs and tribesmen. Traditional authorities of all kinds had to be brought to acknowledge the new rulers, elements of British law and justice had to be made known, tax registers had to be compiled and a foundation laid for a whole new system of government. There was little opportunity for development and welfare in the new areas in the short decade before 1914.

In South Africa the most dramatic political venture was the attempt by Britain to channel Afrikaner nationalism into constructive co-operation. On all sides in Britain a new and at times romantic conception of the Boer and the Boer War grew and was fostered. This image was at marked variance with war-time propaganda but the post-war desire for reconciliation on the part of British people was real enough, and natural enough if social psychology be a guide. Kipling and Buchan put into verse and prose the new feeling for the simple, homely, gallant people who had taught the mother country "an imperial lesson", and brought into the fold of empire a stock of whom none was thought to be "stronger and finer than this one which turned defeat into victory and led captivity captive". The actions of Botha and Smuts at the time of Vereeniging, reinforced later by the conversion of Deneys Reitz, laid a firm foundation for new heroes of the multi-national empire. Peter Pienaar became a household figure of English literature.

Emphasis has been laid, and rightly, on the importance of the economic reconstruction of the Transvaal and Orange Free State after the war. Particular attention has been given to railway and tariff policies and to labour questions, including the acute and prolonged controversies over the importation of Chinese labour in 1904 in order to restore the gold-mining industry at a time when native African labour was dispersed and difficult to recruit. The political concessions to the Afrikaners were, however, probably of greater long-term significance than any economic action.

A crucial concession was made in 1902. At the insistence of the Boer generals, Kitchener and Milner accepted as a condition of the peace treaty that there be no enfranchisement of the native Africans until after the Transvaal and Orange Free State had attained self-government. Chamberlain remonstrated at the time and Milner later expressed profound regret over what he called his biggest mistake. Nevertheless, by this action, Afrikaner nationalism was allowed a prospect of power which it might otherwise never have obtained.

Whether any other course was open to Kitchener and Milner in the circumstances of the day—war-weariness, the prevailing general attitudes on racial differences, the determination of the Boers to fight to the bitter end if anything like the first American post Civil War reconstruction was attempted—is difficult to determine. The fact remains that the racial traditions of the Republics rather than those of Victorian liberalism were given a position of immense advantage: to use the terminology of another sphere—it was made probable that the "Black Codes" of the American South would prevail rather than the gradualist emancipation practices of the North.

Such possibilities were perceived by few at the time; among those few there were South African liberals whose minority voice could gain little heed. The general view in Britain was that substantial power must be entrusted to the Boers. Conservatives and Liberals differed over timing, and their differences were important; but once the Liberals assumed office in December 1905 and were overwhelmingly confirmed in power in 1906 the general objective was emphasized and every obstacle impatiently removed. The speech on the Orange River Colony made in the Commons by Winston Churchill, Liberal Under-Secretary of State for the Colonies, is typical.* The policy carried the full support of Campbell-Bannerman and, after the Transvaal and Orange Free State were granted self-government in 1906 and 1907, plans for South African unification were hastily prepared.

In 1908 an all-white constituent assembly was convened in South Africa and by September 1909 the British Parliament had approved a draft constitution. The constitution was unitary as distinct from federal; it favoured the rural, more racist white voters rather than the urban liberals, and it sanctioned frank colour bars, save for the Cape Province. Membership of the powerful central parliament was restricted to whites. On May 31, 1910, the South Africa Act came into force and power was transferred from Westminster and Whitehall to Cape Town and Pretoria.

In retrospect it seems strange that the traditions and lessons of the colonial histories of native policy and administration and race relations were so lightly regarded, including contemporary warnings such as the Zulu Rebellion of 1906, but the mood of the moment in Britain strongly favoured a great act of faith in the Afrikaners and this was echoed, though less certainly, by the British Cape Colonists and Natalians who had suffered substantially during the war, and who felt that they had speedily to discover a *modus vivendi* with their former republican neighbours.

The Union of South Africa was not allowed the span of even one full term of parliamentary life before the Great War began. Wounds barely twelve years old were re-opened and old divisions reappeared abruptly. Hertzog, who had left Botha's cabinet in 1912 to lead the Nationalist Movement, did not go to the extreme of joining the armed Boer rebellion of 1914, but his party was greatly strengthened by a widespread mood of bitter protest against involvement in the wars of the British Empire. Nationalist sympathies

---

* The speech is reprinted in Keith, A. B. ed. *Select Speeches and Documents on British Colonial Policy* 1763–1917, Part 2. pp. 3–24.

lay much more with Germany, friend of the Boers between 1899–
1902. At Versailles Hertzog would plead for the restoration of the
independence of the Orange Free State, in opposition to the British
Empire delegation, which included Smuts. Meanwhile, however,
Botha and Smuts were firmly in command.

South Africa was important to Britain in the Great War. Given
the hazards of history and the uncertainties of attempting to plot
the course of any nation for longer than a decade it was perhaps a
notable achievement of Edwardian statesmanship to have dealt so
well with the problems of Boer and Briton that South Africa could
be counted an ally at the time of critical challenge from Germany
and Austria–Hungary. The mounting tensions in Ireland showed
how grave might have been the consequence of wider disaffection
within the Empire.

Baden-Powell trained the South African mounted constabulary
in the years after 1902, and regiments of the Imperial garrison
shared their knowledge and skills with the local South African
volunteers who formed active citizen force units. In 1912 Smuts
drafted the new Defence Act for the Union and merged the rural
rifle commandos with the urban battalions. His success not only
permitted the Imperial government to withdraw its regular battalions to Europe on the outbreak of war but enabled the Union
Defence Force to be entrusted with major Imperial responsibilities in
German West and German East Africa. The South African commercial ports were freely used by Imperial transports, including those
conveying the Australian and New Zealand expeditionary forces and
Indian contingents, and Simonstown was a principal naval base.

South Africa's associated territories to the south of the Belgian–
German divide experienced relatively slow development. Nyasaland was left in the care of its missionaries and missionary-minded
administrators. Provision was made in the South Africa Act for the
eventual incorporation into the Union of Basutoland, Bechuanaland and Swaziland and of the British South Africa Company
Territories, a detailed schedule being appended to the South Africa
Act. Only the failure of the National Convention to be liberal over
the franchise and other rights of the African, Coloured and Asian
peoples had led Britain to withhold the "Protectorates" from the
Union. It was also the confident expectation of the British South
Africa Company administration as well as of South Africa's
politicians, that the permissive section relating to the incorporation
of their territories, the Rhodesias, would soon be implemented.

In the case of the Rhodesias the original twenty-five-year period of the Royal Charter had some years to run and the Company was still uncertain as to the nature and extent of its mineral resources, though it was becoming clear that the wealth of gold had been greatly exaggerated in the early propaganda brochures. The European settlers of Rhodesia were also restive. The administrative deficit was mounting steadily in Southern Rhodesia and when the Company sought to exploit commercially its control of the unalienated lands it was challenged by the settlers who, since 1898, had been granted increasing representation in the Legislative Council. By 1911 their potential influence was considerable and they were fortunate to secure as their leader the forceful Cape Irish lawyer, Charles Coghlan. It was he who effectively challenged the Company's land claims before the expiry of the Charter in 1914 and who prepared the basis of the settlers' case which was argued eventually, together with the cases for the Company and the Africans, before the Judicial Committee of the Privy Council in 1918. For its part the Imperial government appointed a Native Reserves Commission to delimit African tribal lands. From an Imperial strategic point of view the British settlers of Rhodesia and Nyasaland could be counted emphatically loyal, so also the Africans. There was no difficulty in recruiting local regiments at the outbreak of war and the problem was rather one of persuading a sufficient number of qualified men to remain in key civilian posts.

Egyptian nationalism was the other major political force in Africa with which Britain had to deal in the first years of the new century. In 1914 Egyptian nationalists were as hostile as those of South Africa. Although several thousand Egyptians either responded to Britain's call for artillerymen and labour corps volunteers or suffered themselves to be recruited, many were as suspicious or as bitterly critical of Britain and her allies as were the Hertzog nationalists and Afrikaner rebels. There was no background of recent large-scale bloodshed to dominate the Anglo-Egyptian relationship but there was a similar marked ambivalence in Egyptian attitudes towards Germany, Austria-Hungary and Muslim Turkey.

During the war the anti-British feeling found increasing grounds for expression and at the end of the war there were passionate appeals for political independence, an aspiration strongly nurtured between 1904 and 1914, and one which was in no way stifled at

birth by the international recognition of British supremacy. If anything the Anglo-French agreement strengthened Egyptian
nationalism by concentrating its expression against one power alone.
Before the turn of the century there was for both Egyptian and
Afrikaner nationalism a certain freedom of manœuvre in that
British suzerainty was neither precisely defined nor universally
recognized. But by 1904 British over-rule was more definite, there
were rigid limits to local initiative—hopes of expansion, whether
towards the Upper Nile or the Zambesi, were curbed.

Cromer at long last gave way to Gorst in 1907, as his former
lieutenant, Milner, in the south had done already for Selborne in
1905. Both pro-consuls continued to influence Imperial policy at
home but their immediate successors were as eager to make their
own distinctive impress upon affairs as were the Liberal cabinet
ministers. The concessions to Egyptian nationalist demands, however, bore no resemblance to those in the south of the continent.
There was no question of self-government, no relaxation of the
capitulatory system, no handing over to Egyptian control of the
Suez Canal, nor any prospect of a united Nile Valley under an
independent Egypt. On these central issues Sir Eldon Gorst was at
one with his former master. Where he differed from Cromer, and
from Kitchener, who succeeded him in 1911, was in his endeavour
to improve personal relations with Egyptians. His efforts, however,
achieved limited success: he was criticized by colleagues schooled
in the aloof efficiency of Cromerism and failed to make significant
contact with Muslim Egyptian national leaders.

To what extent his efforts in the latter direction were undermined
by the Denshawy incident of June 1906 is difficult to gauge. But
there can be no doubt that the execution of the four leaders of the
village riot and the severity of the punishments imposed on the other
rioters had an adverse effect. There were those who discounted the
effect in much the same way as the execution of the Zulu poll-tax
rioters was discounted. Denshawy did not lead on to a rebellion so
widespread and bloody as that in Natal in 1906 but the attitudes
of the governing and alien immigrant and minority groups were
much the same and the long-term consequences perhaps equally
unfortunate. In both cases the administrators were urged not only
to punish the immediate offenders but to impose salutary sentences
which would induce a general respect for life and property. Cromer
was temporarily absent from Egypt at the time of Denshawy and he
might possibly have acted differently or otherwise saved the day.

The fact, however, is that his successor inherited an emotionally disturbed population, and Egyptian nationalist leaders a martyr incident of lasting significance.

The assassination of Boutros Pasha Ghali in 1909 and the execution of his unbalanced young Muslim murderer was another serious misfortune for Gorst. The capable Boutros was the first truly Egyptian Prime Minister and he co-operated actively with Gorst in operating the newly revised machinery of representation, notably the legislative council. Boutros was acceptable to a wide range of Egyptian opinion but he was nevertheless a Copt and when he was killed by a Muslim a delicate religious relationship was upset. Militant Muslim societies had grown in strength after the death in 1908 of Mustapha Kemal, the man who had preserved a broad unity for the national movement, and the existence of such societies heightened Christian-Egyptian fears that the cry "Egypt for the Egyptians" was intended to exclude them and to threaten their established interests. During the premiership of Mohamed Pasha Said, successor to Boutros Pasha, the nationalists brought increasing pressure to bear upon the National Assembly, and there were strong rumours of massacres and disorder being planned with a view to overthrowing the British régime.

It was into this situation that Kitchener came on a visit in 1910; in the following year he returned to take over the Consul-Generalship from the ill and exhausted Gorst. This pre-war Kitchener period in Egypt was characterized on the one hand by a series of severe disciplinary measures, on the other by a substantial advance in the system of representation. Possibly only a Sirdar who had led Egyptian soldiers to victory in the Sudan could have succeeded in imposing his restrictions on the Press and the schools and in preserving order during the period of the Italian–Turkish war in Libya in 1912. But he did succeed, and his new constitution of 1913 was a significant step towards self-government. Substantial powers were conferred in local government and, at national level, the Assembly was permitted to suspend or to initiate legislation. Public debate was also allowed. These measures confirmed Saad Zaghloul's desire to co-operate with the British authorities and he accepted the Vice-Presidency of the new Legislative Council.

The outbreak of war and the declaration of a formal British protectorate over Egypt ended abruptly the hopeful Kitchener era. It is arguable that Egyptian political development and the whole course of Anglo-Egyptian relations would have developed differ-

ently if the Great War had not imposed its demands on the
country and if Kitchener himself had not been summoned hastily
to higher office and an early death. Hertzog and his supporters
expressed much the same views about South Africa's involvement
in both the Great War and the Second World War. The Great War
did come, however, and there is much in the view later expressed
by Smuts during the inter-war debates on the Commonwealth and
Empire, that only the response to the acid test of great events allows
judgement as to the true worth or durability of international bonds.
The fact is that "Protectorate" was a hateful word to Egyptian
national sentiment and the new international status was unacceptable. Egypt was in ferment during the years of war and nationalist
leaders entered the era of Wilson and Versailles with a new determination to achieve independence.

Egypt's associated territory, the Sudan, like the associated territories of South Africa, and all the other territories of British Africa
outside Egypt and South Africa, was an area of administration not
politics throughout the period 1904–14. They remained areas of
administration until 1939. This statement in no way implies that
there were not significant political movements or nationalist stir-
rings among Africa's peoples everywhere, whether in the Sudan,
Nyasaland, Nigeria, Uganda, Basutoland or among Africans in
South Africa itself. Such movements have in fact been recorded by
historians and evaluated by political analysts and sociologists, some
of whom have suggested that particular territorial administrations
were seriously at fault in not acknowledging, and acting more
constructively towards, African political and national movements
during both their early and later years of growth. But the fact remains that it was not until after 1945 that African nationalism
became a powerful force in the continent, nor was it until recently
that the various territorial movements achieved organized strength.
Conversely, a necessary prior concern for politics in an essay such
as this should not blind students of the British–African relationship to achievements during the era of administration. The limitation of space does not permit any adequate account of the particular
system of government in any single territory, or detail about the
judiciary, the provincial and district administrations, the police and
army, or the transport, education, health, veterinary, agricultural,
hydrological, forestry, geological and other important services. But
the joint achievements by Britons and Africans working in

partnership in these basic areas of national order, production, welfare and development were of enduring value. The investment of energy in these spheres of endeavour explains in part the relatively slow growth of nationalism. Not until major obstacles to progress such as poor communications, widespread tropical disease and illiteracy were overcome, could regional and national politics prosper.

During the short decade before 1914 the administrations of all territories were engaged in a process of consolidation. It was during this period also that each territory developed a distinctive personality or character which was to endure at least for half a century. Although geography, economic resources, ethnic and cultural composition largely shaped such character it was influenced to some degree by the nature of the Imperial department of state to which each territory was attached. The Foreign Office remained responsible for Egypt and, by virtue of the condominium arrangement, for the Sudan also. South Africa during the period was included with Canada, Australia and New Zealand in the new category of "Dominions" under a section of the Colonial Office. The Rhodesias continued to be governed by the Chartered Company* though with a greater degree of Colonial Office supervision. The remainder of the territories either continued under or were transferred to the Colonial Office's tutelary and trusteeship divisions, which were characterized by a spirit of responsible paternalism, best personified perhaps by Lugard.

The personality of the Sudan acquired a particular flavour during the sixteen years' Governor-generalship of Sir Reginald Wingate, who succeeded Kitchener in 1900. Despite the close ties with Egypt, including a financial subvention which was paid by Egypt to the Sudan until 1913, it was the wish of British administrators in Egypt and the Sudan alike to emphasize the separateness of the Sudan and, among other things, to avoid there the complicated and troublesome system of commercial and judicial privileges and rights enjoyed by different nationalities in Egypt. New river, rail and sea communications contributed to this end. A channel was cut through the Nile Sudd in 1903 and by 1905 the Khartoum–Atbara railway was operating to Port Sudan, where work on the new harbour was begun in 1906. Independent economic advancement was stimulated

---

* Rule by the British South Africa Company ended in Southern Rhodesia in 1923, when the country became a colony under a responsible government constitution; and in Northern Rhodesia in 1924, when a Crown Protectorate was established.

by the introduction of long staple cotton in 1900, by substantial increases in the cotton acreage in 1905, and by successful experiments in the Gezira area after 1911. Wingate's large Gezira loan from the United Kingdom in 1913 helped greatly to assure the country of a reasonably prosperous future. Islam in the Sudan was treated with respect, full recognition being accorded to Muslim law under the Grand Qadi, an Egyptian jurist. Koranic schools continued to occupy an important place in the educational system, but Gordon College, founded in 1902, became increasingly important as the spearhead of modern Western education, and a nursery of nationalism as well as of the civil service. One of the problems of the Sudan at the time was a sense of grievance among Sudanese graduates of Gordon College who objected to the lower and middle ranks of the administrative service being occupied wholly by Egyptians and Lebanese. Not until the mid-twenties were the first Sudanese appointed. Other more general problems concerned the long-continued pacification of the remoter areas such as Darfur, the Nuba Hills and the tribal lands of the Nuer in the far south.

The personality and image of the Sudan which developed during this period was essentially one of the "North", of Islam, of Arabic. That of Uganda, by contrast, was of the "South", of traditional African religions, political systems and languages. The image of Uganda was also centred upon Buganda, the kingdom of the Kabaka, for whose favours, and those of other traditional rulers, Europe's early explorers, missionaries and traders had competed actively during their quest for the source and course of the Nile. The polarity between the northern part of the Sudan and part of the Uganda was never bridged satisfactorily during the colonial era, despite recurrent attempts to deal with the problem of the non-Islamic southern Sudan and its relations with Uganda.

In the early years of the century official attention was riveted on the areas adjoining Lake Victoria. The Lake Victoria Marine Service linked Entebbe and other centres with Kisumu and the coast railway. Economic development was conceived primarily in terms of the lacustrine basin, and of trade through and with Kenya. Indian troops as well as Indian workers and traders came to the Uganda Protectorate—the former played a notable part in suppressing the revolt of Sudanese soldiers of the administration in 1898. It is not surprising therefore that a significant minority of Indians settled in the country and increased in number, as in Kenya and Tanganyika.

White settlement, however, never materialized, even though over the years there were occasional expressions of fear lest European engineers and artisans remain after completing major public works. The great sleeping-sickness epidemic between 1901–4 was an important if not decisive discouragement. Tens of thousands of Africans died from the disease and large areas were evacuated, including extensive tracts ear-marked for agricultural experiment. Uganda's recovery from this disaster and her subsequent development owed much to the immediate and sustained response of British medical scientists and doctors to the challenge of sleeping-sickness and other tropical diseases. The survivors of the epidemic were generously treated and by 1908 a Government Medical Department was in being as a separate division of the administration. In the more directly economic sphere particular support was given to the peasant cultivation of cotton by Sir Hesketh Bell, first Governor under the Colonial Office. So effective was this initiative that Uganda, after 1915, ceased to qualify for United Kingdom grants-in-aid.

Kenya, by contrast with Uganda, was given a determined thrust in the direction of becoming a British "colony of settlement" during the ten years before the First World War. After the Boer War farmers from the South African colonies as well as Britain were encouraged to take up holdings in the more fertile regions along the line of rail. Under the vigorous leadership of Lord Delamere the settlers were soon organized economically and politically through bodies such as their Convention of Associations. They enjoyed the backing of Sir Charles Eliot and other Governors and were regarded and treated as the principal element in the population and the mainspring of the economy. As such they were accorded special consideration over issues of land and labour. African and Asian complaints against such policy did not become articulate or in any way influential until after 1918. On the outbreak of war the European population, then numbering 5,000, supplied a volunteer force which proved of the utmost value, alongside the existing single battalion of the King's African Rifles, in confronting German East Africa until reinforcements arrived from India and South Africa.

Whereas 1944 was the year in which Kenya's first African was appointed to the Legislative Council Africans had been members of West African legislatures since before 1890. This fact is indicative of certain differences in the historical and educational backgrounds of the two zones, the significance of which must be given full weight. It is also necessary, however, to recall that the Western-educated men and women who did so much to create a distinctive British West African personality were largely restricted to particular localities on the coast. Inland from these centres, where there was relatively intensive contact with British administrators and missionaries, and traders and sailors from Merseyside, there were the vast, newly acquired lands where few Britons had ventured. From the viewpoint of all colonial powers there were formidable problems of pacification, not to mention education and development. As in Southern Africa railway construction played a foremost part in facilitating the extension of control and in bringing closer the regions or provinces, though the physical separation of the four colonies prevented the growth of any inter-territorial British West African railway network. At the same time Nigeria alone presented a major challenge of scale. From Lagos and Port Harcourt railways were built inland and by 1911 Kano was linked with Lagos. In Sierra Leone Freetown was joined by rail to the inland Protectorate in 1908. During this period also the Takoradi–Kumasi railway was completed and the produce of the Ashanti gold-fields, forests and cocoa-groves given a more effective outlet.

Below we shall indicate the development of British thought and practice on West African administration. It was in 1922 that Lugard published his influential work *The Dual Mandate in British Tropical Africa.* That study, based on experience in Nigeria as well as in Uganda and elsewhere, provided the leading text on British colonial administration. Until 1914, however, Lugard was grappling with urgent practical problems in the field, not least the problem of uniting under one government Northern Nigeria with the southern regions. This union, like others elsewhere, was in the main formal and administrative. There were great religious and social diversities between the ethnic groups of the regions as well as differences in education and political aspiration. Such diversities provided a principal challenge to British administrators and constitution-makers throughout the next half-century, though it was not until after 1945 that they were adequately recognized and approached with any sense of urgency. Sufficient was done, however, during the years of consolidation to ensure that West Africans from all parts of the four colonies, new and old, inland Muslim and coastal Christian, rallied to the call to arms in 1914.

2

BRITAIN AND AFRICA 1914–39:
WAR AND TRUSTEESHIP

THE First World War was a great historical divide in the story of Britain. In British Africa it was rather the Second World War which brought the end of an epoch. So far as international relations between Britain and the various African territories were concerned, no great or obvious hiatus resulted from the fact that Britain was substantially weakened in wealth and position by the Great War. Britain, relatively, remained rich and powerful, the African dependencies poor and weak. And despite critics like Leonard Woolf, there was sufficient confidence in the colonial mission at the end of the war to ensure support for the principles and practice of trusteeship as enunciated by leaders of the eminence of Milner, Smuts and Lugard.

(i) 1914–18

Although the effects on Africa were not so momentous as on Britain, Africa's experiences during 1914–18 were none the less very important, and sufficient to inaugurate a new phase in the overall relationship. The war drew the British territories of Africa together in a manner which had been unknown before. Soldiers from all parts served as comrades in different theatres. The personality of each territory was deepened by its co-operation with others as well as by its total response to the challenge of conflict. Individuals became aware of themselves as representatives and members of entities greater than their tribe or local area. War-time co-operation also compelled a new appreciation of the resources and problems of the African countries by Britain and by each of the British African territories themselves. Without this experience of the war the relative isolation of the separate countries would probably have persisted and the principal links would have continued to be essentially unilateral between each individual colony or zone and the United Kingdom. The whole tempo of internal social, economic and political change would also have been slower without the spur of war.

All zones of British Africa were engaged directly in local land campaigns during the Great War. Each played its part also in the wider strategy by dealing with enemy installations or equipment which possessed a more than local importance: high-powered radio stations, long-range warships, strategic harbours, facilities for air operations.* The manpower and other resources of each zone were also called upon to make contributions to the principal theatres of conflict in Western Europe and the North Atlantic, and in the eastern and north-eastern Mediterranean.

It is difficult to evaluate the relative worth of the contribution of each zone. East Africa was fully engaged in the campaign against von Lettow from the outbreak of war until after the armistice. First Indians, then South Africans and later West Africans, notably Nigerians, fought in substantial numbers alongside askaris of the King's African Rifles, all being supported throughout by tens of thousands of African carriers during an arduous and costly campaign. From the viewpoint of the Empire of the day however South Africa's response was the most significant. Had the Union defected there would have been serious repercussions for Britain and the Empire in every sector of operations, quite apart from the longer-term political effects on Commonwealth and international relations.

In the event South Africa's overall contribution was substantial, though some 30,000 troops had to be employed until the turn of the year 1914–15 in suppressing the Afrikaner-nationalist rebellion, led among others by the Commander-in-Chief of the Union Defence Force, General Beyers, and Colonel Maritz. Louis Botha, Prime Minister and former Commandant-general of the Burgher forces during the Boer War, was able to leave at the end of January 1915 to conduct a skilful campaign which culminated in the capture of Windhoek in May and the defeat and impounding of the German forces in July. The conquest of German South-West Africa brought together into the field some 60,000. They comprised both English-speaking regiments of the Active Citizen Force and the many Afrikaans-speaking members of rifle commandos who remained loyal to Botha and Smuts. The occupation of Luderitzbucht,

---

* Military aircraft, used by Italy in the conquest of Libya in 1912, were employed to good effect by British forces in several parts of Africa during the 1914–18 war.

and the wider campaign, was undertaken at the request of a hard-pressed Britain.

After South-West Africa 25,000 South African soldiers were dispatched to France, and 50,000 to East Africa, where Smuts in March 1916 was given command in succession to Smith-Dorrien. South African troops were engaged in the advance on German East Africa from both Kenya and Nyasaland. In addition to participating with the Royal Navy and Royal Flying Corps in events such as the trapping of the ocean-raiding battle-cruiser *Königsberg* in the Rufiji River, they gave the closest co-operation to African and Indian soldiers during exacting operations which produced far heavier death rolls from malaria and dysentery than from battle casualties.

Although the gallant von Lettow Vorbeck remained elusive until after the end of the war, not surrendering until November 23, 1918, at Abercorn in Northern Rhodesia, the main operations in Tanganyika were completed in 1917. By that time, when Smuts was sent by Botha to join the Imperial War Cabinet in London, the principal towns and communications were in Allied hands. The majority of white and Indian soldiers were then withdrawn, as much to prevent further heavy losses from tropical disease as to deploy them elsewhere. Van Deventer, South African cavalryman, succeeded Smuts in overall command but the principal tasks remaining in German East Africa were undertaken by twenty-two battalions of the King's African Rifles and by Cunliffe's Nigerian Brigade.

South Africa's main military contributions elsewhere were in the Middle East and France. Apart from minor frontier operations in Egypt's Western Desert the Union Defence Force in the Middle East was engaged primarily in Palestine under Allenby. There were heavy casualties at Gaza, where the Cape Corps, composed of those South Africans of mixed race who are described as "Coloured", fought with notable gallantry. African and Coloured soldiers from South Africa served also in France. Many hundreds of Africans lost their lives when the troopship *Mende* was sunk off Southampton. The main fighting contributions in France were made by men of European descent, chiefly through the South African Infantry Brigade, though many individuals seconded to British formations gained distinction as airmen, sailors and soldiers. Always necessarily marginal, given the size of the great armies ranged against each other, South Africa's expeditionary force nevertheless made its mark on the Western Front. The Infantry Brigade in particular suffered severe casualties and won deserved praise for stubborn actions on the Somme and on the Lys at times when the Allied front was seriously threatened.

Although South Africa's response was specially significant, and though the Union Defence Force was encouraged by Britain to assume a role of leadership in several campaigns on the African continent, the contribution to the war effort by each of the other zones of British Africa was substantial. In West Africa the Gold Coast Regiment dealt promptly with Togoland, silencing the Kamina radio transmitter which was of special importance in the German network of Imperial communications. Mountainous, forested Kamerun offered more serious resistance. The valuable deep-water harbour of Douala fell to the Royal Navy in September 1914 but it took a further $1\frac{1}{2}$ years hard campaigning by Nigerian, Gold Coast, Gambian, West Indian and Indian troops before the resourceful Colonel Zimmermann left the field to evade capture by seeking sanctuary, with his force, in the Spanish colony of Rio Muni. West African troops were thereupon freed to prepare for their new responsibilities in German East Africa.

African soldiers from all Britain's Central and East African territories, including Northern Rhodesia, proved themselves in modern battle against the well-trained white soldiers and askaris of the German East African forces. The King's African Rifles, from the 1st Battalion in Nyasaland to the other battalions in Kenya and Uganda, earned the prestige which, during the inter-war years, encouraged British officers to compete for secondment from leading United Kingdom regiments. General Hoskins, Inspector-General of the K.A.R. before his transfer to Palestine, was perhaps accorded insufficient recognition for his achievement in welding an effective force from so many diverse peoples and territories.

The good discipline and morale of his men was also highly prized subsequently by the civil administrations to whom many went on retirement as messengers and clerks. The loyalty and devotion of the carriers, properly symbolized in the askari war memorial in Nairobi, has been indicated already. Such African auxiliaries, both in support of the army and on the farms, greatly reduced demands on Imperial shipping and other resources and made possible the effective conduct of operations. Karen Blixen's writings convey something of the atmosphere of Kenya's first major war-time effort, an effort which was echoed again when Mussolini threatened in 1939–45. She, together with other European women on their scattered farms in both Kenya and Rhodesia, were directly involved alongside their men, who displayed singular ability and courage as individual scouts or members of reconnaissance units.

Egypt's manpower contribution was substantial. Tens of thousands of Egyptians were recruited to the British forces as soldiers and auxiliaries and Allenby, among others, wrote well of them. They were always subordinate, however, a fact which many resented then as during the Second World War. The immense strategic significance of the country ensured the presence throughout the war of a large standing British army. Seventy thousand British troops were available in Egypt at the beginning of 1915, one-third of a million later. Whether it would have been better to defend positions such as the "Kitchener Line", ten miles to the east of the Canal, against Kress von Kressenstein and his Turks, rather than to embark on costly campaigns such as the advance on Jerusalem in 1917 is a question to be debated by the rival military historians. To them too must be left estimations of the relative military merits of the various African campaigns, and those of Gallipoli and Salonika, as against a concentration of all available manpower and resources on the Western Front. There is point, however, in emphasizing Egypt's historic role in providing a meeting-place for soldiers of the British Empire from every continent, a role which was repeated within twenty-five years.

The Great War confirmed in the minds of Britain's leaders the strategic importance of its bases in Egypt and South Africa and the value of being able to summon forces from the east of Suez, whether from South Africa up the western shores of the Indian Ocean or across from the Indian sub-continent itself. Aden, Mombasa and Durban acquired fresh significance in Imperial defence plans as a result of the use made of these harbours; Port Sudan, Berbera, East London and Port Elizabeth also. On the west coast between Simonstown and Portsmouth, Freetown remained important and the value of lesser harbours such as Walvis Bay and Luderitzbucht on a long and difficult coast was emphasized, especially after the decision to transfer Douala to the French. South Africa's potential as an Imperial arsenal and source of supply was also made more apparent by the realities of war. Though Egypt was a base for stores, South Africa's industrial and agricultural resources made possible a substantial expansion of secondary industry, especially the manufacture of arms and food. To Imperial leaders there was no question but that Egypt must remain under British control even though a substantial military garrison might be required. In self-governing South Africa on the other hand Botha, Smuts, and co-operative Afrikaners as a whole, in company with British South Africans, plainly suggested themselves as the party for Britain to back against Hertzog and Malan.

Whether the remainder of Africa might better have been insulated from involvement in the war is an academic question. Lugard and others might speculate with misgiving on the possible consequences of employing Africans in campaigns where they "learned to kill white men", but many Africans did participate as combatant soldiers and many others from the great heart of the continent were directly involved in modern warfare at home and abroad. In the event Lugard's several particular fears, including the effect on Nigeria's northern emirates of a war against the Islamic Turkish Empire, proved unfounded. For most indigenous Africans in colonial Africa the Great War served principally to compel them abruptly to take note of the reality of the new territorial divisions of their continent and to learn somehing of the nature of the metropolitan régimes to which they had so recently become subject. There were African leaders in each zone thinking in terms of national and international politics, and who were initiating wider political movements, but they were few and the experiences of the First War served chiefly to hasten the education of their future followers.

(ii) 1918–39: TRUSTEESHIP

There is a case for subdividing the inter-war years at about 1929 and treating separately the decades before and after the World Depression, Japan's attack on Manchuria, Hitler's rapid rise to power and alliance with Mussolini. These world events had their pronounced effect on Africa. In terms of purely domestic politics also the Labour Government, with Sidney Webb as Colonial Secretary, initiated certain new tendencies in British African policy. There is nevertheless sufficient unity about the period to warrant treating it as a whole. Throughout these twenty years the dominant attitude towards Africa among all non-African peoples favoured or accepted the continuance of colonial tutelage or rule. This was true of Arabs, Indians and Japanese as well as Europeans and Americans.

This prevalent attitude found expression in many ways. President

Wilson's principle of immediate ethnic autonomy or self-rule for the constituent peoples of the Austro-Hungarian empire was not extended beyond Europe. Outside Africa the Philippines remained under colonial rule and, though Liberia preserved a nominal autonomy, its survival was frankly bolstered by the United States. The fate of Ethiopia in 1936 is also instructive. There was genuine regret but little more over the West's desertion of Haile Selassie. Africa was regarded as being of subsidiary importance during the power confrontations of the mid-thirties, and a proper source of pawns in the politics of appeasement. There was, furthermore, at the time, as there is indeed still in historical literature of today, an unquestioning acceptance of the superiority of Western imperial rule even in this most ancient of Africa's independent states.

The concept of a hierarchy of "races", with the "Caucasoid" or "European" at the top, Asians and Arabs in between, and the "Negroid" or Africans at the bottom, was widespread among Western thinkers. This thought found particularly clear expression in the trusteeship provisions of the covenant of the League of Nations. The Arab peoples formerly subject to the Turkish empire were regarded as substantially more mature than those of sub-Saharan Africa. For them there could be a shorter period of tutelage by the "advanced" nations entrusted with mandates. But for the "backward" races of Lord Lugard, the "child" races of General Smuts or the "non-adult" races of Leonard Woolf a very much longer period would be required before they could hope to "stand on their own feet under the strenuous conditions of the modern world". It is suggestive of the strength of social-evolutionist thought that a principal socialist critic of imperialism like Leonard Woolf should have accepted so completely the conception of a racial hierarchy.

So far as the Commonwealth was concerned, as a separate entity in international relations, the prevalent hierarchical thought of the victorious Western powers was also manifest. The Wilsonian emphases on autonomy or national and cultural freedom for Central Europe were proclaimed by Smuts in respect of the Afrikaners, French Canadians and Irish in his famous speech on the Commonwealth of Nations to a joint meeting of the House of Lords and House of Commons on April 15, 1917. These principles, however, were sounded neither by him, nor by other Imperial leaders, for the non-Western peoples, not even on behalf of India, though there was warm and widespread acknowledgement of the major Indian contribution to the Empire war effort. Certainly there was an immediate study of Indian constitutional reform which initiated the series of commissions and political adjustments which characterized British–Indian relations between the wars and culminated in the Government of India Act of 1935. But India remained subject to British over-rule throughout the period, a fact important for British power in Africa, and significant also for the position of the Indian minorities resident in British Eastern and Southern Africa.

For Britain's dependencies in Africa, as for the indigenous African majority in South Africa, there was general acceptance of the need for thorough-going paternalistic tutelage. Lugard and Smuts'* the two dominant influences on British African policy, were at one in supporting the concepts of the "dual mandate" and "trusteeship" which provided an ethical foundation for the Western presence and supremacy throughout the continent. Africa must be developed for the benefit of the world, Africa's peoples must be advanced to participate in and to benefit from such development.

There were different views on particular methods of African rule, on the organization of separate administrations, and on the review and supervision of policy and practice. There were also at times substantial criticisms of abuses such as the operation of particular colour bars or the neglect of the other protective duties of a trustee. But even liberal Western critics did not foresee the possibility of an immediate termination of their overall responsibility. Members of the enlightened Hilton Young Commission which reported on East and Central Africa in 1929 were in no sense unusual in seeing no early prospect of any African, as distinct from a missionary or other spokesman, entering the Legislative Council to represent African interests. Such assumptions were noted and their institutional expressions analysed in the masterly survey conducted in the thirties by Lord Hailey, who joined Smuts and Lugard as a foremost British authority on African affairs. Hailey's comparative analysis, published in 1938, together with his subsequent separate volumes on *Native Administration*, provide the most complete picture of the areas of administration of British Africa and the philosophy which governed their rule.

Trusteeship principles were extended also to the former German possessions which were incorporated under the different categories of mandate. In West Africa Britain received portions of Togo and Kamerun, in East Africa Tanganyika. To South Africa was given

* See Hancock, W. K. *Smuts* for definitive biography.

South-West Africa as a "C" class mandate which might be administered as an integral part of the Union. South Africa's exercise of trusteeship was to be questioned sharply by India after 1945, and further attacks mounted as the United Nations acquired more Asian and African members, but during the inter-war years there was relatively little criticism. Apart from adding fresh areas of administration to British Africa the ex-German possessions were perhaps notable for providing at last an "all-red" route between the Cape and Cairo. Not until the mid-thirties was the Versailles parcelling out of German Africa between Britain, France, Belgium and South Africa threatened by Hitler, and only after Mussolini's Ethiopian conquest was the actual pattern of colonies disturbed. As a significant subsidiary thread in the new web of relationships brought about by the mandates, there is point in recalling Smuts's personal interest in Palestine and the contribution of South African Jews to the development of a Jewish national home.

Smuts's pre-eminence assured South Africa of a prominent place in British thought and a major, possibly a disproportionate, influence on African policy. South Africa's geographical position, material wealth and other attributes would have assured her always of real importance, but Smuts personally added a significant and, at times, a decisive dimension. His romantic past and his striking personality which impressed Lloyd George, Churchill, Amery and an extraordinary diverse cross-section of Britons, were coupled with a record of distinguished and efficient service within the United Kingdom itself, as well as in the "remoter marches of the Empire". His personal loyalty to Botha and his inheritance of Botha's political mantle on the latter's death in 1919, confirmed his already strong position in the councils of Britain and the Empire-Commonwealth.

Smuts's views on the organization of the Commonwealth prevailed against those of Curtis, a former member of Milner's kindergarten, and the Imperial Federationists, who sought above all a common policy for the whole association; his memoranda on the League of Nations and international trusteeship were largely accepted and supported by Britain, and during his recurrent visits to Britain he was invited by the universities and other eminent associations to pronounce upon central issues of world peace, democracy and government. The authority thus gained reinforced his observations on African policy, whether he was in office or in opposition to Hertzog and Malan. The book *Africa and Some World Problems* published in 1929 provides a convenient source

of his principal views. And it was Smuts who, in 1932, initiated
Hailey's *African Survey* through the Royal Institute of International Affairs.

South Africa's relationship with the United Kingdom until 1939,
and indeed until 1948, can therefore be seen very much in terms
of the fortunes of one man. The territorial canvas can be stretched
also to embrace Southern Rhodesia, for throughout this time her
responsible Government leaders, most notably Sir Godfrey Huggins
(Lord Malvern), were at one with Smuts on major issues.* The
wisdom of Britain's over-reliance on one man has been questioned,
especially since it clouded the perception, and prevented the understanding of Southern Africa's internal problems, but it is nevertheless essential to focus upon Smuts. His relations with Hertzog and
the whole ebb and flow of politics between the overwhelmingly
"European" or white political parties governed South Africa's
destiny. Though urgent questions of "race relations" were ever-
present, Africans, Asians and Coloureds were mainly excluded
deliberately, and by the agreement of all politicians, from "the
arena of party politics"—and power. Disputes over "Non-
Europeans" between the parties turned primarily upon their administration, not their alliance.

South Africa's ties with Britain and her liabilities as a member
of the Commonwealth, the position of white workers in the advancing industrial economy, and the response of the country to the great
economic depression were the main issues in white politics between
the wars. Inevitably these issues touched all peoples and communities and every aspect of national life but little attention was
paid to the African, Coloured and Indian congresses and trade
unions.

Smuts's support for "Crown and Commonwealth" supplied the
main ground for Afrikaner-nationalist charges against him. His
cool response to Lloyd George's exuberant appeal to South Africa
—and to Canada, Australia and New Zealand—for armed support
in the Middle East in 1922 weighed little against his emphatic
personal advocacy of the Crown as the indispensable cohesive
element of the Commonwealth. (Regular consultation on a basis of
equality between the member nations was his second main principle.) Neither did his friendship with Quakers and other humani-
tarians in Britain who had upheld the Boer cause save him from

* See Gann, L. H., and Gelfand, M. *Huggins of Rhodesia. The Man and His
Country* (London 1964), especially pp. 154–5.

D

heated attack as the lackey of imperialism. When Smuts's government was overwhelmed in 1924 by a republican–socialist coalition comprising Hertzog–Malan Nationalists and Creswell–Madeley Labourites the way was open for Hertzog to press upon Britain his demands for the definition of "Dominion status" in such fashion as to make plain South Africa's independence and her right to be neutral in time of war.

To the resultant declaration of the Imperial Conference of 1926, which stated the principles of full autonomy and complete equality, there was added in 1931 the Statute of Westminster. Naturally neither document afforded the absolute assurance which Hertzog sought that South Africa would not again be drawn into Britain's wars. Nor could that aim be achieved by domestic laws and measures, such as the Status of the Union Act of 1934, which Hertzog felt impelled to enact at a time when Smuts was restored to the Government as his deputy in a fresh coalition. Hertzog's only effective course was to combat Smuts's pro-Commonwealth views at every point and to appoint to key ministries, such as Defence, individuals like Oswald Pirow who shared his sympathy for Germany and his desire for neutrality in European affairs.

The "civilized labour" policy of the Hertzog administration provided the principal basis for co-operation between the Afrikaner-nationalists and the predominantly British South African Labour Party. The Nationalists, dependent upon a rural electorate, were always conscious of the plight of the Afrikaans-speaking tenant-farmers and squatters known generally as the "poor whites". When their impoverishment drove them in increasing numbers to the towns their economic and social protection became an urgent concern of their politico-religious leaders. Special welfare measures, such as subsidized wages, housing and health services, were demanded for the poor whites and it was urged that they be given priority in employment over Africans, Asians and Coloureds. Although the English-speaking worker was traditionally better placed than the Afrikaner, through being skilled in the crafts, commerce and other predominantly urban pursuits, his fears had been aroused by the tendency of the mining corporations and other large-scale employers, during and immediately after the war, to introduce lower-paid African and Coloured workers into posts previously regarded as the province of Europeans. Resistant as they were to the lowering of craft standards and the dilution of their trade unions by the unskilled, newly urbanized Afrikaners, most English-speaking workers were even more afraid of the African movement into the cities and towns.

Smuts's suppression of the industrial strike on the Witwatersrand in 1922, an action which included the use of troops and military aircraft against ex-servicemen workers, and the hanging of the white labour leaders Hull, Lewis and Long, provoked the deep and abiding bitterness which found political expression in the sweeping electoral successes of the South African Labour Party in coalition with Hertzog in 1924. Thereafter, until the 1929 "split" of the Labour Party and the economic collapse of the Western world, the South African parliament enacted a series of frankly discriminatory labour and welfare measures aimed at protecting the white workers. The Mines and Works Amendment Act of 1926, more generally known as the "Colour Bar" Act, is the most-quoted piece of dis-criminatory legislation of the period but it was only one such measure. Of particular significance to the British–South African relationship is the fact that the protection afforded by such laws and regulations was regarded by Afrikaner-nationalists and English-speaking workers as being against the British capitalist-imperialist supporters of Smuts as well as against their potential local com-petitors.

The relations of the political parties were dramatically changed by the economic depression and the "gold standard" crisis. Unem-ployment affected all classes and races and the financial collapse brought ruin to many employers and professional families. The economic and commercial knowledge and skills of English-speaking South Africans and the established links with the "City" of London and comparable centres were essential to rapid recovery. Though Smuts's tolerance of the "republican principle" in the constitution of the new United South African National Party* offended many South Africans of British origin, Smuts did not hesitate to become deputy to Hertzog in the fight for economic survival. In the elec-tions of 1933 and 1938 the new coalition party won overwhelming victories against the right-wing pro-Empire Dominion Party of Colonel Stallard and the right-wing pro-Republican party of Dr. Malan. Not until the fateful parliamentary division of September 6, 1939, was there a substantial political re-alignment.

The narrow majority by which South Africa entered the war alongside Britain was secured by the supporters of Smuts and Stal-lard together with the few surviving parliamentary representatives

* Known generally as the United Party.

of the South African Labour Party, notably Christie and Madeley, and the three "Cape Native Representatives". The latter of whom Dr. Margaret Ballinger is best known, were the first members elected under the Representation of Natives Act, 1936, which, together with a revised rural land law, and an amended urban areas Act, expressed Hertzog's policy towards Africans. A few minor compromises had been made during ten years of preparation but the legislation which was finally enacted embodied the substance of Hertzog's "Native Bills" of 1926.

Segregation between African and non-African in all possible spheres, notably ownership of property, residence, employment, the franchise and other civic rights, was the central objective. Although Smuts professed to set great store by the Natives Representative Council which he opened in 1937, it was purely an advisory body which met under the chairmanship of the senior civil servant responsible for "Native Affairs". And though the three representatives of Africans in the House of Assembly and the four in the Senate co-operated closely with the able African councillors and proved themselves exceptionally worthy they suffered always from the fact that the constitution required them to be persons of European descent, that is "white". Africans with modern education, including graduates from the "open" universities of the Witwatersrand and Cape Town, from Fort Hare and other African colleges, understandably felt that they had no voice in national policy. Despite minor administrative concessions they were grouped with their tribal fellows and untutored workers under the "Supreme Chief"—otherwise the Governor-General—in terms of authority deriving from the Native Administration Act of 1927. This measure, which also gave limited recognition to Native Law throughout South Africa, owed much to colonial precedent in Natal, though the growing prestige of Lugardism in British Colonial Africa, where the conditions were very different, was drawn upon to justify certain of its elements.

South Africa's Indian peoples and her Coloureds and Malays were likewise largely segregated from the main currents of political life. Those in the Cape continued to benefit from the non-racial traditions of the Province and preserved their common franchise rights when the Africans were transferred to a separate communal roll in 1936. There were also special efforts made by the Government to improve the lot of the Coloured people who filled an intermediary position in the economic and social structure. The

Indian people of Natal, however, were subjected to increasing disabilities. Unlike the Coloured people, for whom responsibility was acknowledged, Indians were regarded as "unassimilable aliens". Their local government franchise was removed and every pressure mounted to restrict within defined areas their ownership of property. Under the Malan–Sastri Agreement, signed at Cape Town between Hertzog's deputy and the Agent-General of the Government of India, an attempt was initiated to encourage and assist South Africa's Indian population to return to India. In the event very few individuals elected to be repatriated, or "expatriated", as Indians prefer, and increasing emphasis was placed by Indian Congress and other leaders on the "uplift clauses" of the Agreement, which stipulated that educational and other benefits were to accrue to the Indians who were, henceforth, to be treated as an integral part of the permanent population of South Africa.

Smuts was Britain's principal "internal trustee", and the Union the most significant area in British or Commonwealth Africa in which locally resident Europeans were responsible for governing not themselves only but substantial majorities of Africans also, together with important minorities of Indian and other peoples. But north of the Union there were Huggins and his associates in Southern Rhodesia and Delamere* and Cavendish-Bentinck and their associates in Kenya.

Both territories were set in vast areas of British Central and East Africa and in both there was a conscious aim to build up an "officer-class" of British settlers who would supply leadership in times of peace and war. No formal political unification of the East and Central African territories resulted, or of Central Africa alone, despite certain efforts in this direction in the late twenties and late thirties, but between Smuts, Huggins and Cavendish-Bentinck there developed a real understanding which was greatly facilitated by the growth of air services in the thirties. On major issues confronting Britain and the Commonwealth in Africa, leaders of opinion, including British High Commissioners, colonial Governors and other senior civil servants, could meet readily. In this way the Pretoria–Salisbury–Nairobi axis achieved a reality which, always important, proved of the utmost significance during times of international crisis such as Germany's demand for the restoration of her colonies, the conquest of Ethiopia, and the Second World War.

In their approach to administration there was an essential

* Lord Delamere died in 1931.

similarity in principle and method between Kenya, Southern Rhodesia and South Africa. Given the common overall objective of developing countries for European settlement, as well as the historical links between the territories, it was to be expected that institutions and practices developed in the older south, notably in the Cape and Natal in the nineteenth century, would be adopted in the north. Areas for white farmers were alienated, reservations for Africans were demarcated. African chiefs, elders and other traditional authorities were given relatively limited recognition in these reserved areas and frank pressures and inducements continued to be applied to encourage Africans to supply labour to European farmers, miners and townsmen.

There was little serious thought of African participation in politics. The principle of the common voters' roll, rather than communal representation, was given some theoretical approval in Southern Rhodesia, but on the clear understanding that only very slowly over the decades might small numbers of educated and carefully selected men of other races be added to the European electors. In Southern Rhodesia the Europeans were given effective control of affairs in 1923, after they had opted in 1922 for responsible self-government. In Kenya no formal transfer of political control was made but, until the war, and several years afterwards, very substantial power lay in the hands of the settled Europeans.

From Kenya into Tanganyika, and from the south across the Zambesi into Northern Rhodesia and Nyasaland, British "settler" influence extended and strengthened itself during the period under review. The distribution of Europeans was patchy, being confined to specific mining and farming areas in Tanganyika, Northern Rhodesia and Nyasaland, as also in Swaziland and Bechuanaland, but settler influence was real, especially since it was to local Europeans that the home and local governments looked first for productive enterprises which would advance the territorial economies and improve imperial trade. After Ottawa, when "Empire preference" gained fresh stimulus, European producers in Africa acted in an atmosphere of strong approval for endeavours which promised to assist the recovery of Britain, the Commonwealth and the world from economic collapse. In the areas in which they were chiefly present—for example, along the line of rail, or in the new Copper Belt towns of Northern Rhodesia—the predominance of Europeans became as marked as it was in Kenya or Southern Rhodesia.

The Indian communities of British East and Central Africa pro-

vided successive Imperial governments with the same challenge
that those in South Africa were offering to Smuts and Hertzog.
What civic rights, economic opportunities and social benefits were
to be granted to these useful, yet culturally exclusive, peoples whose
main functions were seen as auxiliary to those of the Europeans
and Africans? As in South Africa the Indians rejected a communal
approach which would differentiate them in matters of franchise,
property ownership and the like. They sought a genuine common
electoral roll in Kenya and access to the "White Highlands", demands which alarmed the local Europeans who were outnumbered,
but demands which it was difficult to refuse without giving affront
to the Government and peoples of India. In the event escape was
found in the formulae of trusteeship, notably in the principle of the
"paramountcy" of the interests of the African wards for whom
primary responsibility was acknowledged by the joint trustees—the
United Kingdom and Britons in Africa. Special recognition might
be afforded to Indians, Arabs, Coloureds, Goans, Somalis and other
minorities in the "plural societies" but the principal groups in
matters of policy and development were the Europeans and the
Africans.

Most non-Africans were concentrated in or near the towns. In
the vast areas of East and Central Africa away from the towns,
mines and European farms the administration of the African
peoples was brought increasingly into conformity with the principles of Lugardism. There were some educated Africans, graduates
of Makerere and other Colleges, but far fewer than in South and
West Africa, and the respective governments were not faced as yet
with any major problem of reconciling the interests of African
modernists and traditionalists. In rural Kenya among peoples like
the Masai and Kikuyu it was difficult, quite apart from any settler
influences, to devise a system of "indirect rule" on classical lines in
the absence of "pyramidal" tribal political structures. Authority
was diffused among elders and age-sets, not concentrated in chiefs
and councillors.

Elsewhere, however, notably in Uganda and Tanganyika,
Lugardism became more deeply entrenched as official doctrine.
Uganda with its multiplicity of traditional monarchies provided a
fertile field. Sir Donald Cameron, one of Lugard's lieutenants in
Nigeria, developed Lugard's principles with enthusiasm when he
was transferred as Governor to the mandated territory of Tanganyika, a move which could scarcely fail to win approval from the

Permanent Mandates Commission on which Lugard served for so long as the expert British representative.

From Tanganyika southwards official doctrine radiated into Northern Rhodesia and Nyasaland, where it took root in the thirties and lapped over into Bechuanaland, Basutoland and Swaziland. At Oxford and other shrines colonial service officers on study leave from these territories were initiated into the mysteries of the trinity of executive, judicial and financial elements by high-priests of the cult. The science of anthropology was invoked in support of indirect rule, Rattray's *Ashanti* and Edwin Smith's *The Golden Stool* being widely quoted as texts.

It is a very real and important question whether more critical appraisals of indirect rule, especially the applicability of its precepts in different practical contexts, might not have encouraged greater realism and flexibility, and better overall preparation of the several British African territories for modern economic and political advancement and eventual self-government. As it was, throughout East and Central Africa, and in the Sudan as well as the High Commission Territories, forms of "tribalism" were given the powerful support of the United Kingdom Government and its various agents.

In contrast with Victorian liberal emphases on rights for the individual without regard for race, colour and creed, Lugardism placed value upon the ethnic collectivity, whether in restricted local area, province, region or state. One result was that Africans under "indirect rule" were schooled in administrative and political institutions very different from those of their fellows in areas where "direct rule" prevailed and they tended to develop a different set of political expectations. This point was not sufficiently appreciated by those in Britain and Africa who in the early 1950's forced Northern Rhodesia and Nyasaland into federal union with Southern Rhodesia.

In West Africa, where Lugardism was deeply embedded, the theory of indirect rule was increasingly subjected to fresh appraisal though little was done until after 1945. C. L. Temple, an early critic and one of Lugard's senior lieutenants in Nigeria, received short shrift from his master, a reaction which was perhaps understandable in the immediate aftermath of acquisition. More trenchant, and more urgent, were the views of analysts of the late thirties such as W. M. MacMillan who, though sometimes insensitive to cultural factors, were eager to see modern economic advance. They were chiefly disturbed lest the bolstering of traditional rulers like the Asantehene in the Gold Coast and the Emirs of Northern Nigeria might inhibit the development of the overall economies of the territories.

In Sierra Leone also, modernist critics of indirect rule backed the Creoles whom they regarded as those best endowed by education and experience to supply local leadership. But the warnings of men like MacMillan were largely unheeded. While, in the "plural societies" of East, Central and South Africa, trustees such as Smuts, failed to provide adequately for educated Africans, so too in West Africa Lugardism was seriously defective in its failure to combine in one system the values of progress with those of tradition. Several of Lugard's observations on educated and enterprising Africans were as insensitive and harsh as were those on the "Babus" of India or on partially Westernized Asians and Africans elsewhere.

This serious defect apart, much was achieved by the administrations in British West Africa during the inter-war years. There was no dramatic progress, constitutionally, economically or socially. Nor could there be, given the assumptions of the day concerning the colonial relationship. Lord Passfield initiated a Colonial Development Fund in 1929 but it was essentially a token for the future. There were on the other hand no disturbances or political movements on a scale sufficient to alarm the authorities. Anti-Lebanese riots occurred in Freetown in the aftermath of the 1914–18 war, the Aba Tax riots in Nigeria took place in 1929, and there were from time to time until the mid-thirties uneasy relations with the Asantehene and his supporters in Ashanti. Perhaps the most significant portent was the "Cocoa Hold-up" of 1938 in which the Gold Coast producers demonstrated a marked capacity for combined action, against the advice of the Administration and the opposition of the wholesale companies. But this impressive act took place on the eve of war and it was not until 1948 that the Accra riots and disturbances inaugurated a wholly new approach on the part of the Imperial Government.

Politically the "Guggisberg constitution", introduced into the Gold Coast in 1925, reflected the thought of an enlightened West African Governor. The elective principle was introduced for the first time. Nine of fourteen African unofficials in a legislature of twenty-nine were elected: one from each of the coastal towns, Accra, Cape Coast, Sekondi; the other six from the newly established Provincial Councils, comprising the Chiefs of the "Colony" or the southern region. But no Africans from Ashanti and none from the north were included. Senior British commissioners for these regions were associated with the Governor in his councils but there were no effective political exchanges between elected representatives. Only in 1946 was Ashanti united to the south within the framework of the Legislative Council, only in 1951 the Northern Territories. Essentially the same principles of organization and similar regional divisions characterized the other West African territories. Much the same timing applied also, for only after the war were significant steps taken to bring together the separate "colonies", "protectorates", or regions.

Contact and exchanges there were, nevertheless, principally in market and work places and in the secondary schools and colleges. The vigorous West African Press also played its part in helping to extend awareness beyond the confines of the powerful "Native Administrations". A penchant for the independent liberal professions of law and medicine brought West Africans to the Inns of Court in London and to professional schools elsewhere in Britain and the United States. Increasingly during the inter-war years such professional men, notably the lawyers, gave depth to discussions on the colonial relationship. Several became prominent in the political organizations which were formed, chiefly in the thirties. The tone of such bodies, however, was generally moderate, liberal or gradualist in contrast with the more radical, militant and revolutionary movements which came into being after 1945. The prevailing mood was one which placed value on education and in which individuals found outlet through their school, college and professional careers. Fraser and Aggrey of Achimota were leading educationists and with their colleagues at Fourah Bay, the missionary Colleges of Lagos and other centres, enjoyed the sustained support of influential bodies in Britain and the United States, support which received an important impetus from the Phelps–Stokes Education Commissions of the 1920's.

In the Anglo-Egyptian part of the Sudan, across from Northern Nigeria, on the Pilgrims' route to Mecca, the inter-war years of administration were characterized by much the same thought and actions as were found in the other parts of British Africa south of the Sahara. Britain had come to terms with Islam in her West African territories, the Nigerian Emirs were among the best paid of Africa's rulers and they were insulated in their exercise of power, including their control of Islamic courts administering the Maliki code. In the Sudan too there was a similar emphasis on traditional Islamic authorities. Ordinances were promulgated in the late twenties giving powers to Sheikhs in the urban as well as the rural areas. The conservative tendency was also made evident in the formulation of policy for the southern, non-Islamic areas. Though no actual merging of the south with Uganda was attempted it was largely isolated from the north, and increasing attention was devoted to the structure of authority among the several different peoples and tribes and to a study of the functioning of their little-known social systems. Professor Evans-Pritchard's books on the Nuer and the Azande were notable contributions.

The major activities of government in the Sudan took place in the technological and economic spheres. Communications were improved and surveyors and hydrologists provided the data required for fundamental economic planning. The Gezira cotton scheme benefited especially from scientific research and by 1925 it was fully established as the mainspring of the economy. Typical of the Britons who gave whole-hearted loyalty and service to the Sudan was Arthur Gaitskell.* The world economic depression struck a severe blow but the sound social and economic foundations of the Gezira project ensured its rapid contribution to the revival. In the educational and medical spheres also much work of enduring value was accomplished. Gordon College, despite the rejection of Currie's enlightened conceptions and the substitution of a narrow, restrictive system which alienated educated Sudanese, continued as the principal educational centre. Some important teacher-training ventures were launched. In the south Christian missions continued to bear the main responsibilities for education and medical care and steadily expanded their work.

But although there were resemblances to Nigeria and West Africa, and though much of great and lasting merit was achieved by British administrators, the overall situation of the Sudan differed significantly from that of Nigeria. Senior British policy makers and local officials might share with Lugard a recollection of rule through princes in India and a desire for a similar system throughout Africa, but the political milieu in North Africa—as indeed in South Africa —allowed no more than a partial implementation in the Sudan of the principles of Lugardism. Political pressures, notably those of nationalism, operated more forcefully in countries fronting on the Mediterranean and Arabia than in those facing the Gulf of Guinea. Conservative Muslim rulers in British West Africa might welcome

* See his *The Gezira: a story of development in the Sudan* (London, 1959).

British over-rule but the Muslims of the Nile Valley, rulers and followers, aspired to an early independence.

The form of Sudan independence, whether it was to be in association with or separate from Egypt, was the central point of dispute between the Sudanese nationalists. It bore upon all questions of tactics and timing in relations with Britain and with local British administrations. Support for the alternatives naturally varied also according to local and international events. There were times when the tide flowed strongly in favour of independence for a united Nile Valley. Ali Abd Al-Latif's White Flag League, founded in 1924, accepted the need for co-operation with Egyptian nationalism if British rule was to be overthrown. But significant ebbs occurred in such feeling, especially when Egypt accepted Sudanese exclusion from Anglo-Egyptian negotiations over matters of common vital interest. Sudanese were incensed when they were not involved in the Nile Waters Agreement of 1929. Quite as strong, and even more sophisticated, were reactions when Sudanese representatives were not consulted before the signing of the 1936 Anglo-Egyptian Treaty. Ismail Al-Azhari was able in February 1938 to establish the famous "Graduates General Congress" as a new and potentially formidable local political force. Relatively few Sudanese had been able, like Al-Azhari, to study at the American University of Beirut but there was cohesion and determination among all Gordon College men.

The Sudan Defence Force proved a much more effective military instrument for Britain than the Egyptian army in the 1939–45 war. Sudanese soldiers were determined and hard-hitting in actions against Mussolini's forces in Eritrea and Ethiopia. It was from Khartoum that the Emperor Haile Selassie set out to play his part in the restoration of his empire. In contrast with the Egyptian army the excellent morale and fighting-spirit of the Sudanese was painfully evident, a fact which was not lost upon Egyptian officers of the calibre of General Neguib and Colonel Nasser.

Some of the reasons for the apathy and reluctance of Egyptians are not difficult to suggest. So far as the army and civil service are concerned, it is just possible that Egyptian service morale might have been higher if Egyptian officers had continued to be employed in the Anglo-Egyptian Sudan between 1924 and 1939. But after the murder in Cairo in 1924 of Sir Lee Stack, Sirdar of the Sudan as well as Commander-in-Chief of Egypt's forces, Egyptians were summarily swept from the service of the condominium. Sudanese officers might be obliged to swear allegiance to the King of Egypt, and the flag of Egypt fly beside the Union Jack, but there was little substance underlying such ritual and symbol. British pre-eminence in the Sudan was a constant affront to Egyptian suscepti-bilities.

In Egypt itself British dominance likewise continued almost unabated until 1939; the Anglo-Egyptian Treaty of 1936 was signed too close to the war to permit the growth of any substantial sense of independence. Zaghloul, like South Africa's Hertzog, had appealed at Versailles for recognition of the independent nation-hood of his country, a status accorded to the Hedjaz, Ethiopia and Liberia, but Egypt was deemed too important to Britain, the British Empire and the Dominions to be allowed anything more than the strictly qualified independence which she was granted in terms of the British Declaration of 1922, and by the complementary Egyptian constitution of the following year. Thus though the Wafd secured in 1924 an electoral victory which was as complete as that of Hertzog's nationalists in South Africa in the same year, the powers of the Egyptian parliament were limited and there was for Egypt no question of equality or autonomy of the kind defined in the 1926 Declaration of Dominion status.

In Egypt there was no Smuts, nor any forceful man approximat-ing to Smuts in stature to give the country a decisive lead. Zaghloul, incensed by the brusque authoritarianism of military occupation in time of war, bore some resemblance to Hertzog, but there was no man of comparable eminence committed to a pro-British position in the manner of Smuts. The "loyal Dutch" of the Cape and Natal had few if any counterparts on the lower Nile. Egypt was neverthe-less deeply divided politically between those who supported the King and his associates, and those who favoured the nationalists in parliament. The triangle of forces in Egyptian politics embraced the royalists and the parliamentarians, with Britain occupying the apex position as the occupying power.

The royalists might have been more effective had the people been happier with Fuad, first Sultan to become king. But he was viewed always as an alien and it was not until the seventeen-year-old Farouk came to the throne in 1936 that Egyptians felt that they had a king of their own. Though popular with the people, however, Farouk achieved little harmony of understanding with Nahas Pasha and the other leaders of the Wafd who took over after Zaghloul's death in 1927. The Muslim Brotherhood, similar in many respects to the Afrikaner *Broederbond*, played their part in affairs from behind the scenes.

The uneasy relations between Britain and Egypt were eased in some degree after the outbreak of the Ethiopian War in 1935. The importance of Egyptian goodwill became as apparent as the need to preserve the Suez Canal in friendly hands. Britain sponsored Egypt's membership of the League of Nations in 1937 and though the rejection of Haile Selassie's pleas for effective international action had done nothing to give confidence in the organization, Egyptians were nevertheless pleased by their admission. By the Anglo-Egyptian Treaty of 1936 and the Montreux Convention of 1937 Britain undertook to end the system of capitulations which protected the special privileges of foreigners. Rights of commerce and property in the Sudan were also guaranteed to Egyptians and it was agreed that the Sudan civil service should be opened to Egyptians whenever Sudanese were not available. The Treaty also proclaimed the formal ending of the British military occupation.

The military clauses of the Anglo-Egyptian Treaty were nevertheless decisive. The Imperial Government received the right to station troops in the Canal Zone and to make use of army training areas. Fly-over rights were guaranteed to the Royal Air Force. Given the menace of Mussolini in the Mediterranean and Red Sea, the strengthening of the Fascist empire in Ethiopia and Libya, and Farouk's tendency to friendship with Italy, Britain's rights under the Treaty were of the utmost significance. When world war came again it was to Egypt that men and arms flowed from Britain, British Africa, India, and the wider Commonwealth for the important campaigns in North Africa between 1940 and 1943.

3

BRITAIN AND AFRICA 1939–64:
BASES AND BRIDGEHEADS

T HE period of the Second World War marks the decisive
watershed in the history of Britain's relations with Africa.
While the Great War had the deepest, long-term effect on
the United Kingdom, it was involvement in a second continent-
wide and world-wide war which led to the transformation of British
Africa. Policies adopted towards and by British African territories
exerted in time their profound influence on Britain's metropolitan
and colonial neighbours. It was above all the emphasis on self-
government as the central objective of British colonial theory,
coupled with new awareness of the meaning of democracy, which
impelled or accelerated the change.

This emphasis on self-government was in no way primarily
directed towards Africa. Majority opinion in the Western world in
1945 still accepted for that continent the pre-war assumptions of
trusteeship and tutelage. But the urgent war-time visions of freedom, equality and democracy, together with those of welfare and
development, led to an accentuation everywhere of the ideal of
self-government or independence. Asia, notably India, and the
lands recently under the Japanese, was conceived as legitimate first
beneficiary of adulthood, Arabia being broadly included with Asia
in this generalized conception.

Africa's leaders, however, together with allies throughout the
"Negro–African" world, were not content to allow the continuance
of any hierarchical system of thought which assigned Africans to
the lowest category. Few non-Africans at the time perceived the
new African–Negro mood and fewer still noted its potential significance. African teachers, clergy, lawyers, doctors and editors were
deeply disturbed and provoked by the revival of extreme racist
theories which were enforced, and given the cloak of academic
respectability, by Herrenvolkist régimes. Few outside observers had
understood the shock which had been felt by Africans, again
together with the whole wider Negro–African population of the
Caribbean and the Americas, when Ethiopia was allowed to be
conquered. Ancient, independent Ethiopia, home of the Emperor

Ras Tafari and of an age-old Christianity, was a symbol of the greatest importance to subject and aspiring people of African descent or origin.

Although relatively few in number, those anti-racist Western democrats who understood and encouraged African resistance to racial ideologies were important. Before 1939 they were articulate in analysing and condemning the mounting racism. Alongside African and Negro colleagues it was they who in the early days of the war helped to prepare programmes for post-war Africa. In the United States as well as in Britain there was a sustained pressure on the part of organizations and individuals to present the case for African advancement and independence.

Organizations included small but influential bodies such as the Committee on Africa, the War, and Peace Aims, based in New York, which in 1942 published the volume *The Atlantic Charter and Africa From an American Standpoint*. In their deliberations the Committee, rooted in the Phelps–Stokes Fund which had pioneered educational inquiries and reforms throughout British Africa in the 1920's, drew substantially upon the co-operation of British church and university leaders and others with expert knowledge of Africa. The work of such organizations concerned with Africa was contemporaneous with that of Gunnar Myrdal and his associates who, in 1942, completed the study of American Negro–White relations which was published in 1944 under the title *An American Dilemma*.

The granting by Britain of independence to India, Pakistan and Ceylon in 1947–8 was an event which strengthened African demands for self-government and added weight to the movements for full Negro emancipation in the United States. In African territories possessing minorities of Indian origin even the most untutored Africans took note of the profusion of new flags of India and Pakistan which were displayed during the independence celebrations. Africans observed the predominant mood of jubilation which prevailed over the more sober reaction to reports of division and conflict between Muslims, Hindus, Sikhs and others. Whatever the relative status of Africa in the image of the outside world, Africans aspired to the recognition accorded to Asians, an aspiration which was supported by individual Indian intellectuals and by certain local Indian political associations such as the Natal Indian Congress.

Among the most outspoken individuals to identify themselves

with African demands for freedom and advancement were certain Europeans or whites in Africa. From times of the earliest European colonization such individuals had been present as independent-minded missionaries, teachers and the like. The majority of settled Europeans, however, responded to the new emphases on self-government and independence by demanding further recognition for themselves. In non-self-governing territories like Northern Rhodesia and Kenya there was a confident expectation that the substantial contributions by local whites to the Allied war effort, efforts which had won praise from Britain and the Dominions, would be rewarded by the early concession to them of greater constitutional powers and responsibilities.

Great Britain, notably in the years between 1945 and 1960, was faced with the problems of dealing with and attempting to harmonize the conflicting demands which have been outlined. Genuine gratitude for overseas support underlay the United Kingdom Colonial Development and Welfare Acts of 1940 and 1945 which increased metropolitan aid beyond comparison with earlier endeavours. Genuine concern also imbued war-time consideration of schemes for closer economic and administrative co-operation between neighbouring British African territories. But given the assumptions of the day and prior concern with the urgent problems of British Asia—India, Burma, Ceylon, Malaya—African political development received limited attention. Not until the events of 1948 in the Gold Coast and South Africa compelled the fresh examination of established assumptions, principles and practices was there general awareness of a new "political Africa" as distinct from an "administrative Africa".

During the period 1948–60 there was political activity on a new scale in every zone of British Africa. Under different parties and personalities different policies were formulated and tried by Britain. There was no conscious pursuit of coherence. Empiricism largely governed the metropolitan approach to policy for each territory and zone, though Labour's Secretary of State for the Colonies, Arthur Creech Jones, introduced important new services to ensure the maximum exchange of information. Egypt and the Sudan required a rapid coming to terms with their particular varieties of Arab nationalism, especially at a time when the ending of the war-time truce had unleashed a more determined Zionism in Palestine.

In West Africa the challenge was seen by Britain to be the direction of African nationalism into co-operative channels. Dr. Malan's

E

defeat of Smuts in South Africa raised much the same problem in respect of Afrikaner nationalism. In East Africa the Mau Mau revolutionary movement erupted in Kenya in 1952 to imperil the whole foundation of the colony and the prospects of multi-racialism. In Central Africa the British Government, in alliance with local European political leaders, tried to achieve a new order, based on a conception of inter-racial partnership, which would prevent extremes of race feeling from damaging relations between Africans and whites to the point of inhibiting rapid economic and social development as well as moderate political advance. A *via media* was sought therefore between *apartheid* and Mau Mau. In 1953, after over two years of preliminary investigation and negotiation by first a Labour and then a Conservative administration, the Federation of Rhodesia and Nyasaland was created.

By the turn of the year 1959–60 the United Kingdom Government had come to the conclusion that the facts of contemporary Africa demanded everywhere an acknowledgement of the majority position of the indigenous peoples of the continent. Henceforth, while every influence would be brought to bear on African successor Governments to respect British and other external interests, and British immigrants, the need to safeguard the rights of non-African minorities would be in the hands of African politicians and officials. The process of withdrawal and the transfer of power which was greatly accelerated between 1960 and 1963 continues and several important constitutions have still to be fully adopted or to be applied for a period sufficiently long to permit their analysis over time. But by 1960 the die was cast for all territories under United Kingdom control. In that year, scarcely two decades after the beginning of the Second World War, a continent of colonial dependencies had moved decisively towards becoming independent Africa.

1939–45: PARTNERSHIP IN WAR

Africa was drawn even more fully into the Second World War than she had been into the First. There were no local campaigns against German colonies in each of the zones, as there had been in 1914–18, but the conquest of Western Europe by Hitler and Mussolini led to two consequences of great significance for Africa. First, the overthrow of the metropolitan régimes in France and Belgium gave to French and Belgian African territories a new and historic importance comparable with that of Portuguese and Spanish America during Napoleon's Peninsular campaign. It was in French Equatorial Africa that de Gaulle was first received with enthusiasm on his own soil and an effective base prepared by Felix Eboue for free and fighting France. The Belgian Congo likewise became the heart of Belgium's empire with its manpower and material contributions important to metropolitan morale as well as to the Allied war effort. Despite many assertions to the contrary the fact that their African homelands had assumed importance on the world scene did register upon the indigenous peoples, illiterate though most were and little informed of international affairs.

The second consequence of Hitler's successful *blitzkrieg* and domination of the European mainland was to give neighbouring Africa a wholly new role in Allied military strategy. After the catastrophic events of May and June 1940, when Mussolini cast his lot completely with Hitler, and Pétain and Darlan left overseas France demoralized and divided, the reaction of each territory in Africa assumed a new significance. Until the tide turned decisively at El Alamein the availability of the North African littoral as a spring-board for Allied air forces, armies and navies remained uncertain.

The defection of Vichy added substantially to the burden of the Allies. The Maghreb was closed, or hostile, in support of the German Afrika Korps and the Italian forces, whose first objective was to advance to the Nile and the Canal to choke "the throat of the British Empire". In the Gulf of Aden the position of Jibuti was not settled until after Mussolini's over-running of British Somaliland had been reversed and the Fascist armies cleared from Italian Somaliland, Eritrea and Ethiopia. Vichy armed resistance at Dakar denied to the Allies Senegal and the Senegalese who would have been invaluable during earlier naval and military engagements. The seizing of the harbours and mainland of Madagascar demanded resources which were required urgently in the war against the Axis powers, including Japan, whose submarines co-operated with German vessels off the East African coast.

It might be too harsh to compare the African colonies of Vichy France with those of Germany in 1914–18, and possibly inaccurate also, because no Vichy field commander displayed the spirit of von Lettow or Zimmermann, but certainly Vichy opposition to the Allies was costly and brought military conflict to wide areas of

Africa. Portugal's neutrality kept Portuguese African colonies relatively insulated from the war but they were the only extensive parts of the continent to escape, a fact which has some bearing on their subsequent distinctive development.

The United Kingdom, isolated as never before by the neutrality of the Irish Republic within the British Isles, as well as by the defeat and occupation of all her nearer neighbours and traditional allies on the mainland of Europe, was in special peril from May 1940 until the United States entered the war and American aid and military support built up her strength to the point where invasion by the Wehrmacht was unlikely to succeed. Save for Eire, the Dominions and Colonies rallied at once to Britain, New Zealand, Australia and Canada in the van. That they were all weaker than the mother country seemed to matter less at the time than the fact that the response was virtually unanimous. There were at least bastions on every continent from which the forces of Germany, Italy and Japan might be beaten back.

In Africa, for reasons which have been suggested already, the British territories proved of particular value. Without Dakar, Freetown was vital to Atlantic communications; so also the South Atlantic headquarters of the Royal Navy near Cape Town, Durban, and the other South African harbours. The deep-water base at Kilindini, Mombasa, facilitated entry for troops to defend East Africa and provided a key link with Aden and Bombay, well clear of the Madagascar Channel. In the massive circumnavigations of Africa by the vast convoys required to sustain the defence of Egypt and India, when the Mediterranean was all but closed, these established British foci proved of incalculable worth.

As bases for air operations, air transport and air training all zones of British Africa were of notable value. North African airfields were essential for long-distance raids on Europe, such as the attack on Ploesti, and for air cover in the Mediterranean until 1943. The West African air communication link, via Takoradi, to the Sudan, Egypt and North Africa greatly speeded the supply of equipment and specialist units, while Royal Air Force instructional squadrons trained fresh air crews in South Africa, Rhodesia and Kenya, where good flying conditions reduced cadet casualties and wastage of aircraft. From all British territories coastal command sorties were flown constantly against enemy submarines and surface vessels which were sunk or impounded by action of the Royal and South African Air Forces.

If scientific and technical advance in the design and production
of aircraft gave the British bases in Africa an added dimension of
utility during the war, much the same was true of road and railway
engineering and the development of motor transport, locomotives
and rolling stock. Trunk roads and railways were built or improved
in every territory to speed the movement of armoured and other
vehicles and to reduce the wear and tear on them. The main arterial
system which was developed was the "Great North Road" which
ran from South Africa to Kenya and beyond to the Nile and Egypt.
When shipping and aircraft were in short supply, and sea and air
lanes were imperilled by submarines and enemy air forces, surface
communications helped to tip the balance towards probable success
in the mounting of land campaigns such as the driving back of the
invaders from Kenya and the direct assault on the Italian imperial
forces in Ethiopia. The inland transit of Tanganyika was of great
advantage, obvious especially to those older Southern African
soldiers of all races in the motor transport companies who possessed
memories of columns of slow-moving human carriers in the
German East Africa campaign.

The contributions of men and materials from each British
African territory were substantially greater than in the Great War
though the casualties were proportionately less. It is impossible as
well as invidious to evaluate in retrospect particular contributions
to military operations in which unique, marginal and major actions
by individuals and groups combine and alter over time to produce
the eventual result, whether stalemate, defeat or victory. The addition of one barely trained and poorly armed battalion has proved
decisive in defence; the successful attack on a small feature by a
single unit has turned a battle; tactical gains have borne strategic
fruit. Each of these truisms was exemplified repeatedly in the
Western desert of Egypt and Libya, Eritrea, Ethiopia, the Somali-
lands, Madagascar, and in Italy, Burma and Malaya, where varied
permutations and combinations of British Africans fought. But,
given the fact that Egypt had to be held at all costs, it is probably
correct to suggest that the positive response of the Dominion of
South Africa to Britain's declaration of war on September 3, 1939,
was again, as in 1914, the most important single reaction in Africa
from the viewpoints of both the United Kingdom and the Commonwealth.

The narrowness of Smuts's majority over Hertzog in the parliamentary division on September 6 has been referred to above. But

there was a majority and the Governor-General, Sir Patrick Duncan, one of Milner's kindergarten, did not hesitate to reject Hertzog's demand, as Prime Minister, for a general election. Smuts, to whom a field-marshal's baton was soon awarded by George VI, acted with characteristic determination in mobilizing every resource, despite strong and menacing opposition from those in active sympathy with Germany both in the Union and South-West Africa.

Smuts initiated, with the able support of Hofmeyr and many of South Africa's most competent men, the most thorough-going and constructive set of inquiries into the national economy and the structure and functioning of South African society. Problems of race and colour and the position of the African, Coloured and Asian communities were not shirked. Faced with urgent manpower questions Smuts was frank in acknowledging the weaknesses of traditional policies of racial segregation. The blue-prints of his experts, van Eck, van Biljon, Malherbe and scores of others from industry and agriculture and statistical, educational, and health services promised a new era of welfare, development and dignity for all the "Non-European" peoples comprising the majority of the land.

Though the promise of a new age was blighted in 1948 by the folly of inadequate electoral preparation, and Smuts's defeat at the polls, the war years after 1943 were politically much easier than those before. With an Allied victory seemingly assured there was country-wide support for Smuts at the general election of late 1943 in which the overseas soldiers' vote played a big part. The South African Armoured Division, which voted in Egypt before going to the front in Italy, carried the general good wishes of the country, as now also did the veteran squadrons and ships of the South African Air Force and Navy, and the specialist units of the army which had been engaged alongside Allied formations throughout the war. The more perilous military period had been that of the Axis ascendancy when sabotage, spying and disaffection in South Africa occasioned acute crises of personal and group loyalty and made it a matter of real courage for the individual Afrikaner to enlist in the forces or otherwise to declare his allegiance.

But Smuts in 1939 and 1940 had shown no hesitation in at once committing troops to the defence of Kenya. The First Infantry Brigade, comprising the Transvaal Scottish from the Witwatersrand, the Royal Natal Carbineers and the Duke of Edinburgh's Own Rifles from Cape Town, were rushed to reinforce the handful of East African units stretched along an immense front. They were joined by fighter, bomber and reconnaissance squadrons of the South African Air Force equipped with old-fashioned aircraft. Had the Duke of Aosta's forces attacked with any resolution they must have over-run Kenya and much of British East Africa as easily as they had done the British Somaliland Protectorate.

The initiative was wrested from them quickly, however, and to-gether South African, West African and East African armoured cars and infantry supported by their own field gunners, and Indian mountain gunners, swept across the Juba River through Italian Somaliland, the Ogaden and on to Addis Ababa. From Eritrea and the Sudan Indian, Sudanese and British regular and irregular units conquered the key fortress of Keren after the most severe fighting of the whole Ethiopian campaign, an action in which Coloured South African motor transport drivers operated with gallantry.

As soon as Ethiopia was conquered and restored to the Emperor the South African troops of the East Africa Force were transferred to join the British Eighth Army in the Western Desert, where the Second Division played a noteworthy part in the capture of Bardia but thereafter suffered disaster with others at Tobruk. The more experienced First Division was fully engaged in operations until after the battle of El Alamein. For several reasons, not least poli-tical, the First Division which had been some three years in the field was withdrawn by Smuts to South Africa after the tide of war turned towards Allied victory. The tragic loss of the Second Division was seized upon for more vehement anti-war propaganda by the Afrikaner nationalists but the safe return to the Union for leave and re-training of thousands of disciplined and seasoned soldiers greatly strengthened Smuts's position.

The pilots and other officers who were seconded to the United Kingdom services, the South African squadrons in the Desert Air Force, and other individuals and units of the Union Defence Force who remained with the Eighth Army or other Allied formations deserve as much attention as the numerically larger Army Brigades and Divisions. It is important, however, in this brief survey to emphasize that the technical and supply contributions of South Africa were perhaps as important to the British and total Allied war effort as were any specific military contributions.

The steady growth of manufacturing industry during the inter-war years had brought the Union to the point in 1939 where very substantial war-time industrial production was possible. Food packaging of military and civilian rations, the making of uniforms, clothing and camp equipment, the manufacture of arms and ammunition and armoured vehicles: in these and scores of other ways South Africa produced essential commodities. The well-established dock and loading facilities at ports which were used habitually in peace-time by large vessels of the Union-Castle and other shipping lines were adapted for war purposes; battle-damaged warships like H.M.S. *Barham* were repaired at Durban, which developed into a particularly important naval and troop transit centre.

If senior British assessments after the war gave first place to South Africa's contribution there was no lack of appreciation of the efforts of the other British African territories, each of which in its own way exerted itself to the uttermost in mobilizing its manpower and resources. Southern Rhodesia made a specially heavy sacrifice and was extended to supply men to her affiliated United Kingdom regiments and squadrons, and to West, East and South African formations. The British residents of Southern Rhodesia, like those in Kenya, were scarcely sufficient in number to maintain casualty-stricken units of their own, such as the Southern Rhodesian anti-tank gunners and the Kenya reconnaissance squadron, but they were called upon regularly to send elsewhere officers, instructors and specialists.

The Africans of Southern Rhodesia, like those in the High Commission Territories and South Africa were recruited to the forces in substantial numbers. The fearful Afrikaner-nationalist tradition of restricting the possession and use of firearms by Africans seriously impaired the military contribution which Africans from South Africa would otherwise have made. Zulus who responded enthusiastically for initial artillery and infantry training tended to withdraw when offered only pioneer, labouring work in the Native Military Corps. The Sotho, Tswana and other peoples who attested in tens of thousands were nevertheless armed appropriately when on active service away from Southern Africa and they constituted an integral part of British Corps and Army troops in North Africa and Italy.

The Gold Coast and Nigeria Regiments, the many territorial battalions of the King's African Rifles, the Northern Rhodesia Regiment, together with other West, East and Central African units made up very effective fighting forces. They were well led by British officers and by experienced African warrant officers and non-commissioned officers,* and co-operated fully and in friendly fashion with South African and Indian soldiers. Although it would be wrong to exaggerate sentiment, a frank mutual respect and sense of comradeship was developed, not least on the part of young white South African soldiers for competent and courageous African platoon sergeants, and veteran sergeant-majors. Many Kenya and Northern Rhodesia whites likewise reported a new depth of understanding and respect for Africans who fought beside them in Africa and South-East Asia. The West African divisions made a notable contribution to General Cunningham's East Africa Force and played their full part in alternating in the leadership in attack during the advance through Somalia and Ethiopia. Together with African battalions from East and Central Africa they were posted subsequently to the Burma front, to figure prominently in dispatches from the South-East Asia campaigns.

Though their material contribution may have been relatively limited both East and West Africa underwent domestic revolutions, principally in the organization of production to meet war-time demands. Kenya was in the firing-line and civilians were organized on an emergency basis. There was no panic on the coffee estates or African shamvas and food production was intensified. Some alarm was expressed by private employers about the probable long-term effect of Army and Government rates of pay, rations, clothing and accommodation on the many thousands of specially-recruited Africans. There were also those who seriously questioned the wisdom of permitting white South African privates, sappers, signallers and troopers to labour alongside African soldiers and workers in British colonies dependent on the leadership of a small *élite* settler class. Such "white askaris" could well raise doubts about the established order in the minds of observant Africans. There was, however, no lack of generosity or hospitality for the humblest soldiers on the part of Lady Delamere and the Kenya Women's Emergency Organization or the local residents who provided after-care for wounded and sick from the military hospitals. This mobilization of domestic resources in front-line Kenya was repeated in the other lands of British East Africa—Uganda, Tanganyika and Zanzibar.

* In the Indian Army there were Viceroy-commissioned officers but few holders of the King's commission. Few, if any, Africans were appointed to commissioned rank until after the war.

Through the conquests of 1940–1 the bonds of responsibility in North-East Africa were extended to embrace the Somali lands and Eritrea, which were brought under the British Military Administration. The Emperor was restored to Ethiopia and assisted in the rehabilitation of his kingdom while the evacuation and safeguarding of the tens of thousands of Axis prisoners of war, mostly Italian, was undertaken by the British authorities. Italian vessels under protection of the International Red Cross removed women and children and other civilians from ports like Berbera. Prisoners of war had to be conveyed to camps and hospitals in Kenya and South Africa.* Ships and troops were directed from military operations for these humanitarian activities, the scale of which demands that reference be made to them. The excellent quality of the administration introduced into Eritrea and the Somali areas should also be remembered. Many of the Somalis who subsequently became effective administrative and police officers gained knowledge and experience under British military mentors.

West Africa likewise underwent thorough-going domestic mobilization. The harbour at Freetown worked to full capacity and the other ports of British West Africa were actively engaged in transhipping soldiers and goods. When the air resources of the Allies were sufficient the West African "air bridge", which had bases in Liberia and the French territories as well as those of Britain, became an operation of the greatest magnitude and importance. In West Africa, as in the Middle East, a Resident Ministry was introduced, in 1942, to ensure the effective working of a vital supply route. A Minister of Cabinet rank, Lord Swinton, was at the head of a West African War Council, comprising the four Governors and service commanders. Although a West African Governors' Conference had been approved shortly before the war in 1939, it was equipped with no secretariat and it was the stimulus of war which in fact initiated effective inter-territorial co-operation.

The War Council secretariat was set up at Achimota in the Gold Coast. It was also in the Gold Coast, at Takoradi, that Allied aircraft were assembled in large numbers for dispatch to the Middle East. Nigeria's contribution in manpower and raw materials exceeded that of the Gold Coast but the central position of the smaller territory and its more convenient access to the West gave it importance as a headquarters. One measure both of the appreciation

* German and Italian prisoners of war from North Africa were also taken to camps in South Africa.

felt by Britain for West African war-time co-operation, and her recognition of the needs of her West African territories was the allocation to them before 1946 of one-third of the total sum granted under the Colonial Development and Welfare Act.

Egypt and the Sudan were inevitably involved in the heavy fighting which raged to and fro between the Gulf of Sirte and Alexandria. It is a mark of the difference between the First and Second World Wars that it was on African soil that major land battles involving Western European nations were fought for very much longer than the period of campaigning in Europe itself. From the day of Mussolini's declaration of war, June 10, 1940, until his Commander-in-Chief in Africa, Marshal Messe, ordered all remaining Axis troops to lay down their arms in Tunisia on May 13, 1943, Northern Africa was a principal battle-ground, comparable in importance with the Russian and Far Eastern fronts.

At the crest of the Axis wave in August 1942 there was the prospect of a fusion of victorious German, Japanese and Italian troops in the lands of Arabia. The Germans were in the Caucasus and at the gates of Stalingrad; the Japanese still in a position of strength on the borders of India. Rommel faced a mere sixty-mile gap between El Alamein and Alexandria. Had the Afrika Korps broken through the war would have taken a dramatically different course, no matter what the determined Russian defenders might have been able still to achieve along the Volga. But the British Commonwealth line held and on the night of October 23 the Eighth Army struck the powerful blow which rolled the enemy back from the Nile and the Canal and across the Egyptian frontier. Past Tobruk, Benghazi and El Agheila the Eighth Army drove to unfamiliar Tripoli and Tunisia, where a junction was effected with the British–American First Army. With the Maghreb regained the Fighting French were able to organize the Moroccan and Algerian divisions which fought so well in the Italian campaigns.

Given the precarious balance of forces and the recurrent prospect of Allied defeat in the Western Desert before October 1943, it is not surprising that there was little sense of positive commitment to the Allied cause on the part of Egyptians eager for independence. Where Hertzog and his associates felt kinship for the Germans, so Farouk and several leading Egyptians were friendly towards Italy and were, like Aly Maher Pasha, and many students, in no way averse to contemplating possible escape from British overlordship through alliance with Mussolini and Hitler. Not until after

Alamein did the position ease to the extent that there could be relatively unguarded co-operation with Egyptian army units in desert manœuvres and other military training exercises.

Before Alamein there was constant awareness of a revolutionary, nationalist element in the Egyptian army and of the Muslim Brotherhood. After September 1939 and before Italy brought neighbouring Libya into the war, however, Egypt's politicians reacted correctly in according Britain the use of all necessary services and defence facilities, as required by the Anglo-Egyptian Treaty. The same was true after June 1940 when first Hassan Sabry Pasha and then Hussein Sirry Pasha were appointed to fill the prime ministership in succession to the suspect Aly Maher. But it was not until after Farouk was subjugated in February 1942 that Nahas Pasha was called upon to form a government, and it was only after his Wafd were sweepingly successful in the March general election that the internal political situation became reasonably satisfactory from the British point of view. There were alarums but no major troubles from dissidents during the tense months at Alamein.

As reward for such co-operation—whether grudging, passive or active—Egyptians were almost at one, after the Axis were cleared from North Africa, in demanding total evacuation by Britain and the incorporation of the Sudan into an Egyptian–Sudanese Union. As a step towards ensuring recognition of her full independent personality in the peace deliberations Egypt, now under Ahmed Maher Pasha, made her own declaration of war on the Axis powers shortly before the end of the conflict in Europe. Though Ahmed Maher was assassinated by a fanatical extremist for this act, which some alleged would lead to a 1914–18-type labour conscription for the Far Eastern War, Egypt was, nevertheless, made eligible to participate fully in post-war councils. In particular she was given a lever to prise full independence when, after 1945, the vast Allied military encampments and transit centres were largely cleared of Commonwealth soldiers and their equipment.

The Sudan did not become a full-scale area of politics until after the war. Though within twelve years full independence was to be declared by Ismail el-Azhary, it was only in 1944 that an Advisory Council for the Northern Sudan was appointed, and only in 1946 that the Governor-General summoned a largely Sudanese conference to consider further constitutional advances from this slight beginning. Reference has been made already to the effectiveness and value of the Sudan Defence Force in the campaigns against

the Italians in Eritrea and Ethiopia. The civil sphere also was
marked by a readiness on the part of the Sudanese to co-operate in
increasing production whenever possible and in facilitating the
efficient transit of troops and supplies to and from the battlefronts.

1945–60/3 : NATIONALISM—AFRICAN, AFRIKANER, ARAB

It was remarked above that the period 1948–60 was characterized
by political activity on a new scale throughout British Africa. Nine-
teen forty-eight was in fact a fateful year. Events in Palestine, Gold
Coast and South Africa directly affected three centres of British
power in Africa while the first full year of Indian and Pakistani
independence changed some principal assumptions of Imperial
organization and strategy in respect of East, North-East and
Northern Africa. The post-war years before 1948 were important
in themselves but seen in terms of an overall pattern of British–
African relationships they were primarily years of readjustment
after the war. The implementation of armistice arrangements, prep-
arations for peace settlements, the foundation of the United
Nations, demobilization, the adjustment to a new peace-time metropolitan government dedicated to a new ideal of welfare at home
and abroad : these were the matters which occupied attention. Overseas, the Indian sub-continent rather than Africa demanded priority
within the Commonwealth.

In Africa too between 1945 and 1948 governments and political
leaders were naturally concerned about the major questions of world
peace and international organization. This was especially true of
Egypt and South Africa. In both these countries, however, and certainly in the area of administration, more time and effort might well
have been devoted to grappling in more vigorous and constructive
fashion with the domestic problems of peace, notably in providing
for the fullest possible utilization of the new skills, knowledge and
ambitions of thousands of ex-servicemen and workers from key
war-time industries.

In British East and West Africa there were also many ex-soldiers.
One rough indication of the numbers involved is supplied by the
Colonial Office estimate that 228,000 were on the strength of the
East African military forces in May 1945, compared with 11,000
in September 1939. The respective West African figures are
146,000 and 8,000. Intelligent plans were devised by perceptive

officers and officials for the employment of such individuals in post-war development, but fulfilment fell far short of even modest objectives. War-weariness, coupled with the inertia induced by old habits, assumptions and the hoped-for resumption of pre-war patterns of behaviour and practice inhibited action. Critical opportunities were wasted.

The flare-up over Palestine and the involvement of Ernest Bevin and the Labour Government in negotiations with Arabs, Jews and the United Nations dominated British public thought in 1948, but what happened in the Gold Coast and South Africa was of equal, possibly even of greater, long-term import. Certainly where defeat and humiliation in Palestine brought new depth and determination to Egyptian nationalism, so African nationalism and Afrikaner nationalism were each given new prospects and significant initial power after the riots of ex-servicemen in Accra in February 1948, and the narrow but all-important defeat of Field-Marshal Smuts by Dr. Malan in the election of May 26, 1948.

Events in each zone had their influence on the other zones. The overthrow of Farouk and the Egyptian revolution led by the Free Officers in 1952, Sudan's declaration of independence at the beginning of 1956, the attack on Nasser and the abandonment of Anglo-French-Israeli intervention in Suez in 1956 were inter-related events of Northern Africa which were closely observed by leaders in other parts of Africa. Yet events in Commonwealth and colonial countries south of the Sahara and in the Indian sub-continent had perhaps their more intimate interaction and direct effect.

No event in Africa was more decisive than the publication of the report of the Watson commission of inquiry into the Gold Coast disturbances of 1948. A subsequent, constitutional reform committee composed wholly of senior Africans of the Gold Coast under Sir Henley Coussey, an eminent African judge, attempted to modify the radicalism of the report. The Labour Secretary of State for the Colonies, who possessed a profound knowledge and experience of colonial issues, applied himself towards the same end. There was a general desire on the part of the Labour administration to encourage West African constitutional advance. Various steps towards this end had been taken and were in plan. The 1946 "Burns Constitution" for the Gold Coast was clearly too limited to provide long-term satisfaction. But the Riots Commission, composed of a chairman from the United Kingdom with little previous experience of Africa, together with an Oxford College head, precipitated developments by their wide-ranging analyses of the underlying causes of the relatively minor local disturbances and by their far-reaching recommendations. Major constitutional provisions were called into question along with other political, economic and social arrangements and many challenging *obiter dicta* were included in the report.

If a militant radical had not been available among the African nationalist leaders the course of Gold Coast and African history might have been different. Dr. Danquah and his liberal-traditionalist colleagues could well have prevailed in the Gold Coast and brought to eventual victory their distinctive brand of African nationalism. Had this occurred they would have been reinforced by similar groups in Nigeria, Sierra Leone and the Gambia. But Kwame Nkrumah was back home and already in a position of potential power as secretary of Dr. Danquah's United Gold Coast Convention. With an essentially political as distinct from professional background, and as one whose nationalist fervour had been quickened and given single-minded direction by life abroad in the United States and Britain, Dr. Nkrumah at once saw the opportunities opened by the Watson report. Like the quick-minded Prince Obolensky, whose try at Twickenham is part of history, Kwame Nkrumah had most of the field still to traverse when he seized the ball in 1949 and embarked on his spectacular solo run. In place of the former members of his own team he was able to count on the popular support of younger radicals of all kinds, not least on certain disgruntled ex-servicemen whose military experiences had given them disciplined determination and confidence.

Kwame Nkrumah had been a leading participant with the West Indian, George Padmore, at the Pan-African Conference at Manchester in 1945. Jomo Kenyatta, Julius Nyerere and Kamuzu Hastings Banda were also present at this meeting which, for the first time, included significant African as distinct from American Negro and British West Indian representation. Whereas Dr. Du Bois and the others who conferred in Paris in 1919—and who attempted unsuccessfully to secure Versailles approval for a Pan-Negro administration of the former German colonies—were mainly Americans or West Indians of African descent, the 1945 Pan-Africanists spoke from within the context of their own continent. Tempered by their disheartening experiences with Soviet and international Communism in the thirties they were now more hardened nationalists.

By the time that the first Pan-African conference was convened by Dr. Nkrumah on African soil in 1958 the new nationalism had an independent base of some strength and had already exerted an influence throughout neighbouring French Africa and other parts of the continent.

Ghana, herald of the new independent Africa, was born out of the Gold Coast on March 6, 1957, after Dr. Nkrumah and his Convention Peoples' Party had won elections in 1951, 1954 and 1956 and had advanced rapidly through successive constitutional stages. At each stage it became clearer that a strong centralist government was the objective and that little consideration would be given to regional, ethnic and cultural traditions. The Ashanti in particular were subjugated. By 1960, when the new authoritarian republican constitution replaced that of 1957, control by the President and his dominant political party was already virtually complete.

The triumph of the new African nationalism or Nkrumahism after 1951 had a many-sided influence. The constitutional advance of Ghana was seized upon, not always from the best of motives, to justify the acceleration of constitutional advance elsewhere. In Middle East and Mediterranean countries and South-East Asia the point was made openly that Arabs, Greek Cypriots, Maltese and Malayans invited priority over Africans. Among Welsh and Scottish Nationalists bent on home rule or independence there were echoes of this opinion, an opinion which was even more vigorously expressed by many Britons overseas in Africa. More emphatic still was the reaction of the recently victorious Afrikaner nationalists. Among Africans elsewhere in Africa, however, whether in predominantly "African states" or the "plural societies", including South Africa, there was frank delight at the progress of the Gold Coast into Ghana. Like Negroes in the United States and the Caribbean they were moved to a new hope and a growing impatience with their civic disabilities.

The opposed force of white or European nationalism or racism in Africa was, like African nationalism, given unexpected opportunity in 1948. The success of Dr. Malan's Nationalists in May 1948 owed little directly to events in the Gold Coast. Internal issues of race relations, notably reaction to the report of an enlightened commission of inquiry into African affairs under Mr. Justice Fagan, provided more obvious and ready-to-hand reasons. But after 1948 developments in the Gold Coast and West Africa, and the whole strengthening of African determination for rapid change through-out the continent, had its obvious effect on the political thought and organization of the locally resident Europeans.

Until 1960 Europeans in the plural societies were largely assured of the continuance of United Kingdom support for them as co-trustees, or equal senior partners, but there was nevertheless throughout the fifties, growing apprehension at the nature and im-plications of the rapid constitutional advance of the African states. The eruption of Mau Mau in Kenya in 1952 reinforced this appre-hension and, among the dominant Afrikaners in the south, it hardened determination to retain power in the hands of European rulers in a land where Europeans were more numerous than any-where else on the continent and were conscious of having been resident for three centuries.

The 1952 Tercentenary celebrations of the landing of Jan van Riebeeck and his Dutch East Indian Company settlers served as a powerful symbolic occasion which was exploited with skill. Though natural emphasis was laid on the Dutch–Afrikaner heritage, British achievement since 1795 was acknowledged in ceremonies which directed attention also to the range and quality of the overall European contribution to every part of Africa. By such means Afrikaner nationalism drew support from many insecure Europeans settled elsewhere in Africa—Belgian, French, Portuguese, Italian as well as British—and from sympathetic elements in metropolitan Europe, the United States and the "White Dominions" of the Commonwealth.

Afrikaner nationalism's electoral triumph in 1948 was not, how-ever, received in Africa at the time with any enthusiasm, either by the majority* of white South African voters, who supported Smuts, or by most white Central and East Africans. Many whites in British Africa, including the Union of South Africa, were in fact more outspoken in their regret and alarm than leaders in the City of London and other United Kingdom centres who possessed close, traditional bonds with Johannesburg, the Cape and Natal. To such United Kingdom interests there seemed to be danger to the profita-bility of their investments in the proposals of Mr. Justice Fagan's Native Laws Commission of Inquiry, which sought to transform the whole system of African employment from one based largely on the temporary migration of rural tribesmen to a new policy which

---

* The favourable underweighting of rural constituencies enabled Dr. Malan to be returned by a minority of votes.

F

placed first emphasis on stabilization, including the recognition of property and other rights for permanent townsmen. Lever Brothers and other companies who tended to welcome African stabilization on economic and social grounds, were in a minority. Locally resident Europeans were far from agreement on the Fagan Commission's proposals but there was confidence that Smuts would never accelerate African advance to the point of danger. The recent record of the Afrikaner-nationalist opposition during the war still dominated their outlook in a way which many in metropolitan Britain, faced with multiple international problems of seeming greater magnitude and urgency, found difficult to understand.

Southern Rhodesian reaction to Dr. Malan's victory over Smuts was characteristically rapid and vigorous. Sir Godfrey Huggins (Lord Malvern), who had been in imminent danger of defeat for reasons similar to those which had contributed to Smuts's downfall —war-weariness, post-war disgruntlement and apathy, desire for a change—was returned with an overwhelming majority in the general election which was held a few months after Dr. Malan's triumph. Afrikaner nationalism, notably republicanism and the *baasskap* elements of *apartheid*, was then seen as a more acute danger than African nationalism by the almost wholly white electorate of Southern Rhodesia; but they responded soon enough to Huggins's warnings of a new African militancy from the north, and supported him in his endeavours to found a British Central African state which would stifle racism and deflect and harmonize the conflicting nationalisms.

The Federation of Rhodesia and Nyasaland represents an important attempt to achieve co-operative "multi-racialism" or interracial "partnership". It is specially significant to the Britain–Africa relationship because its creation was so deliberately supported by both Labour and Conservative ministers and by the forceful senior officials of the Colonial Office. Because of the favourable publicity which Central African partnership received by contrast with South African *apartheid* and Mau Mau racism in Kenya, the importance of the Federation extended beyond Africa to the Commonwealth and the United Nations. From the time when the inter-war idea of formal closer political association between the three territories was resurrected and given open official publicity in March 1951, and official support, until the virtual abandonment of the experiment after the report of the Monckton Commission in October 1960, the

Federation in its pursuit of partnership was presented to the world as a supreme venture in imaginative statesmanship.

Although it is tempting to condemn Central African Federation as a total failure, especially at a time when its formal dissolution is accomplished, it is still necessary now, as it was in the years before the making of the Rhodesia–Nyasaland Order in Council in 1953, to avoid hasty judgements and decisions. For those who, like myself regretfully decided in 1951 and 1952 that significant flaws* in the draft constitution, and the method of its preparation and proposed implementation, offered little prospect of success, it is specially necessary to recall the positive as well as the negative aspects of an important experiment which was backed by many eminent Britons.

In so far as interactions within Africa were concerned, however, the Federation during its brief existence both suffered from its neighbours and occasioned misgiving and alarm among them. The Europeans of the two Rhodesias and Nyasaland, on whom the substance of power was conferred by the 1953 Federal Constitution, were made increasingly apprehensive for the safety of their families and security of their property by the reports of Mau Mau atrocities in Kenya. The long duration of Mau Mau and the cost and difficulty of its suppression, even with full United Kingdom financial and military aid, made a deep impression on many Colonial Service officers as well as permanent residents. There was among all of them a visible stiffening of determination to preserve law and order.

This reaction of the Europeans, understandable in itself, was one which had the equally natural effect of arousing resentment among the educated and law-abiding Africans who composed the majority of the population. There was resentment among the Africans of Southern Rhodesia, but resentment was felt even more strongly by the Africans of Northern Rhodesia and Nyasaland who suffered the principal shock when Federation was imposed against their wishes and in direct opposition to the political expectations which past Colonial Office pronouncements had encouraged among them. Such African discontent was communicated to their fellows beyond

* To cite one example, it seemed clear to me at the time, given South African experience over the "entrenched clauses" in the Union's constitution, that Africans in the Federation should be at the very least assured of more than one-third of the representation in the legislature if the amendment of the Federal Constitution could be decided by a two-thirds majority.

the borders and had the effect in East Africa of making any consideration of closer political association between Kenya, Uganda, Tanganyika and Zanzibar unacceptable. There was, for example, too little rational consideration of the report of the East Africa Royal Commission 1953–5 which recommended an increase in inter-territorial co-operation in the interests of economic and social advance for all. The mere mention of "Federation" in Nairobi by a visiting Secretary of State provoked vehement hostility among Africans in Uganda and throughout East Africa.

After 1957 and Ghana's admission to full membership of the Commonwealth and United Nations the confrontations between African and European politicians became increasingly clear-cut. Every conception of trusteeship was challenged by African leaders and gradualism was utterly rejected. Mounting pressure was applied by Ghana, supported by Ethiopia, Liberia, Egypt and the Sudan, to hasten the independence of all territories under European rule. From their different standpoints the United States and the Soviet Union threw their weight behind this pan-African initiative.

In Tunisia and Morocco, though not Algeria, France had accepted independence, and in 1958 the whole of French West and French Equatorial Africa and Madagascar were granted autonomy by de Gaulle in a single dramatic gesture which transformed the political map of the continent and brought thirteen new African states into international councils. With the balance tipped so decisively and precipitately in favour of African independence there was an intensification of efforts by all other metropolitan powers, save Portugal, to capture African goodwill by accelerating the advance to self-government. Belgium became convinced that she could not hope to hold on when her two powerful European and African neighbours, France and Britain, had decided on immediate African independence, so she too hastened to abandon her long-established traditions of halting gradualism in the Congo and Ruanda-Urundi. During 1959 the conviction grew that independence in North-East, East and Central Africa must accompany the advance in West Africa, and Mr. Macmillan's "wind of change" speech in Cape Town in February 1960, after his visits to Ghana and Nigeria, was a general proclamation of the new United Kingdom attitude.*

The Congo breakdown had a profound effect on the Europeans

* See Lord Kilmuir's *Political Adventure* (London 1964) for observations on the then Prime Minister's "wind of change" speech.

of South-Central Africa but it did not lead to a reversal of European metropolitan policy. In the minds of many responsibility was now to be transferred to the United States and the United Nations. By the end of 1960 the new era in British–African relationships was fully initiated. Governmental responsibilities in Africa were to be abandoned as speedily as possible. Commonwealth ideals and objectives were subjected to detached, critical, even hostile, appraisal of a wholly new kind. South Africa's withdrawal from the Commonwealth left it to Nigeria and the other African members to produce leaders who might give to the "multi-racial Commonwealth" the thought and attention and leadership given to the older Empire-Commonwealth during the inter-war years by Smuts.

Meanwhile Britain's leaders were content to explore fresh conceptions such as "Europe"—with Frenchmen resigned to the evacuation of Algeria and with Belgians, Hollanders, Italians and other Europeans equally disenchanted by their recent experiences of overseas settlement, colonial rule and "decolonization". Wider alliances were also examined, notably the idea of a new "Atlantic Community" integrating Europe and North America, possibly with the addition of Australia and New Zealand. Though links between Britain and Africa were not to be severed or wilfully attenuated they would henceforth increasingly become the concern of the Department of Technical Co-operation and the Foreign Office. In an age of fierce affirmations of independence by African leaders, coupled with sharp criticism of their former metropolitan rulers, the British Prime Minister was moved to assert in 1963 that Great Britain, too, was independent. Yet, like Egypt's independence in the early 1920's, Britain's independence in the 1960's could be no more than strictly "qualified". Centuries of history have never been discarded overnight and in an increasingly interdependent world established bridgeheads must not be abandoned. In the chapters which follow we attempt to examine in turn Britain's several bridgeheads in Africa which, since de Gaulle's rejection of Britain's application for membership of the European Common Market, have received warmer and more hopeful attention from those who had previously assigned to them, and the Commonwealth, a subordinate importance.

4

BRITAIN AND SOUTHERN AFRICA

THE British mode of Western civilization has its most powerful African bridgehead in Southern Africa. Success in preserving established bonds with West and Eastern Africa will turn in large part on the degree to which British influence in Southern Africa succeeds in assisting the present sharply conflicting racist-nationalisms to move decisively towards mutual tolerance and co-operation. A slow synthesis of traditional African, Afrikaner and British civilizations, the product of centuries of living together, supplies a hopeful groundswell but menacing upper currents and surface waves threaten the present and the immediate future. Many opportunities to exert constructive influence have been missed by Britain, primarily perhaps because it has proved impossible to give adequate attention to the complexities of Southern Africa, and also because there has been pragmatic contentment with important short-term economic, strategic and other gains.

Numerous opportunities remain open to Britain, however, and with the support of Western allies, notably the United States, they can be used to the benefit of the world, not least the African peoples who predominate and the Afrikaners who presently control the major part and resources of the zone. But success demands a new depth of analysis and understanding and a determination to sustain coherent action over time. Above all there must be an earlier perception of tendencies and trends so that policy and action may be better founded. Too frequently ill-founded and destructive pessimism has followed upon facile optimism.

Southern Africa in this chapter embraces the present Republic of South Africa, with South-West Africa, Southern Rhodesia and the three High Commission Territories of Basutoland, Bechuanaland and Swaziland. As originally organized British Central Africa constituted a separate section, but since the decision was made to dissolve the Federation of Rhodesia and Nyasaland it has been thought best to treat the lands south of the Zambesi as Southern

Africa and those north, including Northern Rhodesia and Nyasaland, as parts of Eastern Africa.

(i) SOUTH AFRICA

Given the experiences of fruitful British–South African partnership between 1939 and 1948 and the almost obsessionally optimistic regard for Smuts, it is not surprising that the United Kingdom was slow to awaken to the realities of Afrikaner-nationalist
intentions after Dr. Malan's electoral victory. For British Conservatives, shocked by the election of Labour in 1945, it was particularly easy to draw a false analogy between the defeat of Smuts
and the rejection of Churchill. The restoration of Churchill in
1951 played its part in heightening the illusion. Few observers distinguished between the politics of a mature and united country
and those of a youthful political union of divided peoples and
provinces.

Those who, in 1946 and 1947, predicted that any change in
South Africa's government would lead to constitutional and
political developments which would radically alter the pattern of
life in South Africa were regarded as alarmist. The inertia of
thought which underlay this attitude continued well into the new
Afrikaner-Nationalist régime and played its part, for example, in
encouraging a lack of sympathy in the United Kingdom for the new
and large organization of South African ex-servicemen and women
which sprang into being in 1951 to protest vigorously against the
threat to the constitution, notably the method of enacting and
enforcing the law to remove from the electoral rolls Coloured voters
whose rights were supposedly protected by one of the entrenched
clauses of the South Africa Act of 1909.

Complacency persisted in London until well after the re-election
of the Nationalists in 1953. During the next decade it did alter,
though only slowly, as the strength of Afrikaner-nationalist determination was borne in upon British observers. But it required Dr.
Verwoerd's withdrawal of South Africa from the Commonwealth
and the establishment of the Republic to bring final conviction that
a new era had been launched.

Boer and Briton in South Africa have tended to divide principally
over the issues of Crown and colour. Many British South Africans,
concerned to preserve their language and their established links

with their former homeland, were more keenly aware of the reluctance of the Crown and Commonwealth to their interests, than of their responsibility to Africans, Asians and Coloureds. Repeated emphasis by historians as well as Afrikaner-nationalist politicians upon the injustice of the Anglo-Boer War has also tended to encourage British South Africans not to question their secondary position in the national political life. Content to rely externally upon Britain and internally upon pro-British Afrikaner leaders like Smuts, most English-speaking white South Africans were unprepared for the vigorous and systematic stripping of British symbols and the fundamental underlying changes upon which the Nationalists embarked immediately after their return to power in 1948. Few had treated seriously the pre-war portents or the blue-print of an authoritarian republic which had become known in the early years of the war. Very few were prepared at the time to be more than wryly amused by the predictions of Arthur Keppel-Jones in *When Smuts Goes*, published in 1947. Not until mid-1951 did most British South Africans become alarmed and it was by then too late to challenge effectively the entrenched governing party.

The series of enactments which aroused strong opposition were carried out with increasing determination between 1948 and 1951 by Dr. Malan and his associates, who possessed the confidence of a disciplined group whose cohesion and plans had been forged with care over a long period of time. The war-criminals who had supported Germany and engaged in sabotage were released from prison and the uniforms and organization of the army were quickly reformed by Erasmus, Minister of Defence in succession to Smuts. Service dress was given a non-British appearance and new military decorations were substituted for the honours and awards hitherto prized by South African soldiers in common with other British and Commonwealth armed forces.

The control and training of the police, an important arm under the Defence Act of 1912, was also taken in hand at the centre and police relations with local university extra-mural and adult education courses were abruptly stopped. Discussions on race relations were henceforth to conform to *apartheid* doctrine.* An atmosphere of police watchfulness and suspicion became general. Judges and

---

* Police, as Gunnar Myrdal observes in *An American Dilemma*, occupy a front-line position in race relations. Their training on race questions, and their race attitudes, can be decisive in any national or local community.

magistrates withstood the pressures from politicians and from over-zealous policemen of Nationalist persuasion, though the link with the Judicial Committee of the Privy Council was severed by Dr. Dönges in 1950. The Civil Service Commission protested against irregularities in recruitment, most notably perhaps in the case of Professor Eiselen's appointment as Secretary for Native Affairs in place of a recommended English-speaking candidate with a long and distinguished career in the service. The executive insisted on a convinced supporter for this key post and Professor Eiselen was a leading *apartheid* theorist and advocate.

The determined emphasis on the Afrikaans language in every branch of official policy was a hallmark of the new régime. The objective was to place the imprint of Afrikaner culture on every aspect of South African life. So far as it could be done, the process of Anglicization was to be reversed and all people, including Africans, were to be brought under Afrikaner influence. In short, the ghosts of Milner and Rhodes were to be exorcised by the Afrikaans-speaking whites, whose proportion of the white population had remained at about two-thirds, despite Milner's determination to reverse the fractions. Every pressure was exerted on the non-nationalist Afrikaner to abandon his wider loyalties and to sub-scribe to the ethnic-national idea. Education was the principal means chosen, and from the earliest days of Malan's administration official action was taken to separate Afrikaans from English-speaking white boys and girls in primary and secondary schools. The Transvaal Language Ordinance of 1949 was a provincial measure but it was in accord with the "Christian National Educa-tion" policy devised for the whole country. The dual-medium ex-periments of E. G. Malherbe, which had commanded the support of Smuts and which were increasingly proving their worth in removing language, educational and social barriers, were cast aside. The sur-vival of the "Volk" demanded the abandonment of mutual toler-ance and the mobilization of the Afrikaner youth, who outnumbered their English counterparts. To make full use of their political power the age of the electoral franchise was reduced to eighteen years.

By means such as these the Afrikaner-nationalists progressively weakened the British tradition and the political and related powers of the English-speaking white South Africans who comprised their principal immediate adversaries. In the arena of colour, Malan, Strydom and Verwoerd in succession sought through *apartheid* a final solution to the problem of the African and Asian peoples and those of mixed racial origin. Of the three *apartheid* prime ministers, Johannes Strydom expressed himself most crudely in making frequent use of the term *baaskap*, with its frank connotation of "master-race" and "domination", but there was among all three close harmony of thought.

Apartheid intellectuals are perhaps to be distinguished from the politicians. Men like Eiselen and Olivier, and practical administrators like De Wet Nel, hold a genuine conviction that the Indonesian *adat* principle of "like over like" is not only merciful but best in theory for culturally and racially mixed societies. Such intellectuals or idealists have been ready to accept the probable discomforts and material losses which would attend the honest implementation of *apartheid*. In this they have been supported on Christian ethical grounds by assemblies of leading Dutch Reformed Churchmen. But great harshness has attended the official implementation of *apartheid*. It has arisen mainly from the practical enforcement of the many new laws and administrative arrangements which comprise an intricate, interlocking structure of complex, detailed measures designed to regulate almost every aspect of human contact between peoples of the different ethnic groups. Only a people wedded to the legalism of the Roman–Dutch tradition would have embarked on such detail; only a people put on their mettle by the thrusts of pragmatic opposition critics would have acted so strenuously and ruthlessly to prove that it could be applied. The errors of history were to be amended, social and economic forces were to be withstood, policy trends in race relations reversed.

The Group Areas Act of 1950 typifies *apartheid* theory. Other acts affecting Africans, Asians, Coloured and Europeans were passed before it, many other racial laws have been introduced since, but the principle of racial and ethnic separation received perhaps its most emphatic expression in this statute which prescribes the separate ownership and occupation of land and property by the different racial groups as defined in the Act. The Group Areas Bill was given eloquent support in and out of Parliament and affirmed at length in explanatory official memoranda. The extent of established segregation was acknowledged but Cabinet Ministers declared that *apartheid* was to go far beyond anything known in the past.

Dogma insisted that social friction characterizes inter-racial and inter-cultural contacts; hence people must be physically separated. African–Indian riots in Durban in 1949 were seized upon to drive home the point.* Natal was vulnerable on the Indian question and Nationalist propaganda played cleverly and insistently on "Indian penetration" in Durban and other "English" centres in order to weaken opposition. The widest powers of inquiry, decision and enforcement were given to the executive, and in many cases compensation for the loss of residential property was inadequate. Among Africans, already long subject to strict territorial segregation, new ethnic or tribal principles were enacted and given effect. The Bantu-speaking peoples, the majority racial group, were thus subdivided into Zulu, Sotho, Xhosa, Tswana and other groupings.

The Natives' Representative Council, set up under Hertzog's law of 1936, was abolished and a system of tribal, regional and territorial "Bantu authorities" was created to take the place of the earlier forms of modern African local council government, initiated by Cecil Rhodes in the Cape in 1894 and made permissible throughout the rest of South Africa by the Native Affairs Act of 1920. For Indians the same principle of closely controlled local government was mooted. To the distress of many individuals of all races, separation was imposed also upon the Coloured peoples who for over a century had shared franchise and other civic rights with Europeans in the Cape Colony and Province. The political rights of the Coloureds were not altered when the Cape African voters were separated by law in 1936. To Afrikaner-nationalists of Hertzog's persuasion it was in every way desirable, not least from the point of view of white security, that the substantial Coloured minority, people of part-European descent and of European culture, should continue to be associated with the white population. The termination of the traditional rights of the Coloured communities of the Cape and Natal served above all to underline the meaning of *apartheid* in contrast with past forms of segregation. From a purely electoral point of view the Afrikaner nationalists gained substantially by the removal from the rolls in several constituencies of the thousands of Coloured voters who traditionally voted against them. *Apartheid* apologists argue that the special representation which has been accorded to the Coloured population more than compensates for any loss but this view is difficult to accept in the face of the history of African franchise and representation.

* The report of the Commission of Inquiry into the Durban Riots is a remarkable document, revealing in its attitude towards Britain and British democracy as well as questions of race relations. The chairman was Mr. Justice van den Heever.

Apartheid has been enforced in every aspect of life in addition to politics. The Prohibition of Mixed Marriages Act of 1950 is an outstanding example. This measure was scarcely required in view of the small number of inter-racial marriages which were contracted in any year. Its introduction brought hurt and anxiety to families, including missionary couples, who had married in the less race-conscious days of the earlier Cape and Natal. But the tolerance of inter-racial marriages was seen as an affront to exclusivist ideology. The absence of specific legal sanctions against extra-marital relations between "whites" and all "non-whites", Asians and Coloureds as well as Africans, was also regarded as dangerous. The Immorality Amendment Act, introduced to repair the latter omission, deserves special study for its revelation of the emotions underlying *apartheid*. These laws which seek to govern the most intimate personal relations are but two of a vast complex of new *apartheid* measures. The law to enforce separation in public places such as railway stations, passageways and foot-bridges might also be mentioned because nothing is more apparent in South Africa today than the obtrusive notice-boards whose prohibitions are enforced by alert officials and policemen.

No act of *apartheid*, however, was more significant and retrogressive than that which terminated the non-racialism of "open" universities. After enjoying, and exercising, the freedom to accept members of any race the Universities of Cape Town, Witwatersrand, Natal and Rhodes have been deprived of this right. The African, Asian, Coloured and European students who, over decades, had learned much from one another in libraries, lecture-rooms, laboratories and common-rooms have now been separated and a series of ethnic universities brought into being. At school level the principle of separation to which reference was made in the case of Afrikaans and English-speaking white children, has been extended to apply with equal force to language, tribal and racial groupings of African, Asian and Coloured pupils, for whom special curricula have been devised. There was a great deal to criticize in the provision made for African, Coloured and Indian education before the *apartheid* era, but the curricula and examinations were the same and held promise of equal opportunity in a common society. "Bantu education" has brought about a fundamental change.

We cannot refer to every act of the Nationalist régime during the sixteen years of its existence, nor have we space to detail the history of the opposition to it, whether by political parties and movements or by Church, University and inter-racial organizations. What must be emphasized is the fact that resistance to narrow nationalism continues to be alive in South Africa even though the present régime has strengthened its immediate control by means of the harshest, authoritarian measures.* Faced with the fact of the appalling disregard of the rights and dignity of the African, Coloured and Asian peoples, some opponents of *apartheid* outside as well as inside South Africa have resigned themselves, albeit reluctantly at times, to working towards the revolutionary or forceful overthrow of the Afrikaner-nationalist Government by means of blockade, boycott or armed support for anti-government organizations. Others have chosen to concentrate upon ways and means whereby a more peaceful and less destructive change might be brought about, through educational support for and co-operation with those opposed to *apartheid*, and appeals to the Afrikaner conscience which will convince Afrikaner nationalists of the desirability of inter-racial partnership.

If the latter approach should prevail, and it is the one which a majority of Britons support, Britain as a nation will be faced with a task of the utmost difficulty. The constructive and acceptable aspect of Afrikaner national feeling will have to be shown sympathy. African nationalism at the same time will demand equal understanding and co-operation. The traditions of the important minorities of English-speaking whites, Indians and Coloureds must also be respected and safeguarded. Stated thus the challenge of South Africa might seem even more complicated than that of Cyprus and impossible of solution. There are grounds, however, for hoping for a change in Afrikaner outlook and the eventual acceptance throughout South Africa of a universalist, non-racial ethic.

In order to come to terms with Afrikaner nationalism, the reigning ideology, its prime elements must be understood. They comprise a determination both to avoid cultural or national extinction and to achieve and to preserve social and economic standards of the kind enjoyed in Western Europe and North America. Both aspirations are buttressed by Calvinist-derived political convictions. Many Afrikaners consider themselves an elect people possessed of a divine mission in Africa. The fear of cultural extinction, notably the obliteration of the Afrikaans language, derives chiefly from the history of British–Boer, not Boer–Bantu, relations. So far as Africans and Asians are concerned Afrikaners believe that their

* See *Postscript*.

tongue will prevail over the several Bantu and Indian languages spoken in South Africa. But the world position of English has allowed no such confidence in respect of the English language which is generally preferred by Africans and Asians. British and British South African attitudes towards Afrikaans have also been generally unfavourable. There has, it is true, been sympathy for Afrikaans on the part of a few Britons. Sir Thomas Holland of Edinburgh and Sir Fred Clarke of London, by their sympathetic understanding of Afrikaans and Afrikaner culture, have resembled Lord Dorchester in Quebec and President John Hyde of Eire, who gave support to French and Irish languages and traditions. In South Africa Alan Paton has long urged the study and use of Afrikaans on fellow-Anglicans of the Church of the Province of South Africa. More prevalent, however, for most of South Africa's history since unification, has been an attitude of imperious ethnocentrism stemming from Milner and his Anglicization policy in the schools of the conquered Boer republics. Milner's insistence upon English undermined the otherwise excellent work of his imported educational administrators and school-teachers, many of whom are remembered still with affection by Afrikaners of an older generation.

As a result of victory in the South African War and the English language policy of the reconstruction period, most British South Africans have been uninterested in the Afrikaans language movement, which was launched in the 1870's, and insensitive to Afrikaner feelings for their language. The mood of tolerance at the National Convention in 1908–9 encouraged the speedy acceptance of Dutch as one of the two official languages for the Union but there was less than enthusiasm for Hertzog's insistence in 1925 that the Constitution be amended to substitute Afrikaans for Dutch. The beauty of the Afrikaans translation of the Bible which appeared at the time was recognized but its appearance was marked also by wounding observations from Dutch- as well as English-speakers ignorant of the growth and structure of languages, including their own. Such observers could see little prospect of the "new" language serving as a worthy official medium.

Though Welsh is more ancient something of the feeling of Afrikaners for their language can be gained from discussions with Welsh nationalists. There is a real similarity between them and those Afrikaners who refer with passion to their "mother-tongue", and to the "soul of their people", their "language of prayer", their "language of poetry and love". Isolated far from Europe, Afrikaners feel more fiercely the need to preserve their pedigree. A Kruger Professorship of Afrikaans Language and Literature at Oxford might do something to reassure Afrikaners that their right to cultural freedom is respected. The more thorough-going acceptance of Afrikaans by English-speaking South Africans which is taking place could reinforce such initiative. Certainly developments of this kind are essential if Afrikaners are to be reassured about the future of their language and culture. And only when they are reassured are they likely to accept substantial political change.

"Poor Whiteism" has been a spectre among Afrikaners since the acceleration of South Africa's industrial revolution. There were many impoverished whites in the old pastoral republics and in the interior of the Cape Colony but they were preserved from extreme indigence by a close-meshed social safety net held beneath them by dominies and elders of the Dutch Reformed Churches, together with the more well-to-do farmers and their wives, who were conscious always of the obligations of kinship and the necessity of social cohesion on a frontier. During and after the 1914–18 war, when more efficient agricultural and industrial production were demanded, many landless and unskilled Afrikaners drifted increasingly to the cities and towns where they aggregated in distressing conditions not dissimilar from those of comparable groups of Africans. The world depression then accentuated an already bad situation which was documented in detail by the volumes published by the unofficial Carnegie Poor White Commission. These reports naturally received close attention from Afrikaner leaders though it is to be regretted that they gave wholly inadequate attention to the contemporary official "Native Economic Commission".

Afrikaner nationalists, always ready to be incensed by the relative economic prosperity and the better educational and social facilities of British South Africans, determined upon a more vigorous economic and social programme which would ensure for their people a position of comparable strength. Under political guidance a pyramidal plan of organizations of every kind was devised and brought increasingly into operation in the 1930's. Specifically Afrikaner trade unions, banks, insurance companies, savings clubs, chambers of commerce and welfare societies were created and interlocked with Afrikaner cultural and religious bodies. The Voortrekker Centenary celebrations in 1938 set the seal on a new militant, consciously corporative nationalism which developed under the leadership of Dr. Malan and other nationalists, all more narrowly single-minded and fiercely ethnocentric than General Hertzog, whom they overthrew and who died a disappointed and disheartened man in 1941.

Today, after sixteen years of nationalist rule, Afrikaners enjoy an economic and social position which was unknown to them before. A new urban bourgeoisie is in being and international trade has brought to many men and women an increased association with London, Paris, Amsterdam, New York, Hamburg and Geneva. The leading newspaper, the long-established *Die Burger*, though determinedly nationalist, is nevertheless self-critical and mature. In its columns frank discussions of *apartheid* have taken place side by side with consideration of the directly related issues of capital investment, the optimum use of domestic manpower, location of industry, international trade. One of the regrettable aspects of traditional non-Afrikaner attitudes to Afrikaans language and culture is the virtual closing to themselves, notably by Britons and British South Africans, of Afrikaans newspapers, journals and broadcasts. Only in 1956, for example, did the Bodleian Library in Oxford begin to take *Die Burger*. Other libraries and archives are also deficient in the material essential for understanding. The news and comment on Afrikaners in even the best English newspapers and journals tend to be fragmentary and one-sided. Yet Afrikaners continue to value the opportunities in Britain for scientific, industrial, commercial and other training and through those who study in British, European and American universities, colleges and research institutes there can be more sustained and constructive dialogue than hitherto has been conceived or attempted.

The Calvinist-derived and theologically reinforced political convictions of Afrikaner nationalists are complementary to the cultural, economic and social objectives of their creed. No effective dialogue is therefore conceivable unless the theology of Afrikanerdom is mastered and the effects of history on doctrine are more fully grasped. Anglicans and other English churchmen thus far have been notably unsuccessful in their approaches to the Dutch Reformed Churches and the theological seminaries. The heavy weight of history is perhaps such that Christian initiatives are best left to individuals like Dr. Visser t'Hooft and to organizations like the World Council of Churches rather than to Anglican leaders and agencies. Yet such initiatives can and must continue to be accompanied and supported by South African Anglicans as well as by Presbyterians, Methodists, Congregationalists and members of other churches of British origin represented in Southern Africa.

Important bridges have been built outwards from the Dutch Reformed Churches by several courageous Afrikaner Christians in recent years, in the face of fierce political hostility, as well as strong criticism from their fellow-churchmen; yet the depth and extent of religious belief among Afrikaners as a whole is such that these men represent perhaps the most hopeful of all tendencies in contemporary South Africa.* They have subjected dogmas of *apartheid* to close and reasoned analysis from within the framework of Calvinism and, despite feelings of strong sympathy with their fellow-Afrikaners they have been fearlessly explicit in their rejection of unacceptable ethical positions and ecclesiastical arguments of expediency which are adopted to bolster official racial policies. Churchmen based in Britain have seldom refrained from angry attacks on Afrikanerdom and *apartheid*. Such is human nature, including Christian human nature, that the acceptance of other approaches may be impossible, especially when so much of Afrikaner Christian thought and practice on racial matters is indefensible. But a more charitable approach by British Christians is very worthy of consideration. It would at least be guaranteed the effect of surprise and might even prove successful.

Viewing Afrikaner-nationalism as a whole, it is not suggested that an approach by way of persuasion to improve, rather than intermittent punishment to correct, will be easy to adopt. The brutalities and absurdities to which fear of cultural extinction and physical submergence have carried Afrikaner nationalism are impossible to condone. They are also very difficult to live with either in South Africa or in international association, even when the immediate object is one of therapy and change. There is also the supreme difficulty of seeming in African eyes to tolerate evil and abhorrent colour bars. It is in fact this last difficulty which has deterred many from attempting a more constructive approach to Afrikanerdom. This has been specially true since the Sharpeville shootings of March 1960. If, however, we look at the important point made by a discerning left-wing analyst that the African peoples do in fact enjoy a sense of confidence in the future which

* The point is often made in respect of the Sudan that the Muslim Arab conscience of the Northerners provides the best hope of improvement in the position of the African Southerners. The same point holds for the Christian Afrikaner conscience.

is unknown to the insecure white minorities, we are perhaps brought nearer to a position where it is possible to contemplate both the vigorous co-operation with the more hopeful aspects of Afrikaner nationalism and, *pari passu*, vigorous co-operation with similar elements of African nationalism.

Side by side with co-operation with Afrikaners Britain must therefore co-operate in every way with Africans. Education is a pre-eminent need of the African peoples of Southern Africa and it is open to Britain to make in the educational field a contribution of urgent and supreme worth. Emphasis on education in no way implies neglect of political co-operation with African leaders. That too is essential. But given the traditional Commonwealth Relations Office fear of anything but formal relations with the Government in office even educational aid has been grossly neglected. Scarcely any university scholarships for Africans from South Africa have been available since 1945 from either the United Kingdom Government or British foundations and trusts. It has been left largely to independent university initiative by means of voluntary subscriptions or personal endowment to bring to Oxford and other centres the few Africans who have gained admission to British universities. Little has been done for the High Commission Territories either until very recently, though the needs of these countries are also acute.

Political relations with African organizations and with Coloured and Indian bodies must be created and kept in good repair by Britain if she is to be true to her own traditions and if she is to strengthen her position in South Africa and her bridgeheads throughout Africa. The over-cautious Commonwealth Relations Office policy has not helped to strengthen the important concept of a loyal or non-revolutionary opposition—a British political institution of incalculable worth. Albert Luthuli and leaders of the African National Congress, together with many other extremely able and highly responsible African politicians and journalists, have through the years received comparatively little attention from representatives of the United Kingdom in South Africa. While individual officers have privately deplored the official restraints to which they have been subjected the outward reality as observed by Africans has been one of reserve and neglect.

In the 1960's there have been most welcome signs of a change in British official attitudes and practice but a great deal remains to be done. Too often it has been left to diplomats of other Western nations to conduct relations with African, Coloured and Indian individuals and organizations. Easy, matter-of-fact relations are undoubtedly difficult to establish with people who do not enjoy the franchise and other citizen rights and who are subject to numerous administrative disabilities, but it should long have been accepted and demonstrated that open diplomatic contact with the African majority was both essential and to be taken for granted. The exceptional success of the few United Kingdom officers who have ventured beyond the bounds of official caution indicates the rich possibilities of increased active co-operation with Africans. The sands of African goodwill to Britain must not be allowed to run out in South Africa. What has been said of Africans applies *mutatis mutandis* to the substantial Coloured and Asian minorities. They have been better prepared and able to invest in community education and other development projects, but their need of British understanding and co-operation is also great.

The lack of genuine contact with Africans, Coloureds and Asians —and with liberal whites, both Afrikaners and Britons—has led to these most hopeful elements of South Africa being ignored in their own country and represented as "dangerous", "subversive" or "irresponsible" in the United Kingdom press. Even a modicum of reasonable contact would have prevented the absurdity of there being any doubt about the integrity or worth of likeable, dedicated and in many ways essentially ordinary and respectable Englishwomen like Helen Joseph or Hannah Stanton. Certainly there are radical, left-wing whites in South Africa, and revolutionary Marxist or racist Indians, Coloureds and Africans, but sweeping misrepresentations of the South African opposition and the tendency towards mass condemnation has prevented Britain's most hopeful friends from being accurately identified.

Commonwealth Press scholarships and exchanges have done much to bring South African and British journalists together in study and working relationships. Such links must be preserved and extended under a different name now that South Africa has left the Commonwealth if South African society is to be adequately analysed and presented to Britain. United Kingdom society and British policy and public opinion must likewise be fully reported in South Africa in Afrikaans and African-language newspapers as well as in the long-established English-medium dailies and weeklies. British journalists with a proficiency in Afrikaans could contribute substantially to a better Afrikaner appreciation of the United Kingdom and Commonwealth. Informed, non-partisan articles submitted in Afrikaans would be accepted with greater frequency than any requiring translation.

The Press in South Africa represents one of Britain's most worthy achievements. From the 1820's, when Pringle and Fairbairn, editors of the *South African Commercial Advertiser*, fought and won, with the aid of *The Times* and *Chronicle*, a notable battle for Press freedom against an autocratic Governor, there has been a consistent tradition of informed and frank comment. The English-medium publications preserve this tradition today and represent a standard which holds its own even against high-level international competition. The South African African, Indian and Coloured newspapers and journals have drawn on this common heritage which accounts, in part at least, for the fact that narrow national, religious or tribal partisanship is not normally found in them.

This reference to the Press, inadequate though it is, must serve as a principal reminder of the depth of the institutional and organizational bonds which exist between Britain and South Africa. Established large-scale financial, commercial and industrial organizations with interests in South Africa operate in the City of London, in Liverpool and Birmingham and other centres. The Stock Exchange, banks* and commercial concerns of South Africa, including Chambers of Commerce and Rotary Clubs, are immediately familiar to visiting Britons. Church and university organizations have built secure bridges during the past century and more. Strong Anglican, Methodist, Roman Catholic and other denominational networks exist. A separate Anglican bishopric of Cape Town was created in 1848 to consolidate growth during the previous half-century. The universities of South Africa,† both Afrikaans and English-medium, derive primarily from the university world of Great Britain, though

---

* *The First Hundred Years of the Standard Bank* (Oxford University Press), published in London, 1963, supplies an excellent record of the history not only of this bank but of many aspects of the mutually beneficial commercial links between Britain and South Africa during the past century.

† In 1829, the South African College (Cape Town University) initiated higher education. Victoria College (Stellenbosch University) began in 1874. Other foundations include: Grahamstown—St. Andrew's College, 1855, and Rhodes University College, 1904; Bloemfontein—Grey College, 1855; Johannesburg—School of Mines, 1904, University of the Witwatersrand, 1922; Pretoria—Transvaal University College, 1908; Pietermaritzburg—Natal University College, 1909; Potchefstroom University College for Christian Higher Education, 1921; Fort Hare, 1923. Four medical schools exist at Cape Town, Johannesburg, Pretoria, Durban; the last is principally for African students.

the Afrikaans universities emphasize certain other West European, notably Dutch, characteristics. The law, in the structure, traditions and practices of the judiciary and the bar retain an essentially English cast even though Roman–Dutch law constitutes a foremost section of the civil law. The Civil Service at national, provincial and local government levels has not yet abandoned all its important British traditions.

An immense catalogue of organizations and practices might be compiled but the main point is made. What has been wrought organizationally and institutionally by Britain in South Africa during the past one and two-thirds centuries largely remains. In addition to the million and more people of direct British origin or descent there are many others who value the historical bonds with Britain and the Commonwealth. The South African Parliament has suffered serious erosion of its Westminster heritage but perhaps as much of parliamentary democracy remains to build on as elsewhere on the continent. Certainly it will be tragic for the whole of Africa if the resources of South Africa cannot be drawn upon freely for development and welfare throughout the continent.

Nowhere else in Africa, for example, is there to be found the wealth of modern scientific research or applied scientific and technical achievement, much of it of direct British origin, that exists in South Africa. Lord Hailey and other impartial British analysts have frequently directed attention to this fact and to the value of South African contributions in the work of the former inter-colonial Commission for Technical Co-operation in Africa South of the Sahara (C.C.T.A.). Individual South African biologists, veterinary surgeons, agricultural and medical scientists have given notable service to Ghana and other independent states. The same is true of teachers, economists and statisticians. Their professional training and experience within an African environment has frequently given their work an immediate utility of a kind which has been appreciated by African Governments eager to command all available expertise in the interest of rapid development.

But to release to the continent the badly needed resources of South Africa the country must at all costs be spared the destruction and chaos of the Congo or the devastation of Algeria. At the same time there can be no toleration of a régime and an ideology which is deeply offensive to independent Africa. Every effort must be directed, therefore, towards guaranteeing internationally the legitimate cultural and other rights of the Afrikaners, who will undoubtedly fight once more to the bitter end, as they did between 1899–1902, if such guarantees are not provided, while equal effort is directed towards bringing to Africans in South Africa political and other freedom.

Two principal steps are therefore necessary if South Africa is to be changed in the manner suggested. Effective international action must be taken, and a political constitution acceptable to genuinely representative South Africans of all cultural and racial groups* must be devised and brought into operation. At international level it will be necessary for Britain to work actively within each of her major world associations as well as independently through her established unilateral links. The four international associations—European, Anglo-American, Commonwealth and United Nations—are discussed in the final chapter. Britain holds a foremost and respected position within each and her sustained pressure for democratic non-racialism in South Africa coupled with full recognition of the distinctive rights of the several cultural communities must exert wide influence.

As for the political constitution, it may well be that a new system of government, along the lines of the "racial-federalist" proposals of Arthur Keppel-Jones in his book *Friends or Foes*, will be decided upon. A substantial re-drawing of internal frontiers would then be required, however. An alternative version of federalism could be one based on the proposals originally made by W. P. Schreiner at the National Convention of 1908–9. Here power would be divided simply between the constituent provinces of the Cape, Transvaal, Natal and Orange Free State and delegated in defined matters to the central government. South African history since union suggests that such a dispersion of power might indeed have been wise. But it is not inconceivable that the original unitary constitution adopted under the South Africa Act of 1909 could suffice provided that African, Coloured and Asian voters are re-admitted freely and on fully equal terms to the Cape and Natal voters' rolls and admitted also on the same basis to the electoral rolls of the Transvaal and Orange Free State. Additional safeguards such as a "Bill of Rights" and suitable provision for the judicial

---

* In private discussion leading Afrikaner-nationalist editors, churchmen and politicians of independent mind make evident their acceptance of the urgent need for thorough-going consultation and negotiation between representatives of all peoples and parties. They deplore the insensitive authoritarianisms of the Verwoerd administration.

protection and enforcement of civic and cultural rights might be incorporated but the existing, familiar structure of government would remain.

From the viewpoint of most, possibly all, groups in South Africa, it is likely that British initiative in international discussions on South Africa will be increasingly welcome. Intelligent Afrikaner nationalists, even those most bitterly critical of Britain in the past, now appreciate the value of British moderation in international debate on South Africa and indicate a new readiness to listen to British suggestions. Africans, Coloureds and Asians with no wish to see their country become a battle-ground, as well as the Europeans in opposition to the Government, are strongly in favour of greater specifically British influence of an enlightened and progressive kind being exerted alongside Scandinavian and United Nations' efforts. In internal matters, including constitutional arrangements, Britain is also more likely to be looked to as honest broker than many Britons believe. The British origin of South Africa's main institutions is acknowledged, and there is a respect for British administrative and judicial experience. Britain's bridgehead in South Africa is strong and must not be neglected.

(ii) SOUTH-WEST AFRICA

One of the questions which is uppermost in the minds of students of African affairs at the present time is the likelihood of effective United Nations' intervention in South-West Africa, possibly by armed force, if the International Court of Justice at the Hague should rule that South Africa has defaulted in regard to her administration of the mandate of the League of Nations and her failure to place the territory under international trusteeship. Many who favour the enforcement of any such decisions by means of international police action see South-West Africa becoming a base for further United Nations' intervention throughout Southern Africa in order firstly to overthrow the Afrikaner-nationalist Government and *apartheid* in South Africa, secondly to remove Portuguese rule in Angola, and thirdly to transform the present system of government in Southern Rhodesia. It is assumed by this school of thought that *apartheid* and Portuguese and Southern Rhodesian rule will be deemed to constitute threats to international peace and security which will justify United Nations' action.

It is tempting to enlarge on this question in respect of South-West Africa, but it is one which has become increasingly a general international issue in which Britain's voice, though important, especially in the Security Council, is but one of many. For the historical reasons explained elsewhere in this essay, Britain has stronger and more direct links with the High Commission Territories, Southern Rhodesia and South Africa and it is through her bridgeheads in these countries that her constructive influence in Southern Africa may best be brought continually to bear. Since 1914, when Britain requested the Government of Botha and Smuts to undertake the military campaign against German South-West Africa as part of the Union's share in the total empire war effort, the United Kingdom has had little direct association with the country. Walvis Bay, the best harbour, which Britain annexed in 1878 and preserved intact from the encircling German annexations, has long since become and remains an integral portion of the Cape Province of South Africa. Like Simonstown, Walvis Bay has repeatedly proved beneficial to the Royal Navy, but the jurisdiction over both areas is and has been South African, not British.

Great Britain, nevertheless, by virtue of her historical association with South Africa and her sponsorship at Versailles of the South African mandate as well as by reason of her membership of the Security Council could have an important, possibly even a decisive, vote in the United Nations if the South-West African and *apartheid* questions are brought forward in the drastic form outlined above. Present indications, however, are that neither a Labour nor a Conservative administration would feel justified in going to the extent of full-scale armed action. Strong moral pressure will almost certainly be exerted upon South Africa by Britain to uphold any ruling of the International Court. But, given Britain's thoroughly justified exercise of the veto in the recent case of Southern Rhodesia, it is difficult to see any British Government being persuaded, save by the most convincing evidence, that international peace and security is sufficiently threatened to warrant experiment with the ultimate sanction.*

There is little point, therefore, in dwelling on facts such as South-West Africa's remoteness from South Africa in physical,

---

* If logic and equity, not mere majority politics, are to govern the General Assembly, there are several other countries and situations in West, East, North and North-East Africa, not to mention the wider world, which constitute at least an equal threat to international peace and security.

geographical and tactical terms. There are vast, arid areas which separate South-West Africa from the principal centres of South Africa. Saying this does not mean that, even if there is no International Court decision and United Nations' action, Britain would be free from the duty of trying to persuade South Africa and the South-West African administration to reform the system of government. It was perhaps understandable that in the circumstances of the day, the original South-West Africa Affairs Act of 1925 should have made no provision for African representation and that this was acceptable to the Permanent Mandates Commission. Other aspects of the Union's interpretation of the League's mandate of 1919, notably Article 2, which gave to South Africa "full power of administration and legislation subject to the present mandate as an integral portion of the Union of South Africa" were also reasonable. But wholly different was the new Nationalist Government's speedy enactment in 1949, at a time when their majority in the Union Parliament was very slender, of an amendment to the South-West Africa Affairs Act which allowed them to strengthen their control over South-West Africa and to introduce from the mandated territory an excessive proportion of European members into the Senate and House of Assembly in Cape Town.

The political, legal and administrative disabilities of the Africans of South-West Africa are as bad as those of Africans in the Republic. Britain must on every occasion support moral pressure intended to improve their position in the mandated territory. That is an inescapable obligation. But if constructive influence on Southern Africa is to be sustained it can probably be applied more effectively by Britain in South Africa itself and through Southern Rhodesia and the High Commission Territories.

(iii) SOUTHERN RHODESIA AND THE HIGH COMMISSION
TERRITORIES

If South Africa provides the strongest bridgehead in Africa still open to be won to Western democracy, Southern Rhodesia continues to represent an area of special significance within Southern Africa. Of the four British territories south of the Zambesi which were left out when the "big four"—the Cape, Transvaal, Natal and Orange Free State—were united in 1909–10, Southern Rhodesia is by far the largest in population, including a settled population of

European descent, and the richest in resources. Basutoland, a wholly African mountain enclave in the Drakensberg, Swaziland and Bechuanaland each possess a symbolic importance and offer a challenge to the free world to assist in economic development of the kind indicated in the Morse report, which will also help to ensure the maximum political autonomy and administrative efficiency.

But for an effective return towards Rhodes's goal of a strong, prosperous and non-racial federation of all eight territories of Southern Africa, Southern Rhodesia's role could be marginally decisive. This possibility has been recognized by several United Kingdom observers, and Southern Rhodesia, with its consciously patriotic British settlers, has been exploited towards this end since 1889, when a royal charter was awarded to the British South Africa Company, who were thereby enabled to prevail over Kruger. In the Jameson Raid, the Anglo–Boer War, South Africa's unification, and the two World Wars, Southern Rhodesia's patriotism proved of particular value in helping to evoke and reinforce support from south of the Limpopo, notably in Natal, the Witwatersrand and the Cape. Seen from within this context, it is a special misfortune that the well-intentioned Federation of Rhodesia and Nyasaland was defective in certain constitutional arrangements, offensive to Africans in its negotiation, and inadequate in its thrust towards inter-racial partnership during the critical first five years.

Post-mortem argument over the Federation has revealed disagreement as to which of the three main causes was most instrumental in compelling dissolution. Those closely involved in constitution-making and the pre-Federation negotiations, have tended to blame Federal leaders like Sir Roy Welensky or his principal rivals for not achieving sufficient success soon enough to convince Africans of the value of a united Central Africa under a joint European–African partnership in which experienced Europeans exerted the major influence. It is, on the other hand, all too easy to point to the now universally acknowledged strong African opposition to Federation which existed throughout Central Africa, both at the time the Order in Council was imposed in 1953 and for decades before. Between 1951 and 1953, however, the fact of African opposition was either emphatically denied at the highest level by Ministers of the Crown responsible for Central Africa, or it was held by them to be of little or no account because Africans lacked understanding of the concept of "federation".

It was equally difficult between 1951 and 1953, in the face of a solid front of senior authority, to direct attention to certain obvious weaknesses in the constitution. To anyone acquainted with political tendencies in plural societies, not least in the South African Union, it seemed necessary above all to give Africans a voice sufficient at least to block constitutional amendments or other principal draft laws which vitally affected their interests. Suggestions that African representation should comprise at least "one-third plus" in a legislature where a two-thirds majority was required for amendment were, however, brushed aside as unrealistic. There can as yet be no final assessment as to where the main culpability rests for the breakdown of the Federation but each cause has been important. Inadequate and clumsy negotiations prevented the winning of much wider African support and the limitation, and weaknesses of the constitution added their own substantial burden to those in authority who were faced with the virtually impossible task of changing long-established policies and expectations within a few short years.

There were moments in the history of the Federation when the balance inclined towards success, but such opportunities could have been seized and acted on only if there had been complete mutual understanding of objectives, notably of the meaning of "partnership" and the most vigorous co-operation between the Government of Great Britain and the Federal Government in Salisbury. More certain success would have followed acceptance of the reasonable requests of African leaders who asked, *inter alia*, that "partnership" be defined and agreed before Federation. The substitution of the method of patient persuasion for imperious haste would also have helped greatly. Today it seems obvious that they were more right who argued ten years ago that the Federation could never be brought to fruition if African views were ignored, if more courtesy was not forthcoming,* and if serious efforts were not made to meet the constitutional and other criticisms of students who had devoted the time and effort required to keep abreast of local affairs. The vice of looking to the eminent and pliable rather than to the informed and consistent was seldom more evident than during 1951–3, the years of decision.

The most fundamental error sprang from the failure to apply to British Central Africa elementary principles of understanding

* The curt dismissal of the requests of delegations of chiefs and African political leaders to be allowed to present petitions to the Queen was a needless affront to those brought up in a tradition of personal loyalty and among whom were lively recollections of Queen Victoria and her successors.

derived from history and the analytical social studies. No one acquainted with the recent history of the British territories to the north and south of the Zambesi, and more particularly with the very different policies applied to Africans, could expect there to be any easy fusion. Some members of the Hilton Young Commission in their report of 1929 had aptly summarized the main reasons why the close association of Northern Rhodesia and Nyasaland, on the one hand, with Southern Rhodesia on the other, could not succeed, whether under a federal or a unitary constitution. But the Hilton Young Report was wilfully swept aside as irrelevant to the 1950's by over-confident men of the Colonial Office, the Cabinet and Parliament.

The same lack of social and historical awareness to which Karl Mannheim directed attention in the post-war years also goes far to explain the irresolution which attended Central African policy once Federation was introduced. In the brief span of six to seven years between 1953 and 1959–60, Central African policy was subjected to the full force of contradictions which sprang from the United Kingdom's attempt to adapt strategically to the changing political circumstances of the world, notably the new Afro-Asian world after Bandung in 1955, and tactically to the internal needs and pressures of the two Rhodesias and Nyasaland under the system of government which had deliberately entrusted local Europeans with the greater substance of power.

Increasingly Britain's relative weakness in the modern world was emphasized by certain British scholars as well as by politicians who pointed repeatedly to the anti-Mau Mau campaign as an example of the severe draining of resources and energy which might be expected to recur in Central Africa. The Nyasaland disturbances of 1959 were both a consequence of such irresolution and in part a cause of the eventual policy which was announced in the "wind of change" speech in February 1960. Only a confident Britain determined to see Federation through to the fulfilment of partnership over the space of from two to three decades could have made the 1953 constitution work. If the task of persuading the Northern Africans to abandon the expectations built up in them by decades of Colonial Office policy was formidable, so also was the task of effecting a rapid change in outlook among the hitherto completely dominant white minority of Southern Rhodesia, many of whom were confirmed in their trustee or paternalist attitudes by Britain's action in 1953.

Given Britain's inability or unreadiness to control and co-ordinate the progressive advance of the three territories and their diverse peoples to partnership, it is specially unfortunate that Southern Rhodesia's potential role as a liberal lever on South Africa was dissipated by Federation. Seen in contrast with developments in the "African States" of British Africa, to which Northern Rhodesia and Nyasaland looked naturally for precedent, Southern Rhodesia appeared reactionary or illiberal. Within the context of Southern Africa, her appropriate historical framework, however, Southern Rhodesia, with her traditional commitment to common franchise and other rights as well as to the English language and traditions, had a more liberal image. Now that the follies of Federation are acknowledged and the political framework has been dismantled, it is to be hoped that Southern Rhodesia may be allowed to regain something of her former position.

Current pan-Africanist and international pressures are directed towards the complete overthrow of the system of government which has existed since 1923, or earlier if part of the Company period is included, and towards the incorporation of Southern Rhodesia, or "Zimbabwe", into the body of African states to the north of the Zambesi. But if the non-violent transformation of South Africa, together with the relatively undamaged preservation of her re-sources and services is aimed at, then the present grossly exag-gerated condemnations of Southern Rhodesia must be halted and the country given every support to move as smoothly and rapidly as possible towards a genuine non-racialism acceptable to Africans, Europeans and others. Contemporary inter-racial participation in government in Southern Rhodesia is at present in advance of South Africa. Despite South African example the African parliamentary representation which was brought about in 1963 is likely to be preserved.* There is therefore a basis for further adjustments within the foreseeable future to the point where Africans will have an effective share of power.

One of the undoubted advantages of Federation was that it thrust Southern Rhodesia more rapidly towards the acceptance of a wider African political franchise and African membership of parliament than was otherwise likely to have occurred. Although several of the country's leaders were mindful of the non-racial franchise tradition of the parent Cape and critical of *apartheid*, they were nevertheless

* See *Postscript*.

dangerously slow in encouraging greater African participation in the processes and responsibilities of democratic government. The presence of African members of the Federal Assembly in Salisbury greatly facilitated the admission of Africans to the territorial legislature. Given the history of Southern Africa it was a substantial step forward when African members of parliament joined men of the calibre of Sir Edgar Whitehead in opposition to a right-wing Southern Rhodesia Government.

Another major contribution was made during the years of the Federation by the University College of Rhodesia and Nyasaland in Salisbury. The 1952 commission under the chairmanship of Sir Alexander Carr-Saunders,* Director of the London School of Economics and head of the Inter-University Council for Higher Education Overseas, prepared the ground well and laid a strong foundation for the new University, which opened its doors in March 1957. High standards and a thorough-going non-racialism were emphasized. The relationship with the University of London has proved of special benefit. Although the tensions of the surrounding political society of the Federation have made themselves felt, sometimes acutely, the University College has a substantial credit balance of genuine achievement which must prove of durable worth to both Southern and Eastern Africa. Africa has need of every centre of higher education. A soundly established and well-equipped university, incorporating new medical and law schools, in one of the important borderlands of Africa promises to be called upon increasingly and to meet wider demands in the future. The teaching and student body is multi-racial, and Africans and Europeans live together in the halls of residence. Few activities at the University College have been more fundamentally fruitful than the Leverhulme inter-African university conferences. The 1964 Conference of University librarians drew representatives from every part of the continent, as well as from Britain.

Southern Africa has never been and can never be isolated or insulated from the rest of Africa. Southern Rhodesia and Bechuanaland, and to a lesser degree, Swaziland, have borders with states other than South Africa and there is frequent and regular traffic across the borders. In the case of Southern Rhodesia and Northern Rhodesia there is a common railway system, the Rhodesia Railways, and a common major source of electric power and water in the

* Cf. Carr-Saunders, A. M., *New Universities Overseas*, London 1962.

Kariba Dam. The acceptance of the break-up of the Federation of Rhodesia and Nyasaland for the organization of this chapter is in no sense, therefore, meant to suggest either that the established traffic will diminish or that it is in any way desirable that it should do so. It is rather hoped that both newly self-governing Northern Rhodesia (Zambia) and Nyasaland (Malawi) on the one hand and Southern Rhodesia (Rhodesia or Zimbabwe) on the other will increase and strengthen their many ties. In trade, employment, education and sport there are numerous rewarding links already and others can be added.

The Zambesi nevertheless is an historical and policy frontier within British Africa. We need not use André Siegfried's emotive and not wholly applicable conception of a "Mason-Dixon line",* but for the reasons given in the earlier chapters there is good cause to think of Southern Africa as an entity. And in addition to the numerous close commercial, administrative, legal and educational bonds, there is substance in some comparison with America from the race relations point of view because the common history of close association between Africans and Europeans through several generations has made Southern Africa more akin to the United States than any other part of Africa. The Africans of Southern Africa are in many respects more "Westernized" and accustomed to modern industrial society and are therefore more like American Negroes than Africans elsewhere. Like American Negroes, the political, economic and social objectives of educated Africans have centred upon equal rights within an overall common society rather than upon separate "African states". These broad objectives are likely to remain despite the creation of Bantustans like the Transkei and other Afrikaner-nationalist endeavours to strengthen tribal and ethnic associations.

Basutoland, Bechuanaland and Swaziland through their close involvement in the South African economy, notably their dependence upon financial relations such as the customs quota and wage remittances, also form integral portions of Southern Africa. They have throughout their history been largely dependent on South Africa for most social and other services and the new, nonsectarian University College in Basutoland, which is being developed from the small Roman Catholic college at Roma, will retain close relations with South African universities, archives,

* In his *African Journey* (London 1950), Siegfried asked whether the Zambesi or the Limpopo would constitute Africa's Mason-Dixon line.

libraries and research institutes. The advance of each of the High Commission Territories to genuine self-government within the immediate future will however be of real significance. With the Basutoland Government wholly African in composition, those of Bechuanaland and Swaziland predominantly so, together with a multi-racial Southern Rhodesian administration there will open the prospect of direct contacts and negotiations on a basis of governmental equality with South Africa which might well assist all eight units of Southern Africa, perhaps with South-West Africa as a ninth, to work out a new and more rewarding and hopeful *modus vivendi*, possibly even in the long term a great federal state.

5

BRITAIN AND WEST AFRICA

THE measure of optimism which facts compel us to allow to Southern Africa and its relationship with Britain must be given equally to West Africa. Britain's bridgeheads along the coast of Guinea are strong and rich in promise. At the turn of the year 1963–4 the Freetown correspondent of the journal *West Africa* could write that 1963 was notable for the fact that "almost alone among West African countries Sierra Leone has had no treason trial, no attempts on its leaders' lives; and almost alone, too, Sierra Leone has an effective parliamentary opposition". But despite this disturbing and not unfounded observation on the present political condition of Ghana and Nigeria, as well as Togo, Gabon, Senegal and other countries, there is too deep a history of common democratic aspiration and too strong a tradition of freedom to justify the weakening or abandonment by Britain of her ties with West Africa. Despair is out of place also in respect of the social and economic challenges facing Nigeria, Ghana, Sierra Leone and the Gambia. They too can be overcome with lasting mutual benefit by a combined endeavour which builds on deep foundations already laid.

Before we examine in turn some of the important political, social and economic problems of contemporary West Africa, it may be helpful to recall the distinctive characteristics of the British West African nexus to which reference was made at the beginning of the first chapter. Traders, missionaries and administrators, according to Mary Kingsley,* comprised the British genus "coaster". Significantly absent from her classification were miners, planters, ranchers and farmers. Though some few British and other Western mining engineers did come to work the gold of Ashanti and other mineral deposits, and though strong efforts were made after the First World War by leading Britons to be permitted to establish

---

* See Stephen Gwynn's *The Life of Mary Kingsley*, 1862–1900, for an account of this gallant, perceptive and witty Englishwoman. On page 31 of the second edition of 1933 there is a concise statement of her views on the wider importance of traders and of trade.

H

plantations in the British West African territories, the essential composition of the European "coaster" population was not changed throughout the period of colonial rule, nor was their number ever increased to a degree alarming to local African opinion.

In pronounced contrast, therefore, with the British territories on the eastern side of the continent, stretching from the Cape to Kenya, the West African colonies, protectorates, mandated or trust territories experienced no permanent settlement. No land was alienated by the administrations to immigrant farmers and ranchers. Applications for concessions to permit companies to operate cocoa and other plantations were likewise rejected. By this rejection the British West African territories were spared many of the disputes and abuses which affected near-by lands under French, German, Belgian and American influence. Land ownership was preserved in African hands and small-scale individual or peasant farmers and growers were responsible for production in a predominantly agricultural economy. Much trade at local level also remained or became African controlled, and so too did the operation of motor transport enterprises. The differences in British policy and practice between South-Eastern and West Africa may thus be briefly summarized, but brevity should not be allowed to obscure the profound nature and consequences of the differences.

There is a distinct quality about British West Africa and a characteristic general outlook among Britons associated with ships and other craft out of Liverpool, London and the Guinea coast which marks off it and them very definitely from their fellows on the other side of the continent. Professor Sir Keith Hancock's description of British West Africa as a "traders' frontier" in contrast with a frontier of settlement perhaps best summarizes the central reason for the difference. But as he and others have shown, British West Africa, after the abolition of the slave trade and slavery, became in the nineteenth and twentieth centuries a traders' frontier of a very special kind.

Philanthropists of the anti-slavery school were convinced of the value and virtue of legitimate commerce as a means not only of eradicating the evil institution but as perhaps the best method of opening Africa to the wider influences of modern civilization. Men of the calibre of Granville Sharp, Wilberforce and Livingstone firmly held this view. Together such individuals and their supporting societies and companies were both able to influence official policy, and at the same time were themselves always responsive to suggestions calculated to regulate trading operations in a manner beneficial to African welfare.

On the Indian Ocean side of the continent the competition of European, Indian and Arab immigrants with Africans at every level prevented Livingstone and his associates from giving full play to the philosophy of Christian commerce. The nature of the traditional economies was different, and so also were the type and distribution of the natural resources. Only in very recent times has Sierra Leone's diamond boom brought something of the flavour and turmoil of the Kimberley "rush". The overall volume of West African trade in comparison with that of Southern Africa might be small in animal and vegetable as well as mineral products, but trade in West Africa was liberatory in the spirit of Adam Smith or of Emerson, if American example is allowable. Despite the dispossession of Amerindians from their lands, and the continued existence of slavery in his South, Emerson undoubtedly spoke also for the enlightened merchants of the British companies trading with West Africa when he wrote that "the historian will see that trade was the principle of liberty . . . that it makes peace and keeps peace".

The gay, brisk and confident market women of West Africa, mistresses of commerce, and the shrewd, good-humoured individualist West African farmers, producers from family holdings of cocoa, palm-kernels, cotton and ground-nuts, provide West Africa with much of its characteristic and attractive flavour. We must not ignore abuses, and abuses there have continued to be on a coast where African suppliers and middlemen had previously engaged alongside Europeans and Americans in the slave trade. Nor must we overlook the impatience, sometimes resentment, of African commercial aspiration in the face of skilful competition from European buyers and sellers backed by large metropolitan concerns and, during the last part of the nineteenth century, from the enterprising Lebanese. The latter, by virtue of their intermediate position, frequently suffered slings and arrows from both Europeans and Africans. Lebanese achievement has been remarkable none the less, and the Christian and Muslim descendants from the ancient Phoenicians are equipped by history and temperament to participate both in trade directed towards the coast, and in trade by caravan across the desert from the emirates and other provinces of Islam in the inland sectors of Nigeria, Ghana, Sierra Leone and the Gambia. Outstanding Lebanese individuals have played their part also in stimulating production in West Africa and West African commerce in Britain.

If trade and economics have been chiefly responsible for fashioning the British–West African relationship and for supplying a distinctive character to the West African countries recently under British rule, the missionaries and administrators, and more recently the secular teachers of trade unionism, co-operative organization, of adult and university education, must be acknowledged, for their contribution also has been substantial.

The work of generations of Christian teachers is everywhere obvious in the coastlands of Guinea and inland, where the middle regions merge into the great belt of Islam. Even in the heart of the Muslim area the life-work of devoted medical missionaries of the calibre of Dr. Walter Miller is reflected in the grateful recollections of the countless men, women and children whom he may not have converted to Christianity but to whose health and well-being he ministered in selfless fashion. The English-speaking "White Fathers" are also to be found in the inland territories, working in simple dwellings in towns like Tamale or walking or cycling along the tracks between distant village communities. But it was the policy of the British administrations not to give offence to Islam and to avoid the friction of competition between major faiths, which could have erupted had eager Christian missionaries been given free access to African rulers and subjects governed by conservative forms of Muslim belief and law.

Towards the coast, however, Christianity is very evident. The edifying sermons and rousing hymns in the Liberian religious broadcasts have their own distinct flavour, reminiscent of the faith of those Americo-Liberians of an earlier day who returned from the United States to Africa. Methodism and Presbyterianism supply major denominational components in Liberian Christianity and they exist in strength also in the other English-speaking West African territories. Wesleyans and Presbyterians are numerous in modern Ghana and the other countries, Presbyterians having in many places taken over from Basel missionary predecessors. The large Quaker interests connected with the cocoa trade reflect also the important concern of the Society of Friends, who have made notable contributions to African welfare. Roman Catholics and Anglicans are to be found in every territory, though the Anglican congregations whether of "S.P.G." or "C.M.S." orientation may not always resemble in their outlook and behaviour those of England, whom Betjeman could describe as conservative and good and slow.

But it is Christianity as a whole to which attention should rather be directed, partly because inter-denominational co-operation has made headway in West Africa, and partly also because each denomination of any size has embarked on essentially similar educational, health and other services in a zone which is still in desperate need of them. Primary schools, secondary schools and teacher-training centres have been established wherever the particular church or missionary society has been able to raise the funds from its home supporters and local members. The education of girls and women has always received some degree of support which has increased steadily through the years. The bleakly named Female Institutions of the Victorian age have proliferated into the happy Girls' Schools of the present, which send forward their due quota to the co-educational colleges and universities. Mission hospitals and nurse-training centres pioneered also both the healing of the sick of both sexes and an advancement in the status of women.

One of the most important contributions of the church in West Africa, notably of the Church Missionary Society (C.M.S.), founded in 1799, was the development, despite vicissitudes, of Fourah Bay College from early in the nineteenth century and the education over the years of a substantial number of outstanding African leaders. Bishop Samuel Adjar Crowther, consecrated Bishop in Canterbury in 1864, was its first pupil and many others who became priests and school-teachers, including headmasters of C.M.S. grammar schools, studied at Fourah Bay. In 1876 a special relationship was entered into with Durham University and the dream of Dr. Edward Blyden for a West African university was given initial reality. The scholarly Blyden, who rose to high office in Liberia, was a West Indian whose colour denied him higher education in the United States, where he was first taken in the hope that he might be trained for the ministry. In 1879 the degrees of the first graduates were conferred by the Bishop.

In addition to the regular output of graduates from the Fourah Bay University College, which from the outset included students from other West African countries, there was a steady flow of West Africans to Great Britain. Many received advanced training at the C.M.S. College in Islington, others studied at Oxford, Cambridge and London, or qualified for the bar at one of the Inns of Court. Dr. John Easmon, who became Chief Medical Officer in the Gold

Coast in 1893, studied medicine both in Brussels and in London before he undertook the research on malaria on which he published a notable, original work. By the end of the century there was an impressive group of eminent West African clergy, scholars and professional men, many bearing European names adopted by their families from former masters or benefactors. From Sierra Leone they radiated to the other territories, some like Bishop Crowther returning from bondage to his native land of Nigeria, where the C.M.S. was once more prominent in education and evangelism.

The early presence in each territory of a significant number of well-educated Africans with first-hand experience of Britain and other Western countries had its important influence upon British administrators. It is true that Lugard was critical and suspicious of educated Africans and that between the wars there was not the expansion in African appointments to the administration which might have been anticipated from past practice and the growth in education. But there were always educated Africans to be encountered by the young British officers, including several eminent in theology, law or medicine, and their effect was such as to reduce the dangers of adverse stereotyped judgements being made of African ability and character. There is no better solvent of prejudice than competent medical treatment from an African doctor or nurse. It is true that the many lawyers of West Africa have sometimes provoked hostile comment from some British administrators but their presence too has been generally beneficial, especially when reflected through distinguished African judges or eminent civil servants and public service commissioners qualified in law.

In every zone of British Africa certain great administrators have stood out in their day to become legends and symbols. We have referred already to Lugard and his associates, all notable for their integrity and thoroughness. Of an earlier age Captain George Maclean, who arrived at Cape Coast in 1830 and served the Gold Coast for many long years, achieved a remarkable reputation. Admiration among Africans for his efficiency in economic development and judicial and administrative work were matched by affection for his fairness and wisdom. The Maclean tradition has been important in the Gold Coast (Ghana), where other men of a later age have also won renown. Sir Gordon Guggisberg, founder of Achimota College and architect of the 1925 Education Ordinance as well as the famous constitution of that year, was outstanding during the interwar years. His far-sighted and realistic plans for preparing Africans

to assume senior administrative offices in the government service
were not brought to fruition as soon as they might have been; there
was much the same pause in West Africa as in the Sudan and elsewhere. But at Achimota the close partnership of the Rev. A. G.
Fraser and Dr. Aggrey created a college whose graduates have
served their country with the same distinction as have those of
Gordon College.

In more recent times the Gold Coast, like Nigeria and the other
territories, has had outstanding men to uphold the tradition and
style of West African Governors. Together with many able lieutenants, these governors and administrative officers were quite as
much "coasters" as any trader or missionary. On the eve of independence, when African ministers required guidance on the
unfamiliar intricacies of their portfolios, many Britons were impressive in their quiet, tactful performance of duty. Some stayed on
after their administrative careers to serve the cause of African
education.

These administrators were some of the principal agents of British
enterprise and endeavour in West Africa. They must serve as
representative because space does not allow consideration of the
agriculturists, foresters, horticulturalists, geologists, archaeologists,
anthropologists and the many others from Britain who contributed
substantially to Africa of themselves—though few of them would
wish to deny that they themselves gained greatly from the challenge
and experience. In the long course of British–West African history,
especially the years since the last half of the eighteenth century,
when slavery began to be progressively overthrown, these men
helped, in company with Africans, to lay the foundations of the
modern states of Sierra Leone, Nigeria and Ghana, together with
tiny Gambia. Their achievement is obvious on every hand to any
visitor to contemporary West Africa, and it would be inexcusable
for any analyst to fail to pay tribute to it.

Inadequacies, however, also marked the colonial period, as perhaps most of the old West Africa hands would readily acknowledge,
and also their newer British colleagues of the post-war age of
accelerated development and welfare who tackled with determination the tasks of "mass education", "education in citizenship",
training in trade unionism and the operation of consumers' and
producers' co-operatives. Given the slow tempo of the generations
before 1945, there was too little time even for armies of "community development" and other officers to ensure full preparation

for the independence which followed so soon after the political explosion of Africa in 1948. But preparedness could have been substantially greater had full heed been given to the voices of the enlightened senior men of the early 1920's who urged vigorous policies of education and progressive Africanization in every British territory. Such men were wholly in tune with the members of the Phelps–Stokes Educational Commission, which toured West, South and Equatorial Africa in 1920–21 under the chairmanship of Dr. Thomas Jesse Jones.

Unfortunately the conservative emphasis of Lugard and Smuts on the prior importance of Africans in the group or "mass" prevailed over the equally valid concern for meeting the needs of the enterprising individual and the wider society during a time of economic and social change. Dr. T. Olawale Elias, Attorney-General of Nigeria and scholar, in his recent book, *Government and Politics in Africa,* has directed attention with some asperity to the fact "that a more liberal spirit in the sphere of senior appointments for Africans informed government policy up to about 1920 than that which was abroad between that date and the end of the 1939–45 war". A progressive continuation of the pre-1920 practice of Africanization would not only have provided self-governing West Africa with a more adequate quota of senior officials but would have had its effect in strengthening the civic framework at every level.

In the event there were too few experienced local men and women available for responsible office in government and political organization. Had they been there it is at least very possible that the course of advance to independence in Ghana would have been more along the lines of evolutionist Danquahism than revolutionary Nkrumahism. As it was Kwame Nkrumah, the politician newly returned from a post-war world of large visions and international Negro–African impatience with colonialism, "Balkanization", and economic and social underdevelopment, came to one of Africa's most significant offices. In 1945, soon after his coming to London from a ten-year sojourn in the United States, he co-operated actively with George Padmore in organizing the Fifth Pan-African Congress, which was held in Manchester in October under the joint-chairmanship of Dr. W. E. B. Du Bois of the United States and Dr. Peter Hilliard from British Guiana.

At the Manchester Congress, according to Dr. Nkrumah's autobiography, *Ghana*,* the ideology of Pan-Africanism "became African nationalism—a revolt by African nationalism against colonialism, racialism and imperialism in Africa—and it adopted Marxist socialism as its philosophy". As this book explains, the composition of the Fifth Congress was much more radical than its predecessors, which "were both promoted and supported mainly by middle-class intellectuals and bourgeois Negro reformists". Prime Minister of the first independent African state of the twentieth century, Dr. Nkrumah wasted no time in organizing, in 1958, the first Pan-African Congress to be held on African soil. Accra became a magnet for Padmore, Du Bois and other radical stalwarts of the Negro-African movement. A stage was in being for the proclamation from within Africa of targets of "African unity" —the sweeping away of colonial boundaries and the rapid political unification of the whole continent; of "African socialism"—to accelerate development and the redistribution of wealth; and of the fullest expression and projection throughout the world of the "African personality".

Yet in his quest for African unity Ghana's Prime Minister, soon President, had no monopoly of leadership either in his own country, in West Africa or in the wider continent. Dr. J. B. Danquah and many senior professional men were present to supply alternative leadership within Ghana. In Nigeria there were leaders of the eminence of Dr. Nnamdi Azikiwe, Chief Obafemi Awolowo, and later the Federal Prime Minister, the quiet, determined Alhaji Sir Abubaker Tafawa Balewa. Sierra Leone's Sir Milton Margai and the younger medical practitioner, Dr. Thomas Karefa-Smart, were no less formidable. In the French-speaking West African territories Leopold Senghor stood out above all by virtue of his distinction as a scholar and poet as well as his notable political position in Paris within the parliaments of the French Union and later his presidency of Senegal. His profound contributions to the concept of the African personality—*négritude*—and the idea of African socialism provided a challenge to all, which has thus far perhaps been met on his level only by Professor Kofi Busia. On behalf of Togo the gifted Sylvanus Olympio demonstrated his talents at the United Nations and at home devoted his wisdom to all-round economic development. Houphouet-Boigny of the Ivory Coast, Modibo Keita of Mali and Sekou Touré of Guinea are others important in the affairs of West Africa who have to be taken into account.

* *Ghana : The Autobiography of Kwame Nkrumah*, London 1957 (Nelson), p. 53.

This mere listing of some of the leaders of West Africa, of the vast French-speaking, as well as the English-speaking area, in which President Tubman of Liberia must be included, reminds one of the diversity of personal political philosophies and itself reveals the virtual impossibility of any simplistically-conceived "unity" either of West Africa as a whole or, still less, of the entire continent. The Emperor Haile Selassie of ancient Ethiopia and President Julius Nyerere of Tanganyika are but two from the other zones to remind us of the diversity of responsible senior leadership in Africa south of the Sahara and north of the Zambesi. That all such leaders will pool their resources increasingly in the overall interests of the peoples of Africa must be the hope and wish of every responsible student, but the evidence suggests few grounds for the many facile expectations of an early attainment of continent-wide unity in the sense of political unification or economic and commercial integration.

Pan-Africanism has yet to demonstrate that it is different from Pan-Europeanism, Pan-Americanism or Pan-Asianism, each with its many well-known difficulties, inconsistencies and contradictions. Viewed more narrowly in ethnic terms, it has again to show where, if at all, it differs from comparable Pan-Slavism, Pan-Arabism or Pan-Celtism. As with each of these other "Pan" movements there is a reality in Pan-Africanism. But, like them or even "Afro-Asianism", it varies in its nature and intensity and becomes operative in specific situations or in response to particular stimuli. It can be meaningfully evoked in terms of voting at the United Nations in opposition to anything savouring of Western *apartheid* or colonialism. But it can be as easily dissipated over the more numerous issues on which Africans are themselves divided.

Whether post-war West Africa has seen more of unity than disunity, of integration than separation, is difficult to determine. Almost all West African political leaders, French- and English-speaking, have been at one among themselves, and with their fellows elsewhere in the continent, in condemning the arbitrary nature of frontier-delimitation by the colonial powers during the days of their exploration, occupation and scramble for Africa. At conferences—for example a well-attended unofficial West African parliamentary conference at Oxford in 1956—whole sessions have been taken up with criticism of colonial boundaries. Sylvanus Olympio in New York won acclaim for his effective eloquence in pleading the case of the divided Ewe. Yet in the eventual United

Nations support for the division of Togoland to allow the British-administered portion to merge with Ghana, there was more concern for the speedy independence of part of colonial Africa than consideration of the plight of a severed ethnic entity like the Ewe. The subsequent barriers erected at the frontier of Ghana and Togo, more difficult to negotiate than in colonial times, and the sharp tensions between the two countries betoken separation rather than union.

The Federal Republic of Cameroun is a happier example of fusion of adjoining French- and English-speaking territories. There were understandable regrets among British administrators and scholars when the British Trust territory of the Southern Cameroons, in which they had worked, opted to leave the Commonwealth by joining the French Cameroons to constitute a new state. But they were aware both of the fear of Eastern Nigerian predominance which motivated the peoples of the Southern Cameroons and of the fact that the northern portion of the Trust territory had chosen the opposite course of becoming integrated into the Northern Region of Nigeria. In the case of the Togoland plebiscite, the United Nations had not allowed, as they did in the Cameroons, the separate segments to make individual and different choices as to their future association.

The fate of Senegambia is not settled at the time of writing, though it does now seem that a federal-type merger which allows British Gambia substantial municipal and cultural autonomy is likely. The Senegambian example is significant in that the "absorption" of the tiny riverain colony and protectorate, Britain's earliest foothold in Africa, has taken very much longer to fulfil than many chose confidently to predict. Equally significant is the fact that, despite supreme tact on the part of the encircling French-speaking state under its distinguished and enlightened head and the objective advantages of integration, the Gambians have found it so difficult to abandon their selfhood. American observers accustomed to the state writ large, and to an anti-European colonial tradition, have been prominent in their predictions of fusion, though several British writers, concerned to see more viable local economies succeed colonial rule, have shared their view.

The dissolution of the Federation of Mali in 1960, after a bare eighteen months of union between Senegal and the former French Sudan, is another instance of the difficulties of political unification even when the economic interests of the two parties would seem to be best served by the joint control of communications. No less acute are the obstacles to unification when attempts are made to bridge the Sahara, as the disputes over Mauritania have revealed. Most of Mauritania's commerce is conducted southwards with Mali, the Gambia and Senegal, but the Moroccan claim to historical suzerainty over Mauritania has been as strenuously asserted in recent years as was formerly the claim of Egypt to the Anglo-Egyptian Sudan.

The continuing disunity of the Maghreb itself is also relevant to our discussion, though we can do no more than point to the friction between Morocco and Algeria which required the recent arbitration of Emperor Haile Selassie and to the barriers which still exist between Algeria and Tunisia. South of the Sahara the Ghana–Guinea–Mali union must be considered because we have here an example of an attempt at unity which was provoked by powerful emotion and common feeling at a time of crisis. The decision of the people of Guinea in 1958 to reject by plebiscite continued association with France led them into a state of immediate financial and other need. Ghana reacted at once in a spirit of generosity to the plight of a near-by African state whose leader shared with Dr. Nkrumah many of the same philosophical and political beliefs. But little significant action has followed Ghana's gesture in offering financial and other aid and the degree of practical co-operation between Ghana and Guinea, and Mali also, has been relatively small. Certainly there is a sense of ideological affinity between the states and a readiness to assist one another on occasion, but it would be inaccurate to describe the so-called union as anything more than a loose league or alliance, unproved as yet by any acid tests.

Our examples could be multiplied, and it would be appropriate to incorporate some discussion of Portuguese Guinea, Liberia and the Spanish territories and of the rival and changing alliances of states which have centred on Casablanca, Conakry and Accra, on the one hand, and Monrovia, Lagos and Brazzaville on the other. But our range of examples has been sufficient to make plain that the reality of West African unity is less evident than the frequent denunciations of colonial frontiers and "Balkanization", and the exhortations to unite, would suggest was likely to be the case. As has been said already, there can be no question but that every attempt at closer regional co-operation in West Africa is to be welcomed and supported in the spirit of the concluding observations of Mr. F. J. Pedler in his book, *West Africa*. A United States of

West Africa is a worthy objective and it is specially desirable that everything be done to bridge the linguistic divides between the French- and English-speaking lands which interlock across the map.

In the pursuit of the goal of total West African unity, however, it would seem that the brick-upon-brick method of steady construction is much more likely to succeed and to endure than any hasty, over-ambitious contrivance. In particular there is need for the individual successor states, who have almost all chosen to retain the colonial boundaries, to set about the task of creating a united nation within their borders. Nigeria, Ghana and Sierra Leone each possess formidable problems of national unity which must be overcome if their contribution to a wider whole is to be sound and reliable. This is the fundamental political problem to which we now turn. We must give some consideration also to the question of how the abandoned inter-territorial organs of co-operation of British West Africa might be re-created in the interests of all.

Each British West African state inherited a major task of nation-building when power was transferred from Westminster and Whitehall. The full magnitude of the task was not recognized by those who drew too sharp a distinction between the "African states" and the European-settled countries. There was the facile assumption that the Africans of the African states would unite rapidly once the alien colonial rulers had withdrawn.* The West African minorities who protested that "African domination" or "black imperialism", as they themselves described it, might be worse than government by a distant ruler were dismissed with little sympathy. According to the prevalent cliché which served to justify precipitate transfers of power Africa's political problems had to be settled by African peoples on the spot, not by people thousands of miles away.

The historian might find our generation of Britons grievously guilty of neglect in respect of the West African and other African constitutions. A wealth of relevant constitutional history from the British Isles alone might have been used more fully. The record of success and failure in ethnic or national adjustments between Irish,

* It is interesting to note that Soviet Russian analysts who shared this assumption, and who attributed ethnic division to capitalist-imperialist machinations, have revised their views. See, for example, the article "Potekhin on African Frontiers" in *The Mizan Newsletter*, a review of Soviet writing on the Middle East and Africa, vol. 6, no. 4, April 1964. Professor I. I. Potekhin then acknowledged the African acceptance of the colonial frontiers and the need for intensive empirical study of African political and ethnic borders.

Scots, Welsh and English is instructive. No less important is the manner and timing of the progressive expansion of the electoral franchise in the United Kingdom and the whole advance from the "rule of law" to "democracy". The late Professor Sir Reginald Coupland and Sir Ivor Jennings are some of the scholars of Britain who must be exempted from criticisms of neglect, and so also Professor W. M. MacKenzie for his important recent work on East Africa, but too few leading men were alert even to the nature of the challenge, let alone to possible solutions. From each latter-day African governor might have come the cry which Milner made from the Transvaal in 1904 for a more thorough combing of Colonial Office pigeonholes for appropriate constitutional precedents.

In fact, before 1939–45, there was little serious thought about African self-government, and after 1945 too little time to make considered preparation for it. In West Africa, first on the constitutional slipway, there were several common problems but a diversity of solutions which were contrived more or less hastily. A foremost common problem arose from the administrative organizational history of each of the territories. The traditional distinction between "colonies" on the coast and "protectorates" inland had led everywhere to barriers between the constituent units. We noted above the case of Ghana, where it was only in 1946 that Ashanti was represented in the Gold Coast Legislative Council alongside the southern region or "colony", and 1950 before the Northern Territories were drawn in—British Togoland also being administered separately as a Trust Territory until 1957. In Sierra Leone a measure of direct representation for the Protectorate in the Legislative Council was instituted in 1924, but it was not until 1951 that it was increased significantly and only under a constitution of 1956 did it come about that a substantial body of elected members from the Protectorate entered the new House of Representatives, constituted for Sierra Leone as a whole.

Nigeria had a similar constitutional history in that it was not until 1946 that a constitution was promulgated making provision for the first time for a Legislative Council for the whole of Nigeria. Hitherto, under the constitution of 1922, the Council legislated only for the colony and the southern provinces, the Governor making laws by proclamation for Northern Nigeria. The 1946 Nigerian constitution must be noted also for the fact that while it aimed deliberately to promote the unity of the country it sought to make provision for its diversity. Regional Houses of Assembly were created in Eastern, Western and Northern Nigeria, with a House of Chiefs for the Northern Region. In 1951 a House of Chiefs was instituted for the Western Region as well under a new constitution which greatly enlarged the membership of the Nigerian House of Representatives and made it substantially elective, in contrast with the mainly nominated central legislature of the Richards constitution of 1946. Those who were elected, however, were mostly returned indirectly by means of an electoral college system. In 1954 yet another change took place and direct elections were introduced for the House of Representatives, the membership of which was increased once more to a total of 184. The 1954 constitution also declared Nigeria a federation.

It is the fact that a definite choice was made of a federal constitution, as distinct from a unitary one for Nigeria in 1954, which we choose to emphasize here. The subsequent review of the 1954 constitution in London in May and June of 1957, some months after Ghana obtained full self-government or independence, will be touched on later, when other aspects of Nigerian constitutional development are discussed. But at this point it is important to recall what very different courses have been chosen by each of the West African governments in their quest for national unity. For Nigeria the solution of federalism was chosen, for Ghana that of unitary centralism, for Sierra Leone a single parliament and a devolutionary administrative system. It is to be hoped that each will succeed in its objective, but it is possible that better results might have been obtained if there had been a more comprehensive and assured comparative appraisal of suitable forms of government instead of a reliance on hurried *ad hoc* adjustments devised in the interests of the personalities involved and to meet certain ephemeral political circumstances.

Ghana's present authoritarian system of government, similar in so many ways to that of contemporary South Africa, raises the same question which we have asked in the case of South Africa: whether a federal-type constitution might have ensured greater freedom and encouraged over time the negotiation of a deeper and more durable unity. In Nigeria in 1946 a foundation for federalism was introduced and, as we have seen, was formally decided upon eight years later. There was keen debate over the Richards constitution of 1946 and many young Nigerians saw in it little more than an imperialist desire to "divide and rule". Student members of the United Nigeria

Association in Britain argued strenuously for a unitary arrangement which would compel groups to work together. But increasingly many of them came to acknowledge that the diversity of Nigeria was a reality which could not be ignored and an ancient one which had preceded British rule. Discussion turned more on the number of regions : whether there should be six, eight, fourteen or twenty-two rather than three, for the population approaching 35 million comprising peoples like the Hausa, estimated at the time to number over $5\frac{1}{2}$ million, the Ibo 5 million, the Yoruba $4\frac{1}{2}$ million and the Fulani over 3 million.

The Ghanaians and Britons who won the day in opposing federalism for Ghana elected to see little in common between the problems of Nigeria and those of Ghana. The most frequent justification for dismissing the federalist case was the small size of Ghana. Argument held that it was absurd to suggest a federal form of government for a state of relatively limited area containing a population of between $4\frac{1}{2}$ and 5 millions. This view gained the widest currency among politicians and press and radio commentators. Authorities on federalism, when approached, directed attention to confederal Switzerland's smaller area and comparable population, and offered the opinion that a federal-type constitution might best meet the conditions of the Gold Coast; but their testimony was barely heeded. Equally unheeded were the pleas from the peoples of Ashanti, the Northern Territories and Togoland, as well as some in the South itself, who were afraid of a future in which a single party or group might dominate all.

Those in the Gold Coast who opposed a unitary system for the country were allowed to be caught in a false position. Given the general desire for self-government, in which they themselves shared, they did not wish to seem to be delaying the day of independence. The new, well-organized and militant Convention People's Party with its doctrine of "Positive Action" and its emphatic cry of "Freedom" played on this point and, by skilful political tactics, weakened and divided the opposition in the crucial years of the early 1950's. Given the records of bodies like the Northern Territories Council, and the Asanteman Council and Press of Ashanti,* the United Kingdom Government and local British administration might well have spared those who sought some real measure of regional self-government the painful confusion of choice which was raised by the posing of the false alternative of independence or

* Notably the *Ashanti Pioneer*.

federalism. There could be little risk of the alleged danger of Ashanti or Northern secession when the produce of the inland regions required outlets through the South.

But only very belatedly, in 1955, was Sir Frederick Bourne summoned to advise on the fundamental question of the organization of the political system. It is significant that the evidence led him to recommend substantial devolution of power from the centre to five regions, and Regional Assemblies. It was, however, late in the day to suggest thorough-going federalism of the kind formally adopted for Nigeria in 1954. The general election of 1956 produced an increase in the opposition to Dr. Nkrumah, and majorities for the Northern Peoples' Party and the National Liberation Movement in the north and Ashanti respectively, but at a time of high political emotion the predominant support was for early independence and "Freedom".

To understand the dilemma of responsible Britons over Gold Coast independence it is important to recall the emotions which prevailed at the time in Britain as well as West Africa. If there was precipitate action over Ghana's constitution it was partly for emotional reasons comparable to those which had led to the rapid passing at Westminster of the South Africa Act. Just as in September 1909 the prevailing United Kingdom mood endorsed a great act of faith in the Afrikaners, so in September 1956 there was a strong desire on the part of Britons to make an essentially similar act on behalf of Africans. World opinion added its weight. Of all British African zones West Africa was best placed to provide the first candidate for independence and the Gold Coast, through its leader, seized upon an opportunity which Nigeria and Sierra Leone were prepared to postpone until they had made more adequate preparation.

The constitution with which Ghana was endowed on March 6, 1957, survived a bare three years. On July 1, 1960, a republican constitution came into force with the President, Osagyefo Dr. Kwame Nkrumah as head of government as well as head of state. Executive power is vested in the President, who may veto legislation and dissolve parliament. There is also presidential control of the armed forces and the civil service. More recently the President has assumed or exercised control of the judiciary. The Chief Justice, Sir Arku Korsah, and other judges were dismissed after pronouncing verdicts not acceptable to the President. Central government control of the regions and districts is strong. The regional commissioners

I

for the eight regions are at the same time the designated regional secretaries of the Convention People's Party. Ghana was in 1964 declared a one-party state. From Ghana during the past few years there have come frequent reports of the denial of civil liberties, of arbitrary arrest, detention, imprisonment, deportation and Press censorship.

Ghana's abandonment of her first constitution and her adoption of a frankly authoritarian system have brought dismay to her friends in Britain, satisfaction to those who emphatically opposed the notion that any African state was ready for self-government. Most of the Press reports on Ghana in 1957 were either too optimistic or too pessimistic and the new state, like others subsequently, suffered from ill-informed and unbalanced comment. The principal point to which attention is directed at this stage, however, is the system of government which Ghana has chosen, not only for its own sake, but as the consciously favoured instrument for the achievement of national unity. Nkrumahism, like Sukarnoism in Indonesia, sees in presidential guidance and single-party control the most effective means of reducing or obliterating traditional religious, tribal and other barriers, so that all citizens may be welded together in one loyalty in the service of rapid economic and social development.

Nigeria's adoption of federalism as the means of attaining unity is not only of the greatest interest but may have a wide future significance in Africa. We have outlined Nigerian constitutional development until 1954, when the formal declaration of the principle of federation was made, and we have looked meanwhile at Ghana's course. It is undeniable that there was impatience in the two southern regions of Nigeria, the Eastern and the Western Region, when it became apparent that the smaller Ghana was to receive independence in March 1957. Such feeling was eased somewhat after the London conference on Nigeria agreed, in May–June 1957, that these two regions were forthwith to be granted internal self-government. The Northern Region did not claim immediate internal self-government, which was in fact deferred until March 1959. The conference furthermore decided to set up commissions to make recommendations on three outstanding problems: the fears of minorities, the fiscal system of the Federation, and constituency delimitation for the election of members to the House of Representatives.

Leaders of the Northern Region were very conscious of their unpreparedness for self-government in comparison with their two southern partners. In particular they were aware of their lack of trained manpower. The Kano riots of 1953, in which forty were killed, had shown how unpopular in the north could be the educated southerners who were filling posts in government and commerce. The fact of religious difference had not helped. In contrast with the Sudan, the Christian and other non-Muslim southerners supplied most educated men and women in a conservative Islamic north. Physical separation of the southerners in the strangers' quarters outside the city walls also made them more suspect, identifiable and vulnerable. Clearly education and training had to be accelerated rapidly in the north if the most populous constituent of the Federation was to play its full and confident part in future independent Nigerian nationhood.

There are substantial non-Muslim populations in the north as well as many peoples besides the Hausa, Fulani and Kanuri. These three together comprise over half of the estimated population of some seventeen million, but ethnic groups like the Tiv of the Benue Province, and the Nupe are numerically significant minorities who on their own outnumber the populations of several of the new states of independent Africa. The same is true even of "overspill" populations such as the Yoruba in the Northern Region, who extend across from the Western Region, in which they predominate. It is the presence of such substantial groupings which has given strength to the repeated demands through the years that at least a fourth, "Middle Belt" region be established south of the Hausa, Fulani and Kanuri and north of the Eastern and Western Regions.*

In the Western and Eastern Regions also there are minority groups whose very size has led to suggestions that more regions based on ethnic principles be created. The Edo in the West, the Ibibio in the East and the Ijaw, who span the Western–Eastern boundary, are examples. But northern fears of southern control in an independent Nigeria made it unlikely that the predominant elements in the Northern Region could be persuaded to accept any drastic redrawing of internal boundaries which might place them at a political disadvantage, especially in competition with the vigorous and enterprising Ibo of the Eastern Region or the Yoruba of the West.

If sufficient time could have been gained by Britain, assuming

* See Buchanan, K. M. and Pugh, J. C., *Land and People in Nigeria* (University of London 1955). On page 93 there is a map showing the "Middle Belt" and its ethnic composition in relation to the other regions.

that it was wanted, it is possible that some six, four or eight regions might have been negotiated. But faced with the desire expressed by many Nigerians at the London conference for an early rather than a later transfer of power to the Federation as a whole, it was decided to accept the existing regional framework as the basis and to propose a variety of safeguards other than political autonomy for the minorities. "Minority Areas" were proposed for the Edo in the West, a Calabar Area in the East, and a Special Area to assist development in the Niger Delta. For the country as a whole, provisions in the federal constitution to protect human rights were suggested and support was expressed for the preservation of the Nigeria Police as a unified force under an inspector-general with regional representation on a Police Council and arrangements for regional recruitment.

The London conference of 1958 speedily accepted most of the recommendations on the minorities and the financial and delimitation arrangements. It was also agreed to set up a House of Chiefs in the Eastern Region. The principle of derivation was mainly adhered to in respect of fiscal distribution, but there was greater acceptance of certain provisions to allocate funds to regions according to their needs. The stage was set for the pre-independence federal elections in 1959. The results were much as expected, with the Northern Peoples' Congress securing 142 of the 174 seats allotted to the North, Dr. Azikiwe's N.C.N.C. (National Council of Nigeria and the Cameroons—later National Council of Nigerian Citizens) obtaining 58 of the 72 seats in the "Ibo" East, and the Action Group of Chief Awolowo 34 of the 63 seats for the "Yoruba" West. The Yoruba and others in the middle belt section of the Northern Region returned 24 Action Group candidates. The Northern Elements' Progressive Union were able to gain eight of the Northern seats, campaigning in association with the N.C.N.C. Two of the three Lagos seats went to the N.C.N.C., one to the Action Group.

It will be seen from the nation-wide distribution of 142 seats to the Northern Peoples' Congress (N.P.C.), 89 to the N.C.N.C./ N.E.P.U., and 73 to the Action Group, with eight Independents, that no party had outright command of the Federal Parliament. A coalition was negotiated between the N.P.C. and the N.C.N.C.; the Federal Ministry, under Alhaji Sir Abubakar Tafawa Balewa, came to comprise 10 members of the N.P.C., seven N.C.N.C., and two Independent senators. Dr. Nnamdi Azikiwe, leader of the

N.C.N.C., chose to remain outside the Cabinet and House of Representatives and accepted the office of President of the Senate. Chief Awolowo became Leader of the Opposition.

On October 1, 1960, Britain's great state in Africa became fully self-governing. There was a special sense of history about the occasion, which was marked by deeply-felt tributes from both Nigerian and British spokesmen. Sir James Robertson, last colonial Governor, an Oxford Scot with a distinguished record in the Sudan, was urged to stay on as first Governor-General, a position which he filled with characteristic balance and competence for a brief period before handing over to Dr. Azikiwe, the turbulent, militant, enterprising "Zik" who for so long, in the United States, Britain and his homeland, had been one of Africa's foremost nationalist leaders. To many observers it seemed inconceivable that "Zik" could be content with a headship of state rather than of government, but the circumstances of Nigerian politics have thus far at least led him to continue his role, now as President under the new republican constitution, which has not altered the fundamental institutional structure and division of powers which were inherited at independence.

Changes there have been, however, some of which have aroused regret and alarm among friends of Nigeria in Britain. The severance of the link between Nigeria and British courts through the termination by Nigeria of the right of appeal to the Judicial Committee of the Privy Council is one source of regret. It is felt particularly by those who have enjoyed close ties with Nigerian lawyers through the years and who have counted on the law to serve as a unifying bond for the Commonwealth. To such men a Commonwealth Court on which Nigerian judges sat alongside colleagues from elsewhere offered special promise. The recent prohibitions imposed against certain eminent British barristers, some of whom have long been in the van of African freedom movements, have occasioned alarm as well as regret. The Chief Enahoro extradition, and the trial itself, caused deep misgiving which was felt also about the arraignment of Chief Awolowo. If there is not freedom to select defence counsel from anywhere there can be little assurance about the procedures of law and justice. Certain reports of continuing bribery and corruption have also troubled those who recall the findings of certain pre-independence commissions of inquiry.

The most disturbing development in Nigeria since independence, however, was the division in 1963 of the Western Region, strong-hold of the official opposition party, into two regions. It has been made clear above that there are objective grounds to justify such action, but it is most unfortunate that the Western Region was seemingly singled out by the other two in coalition for such treat-ment. Far wiser and more statesmanlike from every point of view, not least that of national unity, would have been a comprehensive re-examination of the whole question of the optimum number of regions and the more rational re-drawing of internal boundaries. It may well be that certain politicians have seen in the creation of the new Mid-West Region a first step in a process which will culminate in the reduction of the dominance of the North by its eventual sub-division, but it is doubtful whether the bitterness aroused among those who feel victimized in the West will make the venture worth while. The precedent of scrupulous regard for constitutionalism and respect for an impressive Nigerian leader of the stature of Chief Obafemi Awolowo* could be much more rewarding and powerful.

In his autobiography, Chief Awolowo is both hard-hitting and scholarly in his criticism of the Minorities Commission, which he believes was "deliberately staged in order to provide an authorita-tive excuse for Britain to wash her hands of the matter and transfer responsibility for creating the three proposed states, or any states for that matter, to the majority ethnic groups". The three proposed states to which he refers are the COR State—comprising the Cala-bar, Ogoja and Rivers Provinces in the East—the Mid-West and the Middle Belt States. Proposals for such new regions to be carved from the existing three, to make a total of six, are of long standing in Nigeria, and Chief Awolowo and his supporters firmly took the view that there was an inescapable obligation on the part of the British Government, which had thus far provided the unifying cement of Nigeria, to think things out beforehand and to ensure the best possible conditions for the safeguarding of the many minority peoples and the preservation of democracy before she abandoned power.

Beecause of Nigeria's immense significance in Africa, the Com-monwealth and the United Nations it must be hoped that what was not done before the transfer of powers, or was too hastily done,

---

* See *Awo, The Autobiography of Chief Obafemi Awolowo* (Cambridge 1960) for a summary of his thought. Chapter 12, "Evolution of a Federalist", is of special relevance. See also his *The Path to Nigerian Freedom*.

may be done now and in the future by Nigerians and Britons working on the same problems in closer partnership. It may be much more difficult or even impossible to achieve now, given the demands of politics on the African leaders concerned, but the effort must be made. Nigeria fortunately has no dearth of able men dedicated to the ideals of democracy and the rule of law. Many of her leading thinkers reject emphatically the suggestion that liberal democracy, with its encouragement of an effective and free parliamentary opposition, is inappropriate to Africa. But if such ideals are to be fulfilled there is clearly a need for more trained manpower.

Yet before we look at the manpower needs of Nigeria as an example of Africa's requirements, we must give attention to Sierra Leone and her approach to the problem of national unity. Smaller than Ghana and Nigeria, Sierra Leone nevertheless remains the historic point from which British influence expanded in West Africa, and her recent course of political advance is far from uninstructive. The manner in which she has tackled and is tackling the immensely difficult task of achieving democratic partnership between the hitherto dominant Creole minority and the tribal and other peoples of the Protectorate is of special interest and may have its lessons for neighbouring Americo–Liberians and others farther afield.

The political institutional development of Sierra Leone has its significance; but of equal importance has been the personal example of Protectorate leaders of the distinction of Sir Milton Margai, who died in April 1964, and of Creole leaders who have given a vigorous lead to their people to come to terms with the new world of democratic Africa with its demands of "one man, one vote". The fact of sharing a broadly common skin-colour has possibly played some part in facilitating the adjustment though its importance can be greatly exaggerated, especially by outside commentators of different stock. For the Creoles, brought up in full consciousness of their historic ascendancy and their important contribution to West Africa over several generations, it has been, and is, far from easy to accustom themselves to a position of secondary political significance and declining status even within their own relatively small country. Much has been made of the unfortunate terms used by some Creoles in their reference to the tribal peoples of their country, many of which resemble those used by other similarly placed groups, not least certain European settlers, but there is perhaps greater need for the understanding and perspective given by Professor Arthur Porter of the University College at Fourah Bay in his new book, *Creoledom*, a study of the development of Freetown society.*

An important change in the constitutional development of Sierra Leone came about after the British Government accepted the recommendations contained in the report of the Electoral Reform Commission, the Keith–Lucas Commission, which was published in Freetown in 1954. For some years previously, notably in 1947 and 1948, the Creoles had fought a determined rearguard action, but first the increase in 1951 of the Protectorate representation and then, ten years later, the Sierra Leone (Constitution) Order in Council of 1956 greatly broadened the territorial basis of the membership of the legislature and extended the franchise to virtually all adult men and women taxpayers. Direct elections were introduced for the first time in the Protectorate, from which 25 members were returned to the House of Representatives as against 12 from Freetown and the Colony area. Provision was made also for 12 Paramount Chiefs to be elected by the 12 District Councils in the Protectorate. Substantial executive power was conferred shortly afterwards on the elected representatives, 11 ministers being drawn from among the members of parliament.

Serious conflict could have marred the internal transfer of political power from the Creoles to the peoples of the Protectorate had the leadership of the latter been in less statesmanlike hands than those of Dr. Milton Margai. This remarkable Mende man, born in 1895, was the first Sierra Leonean from the Protectorate to qualify in medicine, graduating from the University of Durham in 1926. After a career in the Medical Service of his country which lasted until 1950 and during which he made important adaptations of traditional health practices among tribal peoples, especially in the field of midwifery, he retired and turned to active politics at national level. He had previously served on a District Council and in the Protectorate Assembly, during which time he took the lead in founding both the Sierra Leone People's Party to counter Creole dominance, and a newspaper, the *Sierra Leone Observer,* published from Bo.

The 1951 general election first brought Margai's party to power

* Christopher Fyfe's monumental *A History of Sierra Leone* (O.U.P. 1962) is also to be recommended as a mine of illuminating information up to and including the 1914–18 war.

in Freetown. In 1954 he became Chief Minister. The 1957 elections, conducted on the basis of the new system, saw him confirmed in office by a convincing majority. With the prospect of independence, "the Doctor", now Sir Milton Margai, brought his own and two other parties into a "United Front" for the London constitutional conference of 1960, which prepared the way for Sierra Leone to become a fully self-governing or completely independent member nation of the Commonwealth on April 27, 1961.

In West African and Pan-African as well as domestic politics, Sierra Leone's representatives, under the leadership of Sir Milton Margai and Dr. J. Karefa-Smart as Minister of External Affairs, have aligned themselves with Liberia and Nigeria and adopted the standpoint of what was the "Monrovia" group. They were never mere endorsers of other policies, bringing always a vigorous, independent, commonsense viewpoint to bear on domestic and international issues. The Sierra Leone Cabinet has worked actively to preserve good relations with Britain, British teachers and civil servants have continued to be welcomed, and the Commonwealth is held in esteem. The death of Sir Milton Margai may well lead to a shift in certain aspects of policy, but there is good reason to hope that his efforts towards an enduring national unity will prevail despite the dangers of inter-tribal friction in the Protectorate; this might now become more acute and so add to the Creole-Protectorate difficulties and the problems which centre on the illicit diamond traffic, in which Lebanese are reputed to play a foremost role.

Our brief survey of the problems of national unity and the various attempts to deal with them has ended appropriately with Sierra Leone, where so many British West Africans have been educated and from where so many set out to work in Nigeria, Ghana and the Gambia. Sierra Leone may best serve also as the starting-point for any discussion both of West Africa's major economic and social problem, the need for more trained manpower, and the desirability of closer inter-territorial co-operation between the Commonwealth countries of West Africa.

From the earliest years of the Freetown settlement education and training were given high priority by British missionaries, administrators, traders and soldiers. Their efforts were more than welcomed by the liberated Africans who worked in close partnership with them and later by the indigenous peoples who had not been uprooted from their traditional social systems and were at first naturally more reluctant to accept new ideas and methods. Through the nineteenth century, Victorian liberalism, unbending though it was in many respects, encouraged and supported those individuals who were prepared to work hard and, if necessary, to make personal sacrifice for their own advance. Reward for successful endeavour was also not ungenerous, as the presence of many senior Africans in government and other service in the late nineteenth century makes clear.

Christopher Fyfe and Dr. Elias among others have pointed out that there was a regrettable lapse in such generosity of outlook and practice after the turn of the century and between the wars, when proportionately fewer Africans received senior appointments, but nevertheless good educational foundations were laid by Britain. And despite the dark period when adverse racial stereotypes were prevalent and militated against the appointment and promotion of Africans, it was always possible for the individual African, boy or girl, man or woman, to secure the highest qualifications if he or she were blessed with the necessary determination and talent. In West Africa and South Africa, and to a lesser degree—for historical reasons—in East and Central Africa, there are numerous examples of individuals whose personal educational histories bear out this observation. Sir Milton Margai, Dr. B. W. Vilakazi and President Jomo Kenyatta are cases in point.

This central quality of British education—English as well as Welsh and Scots—which emphasizes individuality above all else has proved of priceless worth in Africa. The more authoritarian traditions of the Dutch and Afrikaners, of the Portuguese, Italians and Belgians, and even in some respects of the French, with their stress on uniformity, must suffer in comparison. In mission and government schools and colleges in each of the British territories—infant, primary, craft, secondary, and teacher-training—the principle of the worth of the individual and the right of each person to advance to the highest possible point have been accepted, no matter how imperfectly or reluctantly at times. Much of the distinctiveness of the independent countries once under British administration stems from this educational approach, with its emphasis on the self, and upon independence of thought on public issues of politics, economics and society quite as much as on matters of personal philosophy and behaviour.

The golden thread of quality in education was kept in mind during the last years of the Second World War, when Britain sought in determined fashion to build on earlier education achievement in West Africa. The importance of school education was never lost sight of, especially by the new education adviser appointed to the Colonial Office in 1940 and the Institute of Education at London University. But under the stimulus of war-time ideals, thoughts turned increasingly to the provision of more adequate facilities for higher education throughout the colonial empire, by means of colleges of arts, science and technology and university colleges. In 1940 the Colonial Office Advisory Committee on Education—first created in 1923 as child in part of the Phelps–Stokes Commission—took note of a comment on university development which appeared in the proceedings of the West African Governors' Conference. A memorandum by Professor H. J. Channon on the need for a review of the whole question of university development overseas was also favourably received. The Asquith Commission on the more general issues of higher education in the colonies as a whole and the Elliot Commission on Higher Education in West Africa, both set up in 1943, represent the outcome.

We cannot give to either report the space which it deserves, nor discuss the merit of contrasting views on the number and location of new universities in West Africa. Rather must emphasis be given to the fact that, in response to eager opinion in both countries, university colleges at Ibadan, Nigeria, and Legon, Ghana, were incorporated and brought into special relationship with London University in 1948. Money was given generously by the United Kingdom Government, and the universities of Britain gave no less generously of scholars, academic administrators, librarians, laboratory technicians and the many others essential to the successful creation of first-class university institutions. There was no false economy over building and equipment either: Aggrey's dictum that only the best is good enough for Africa was accepted in full, though usually in a deceptively matter-of-fact way, by those in the British universities who responded to the challenge. The medical school at Ibadan, the institutes for social and economic research, and other developments outside the arts and science curricula were also endowed with the best that Britain could provide.

As the United States Supreme Court observed in 1954 in its judgement on the famous desegregation case, it is impossible adequately to define all the intangible and other elements which go to the making of a first-class law school or university as a whole. All that can be said with confidence is that, to a visitor with any comparative experience of British, European, North American and other African universities, the university colleges at Ibadan and Legon were truly first-class. The same mark of quality was apparent at the former colleges of arts, science and technology at Ibadan and Kumasi which, since independence, have been transformed into universities. These centres, together with the pioneer Fourah Bay in Sierra Leone, which became a full-scale university college in 1959, have not only produced many hundreds of graduates but have served to set high standards of scholarship and science. They have also sought always to defend the principles of university autonomy and responsible academic freedom in the interests of the national societies in which they are located.

But the golden thread of quality must be woven into a broader quantity of good durable cloth if it is to be seen to advantage and if it is properly to serve the whole. This became apparent with increasing urgency before independence when the prospect of decades of preparation was telescoped into years. It has received starker emphasis since the new African states assumed full respon-sibility for their own destinies. As integral units of the university colleges extra-mural departments such as those in Ghana and Nigeria sought to prepare men and women throughout their national societies. The headquarters staff and resident tutors in remote centres such as Tamale in northern Ghana maintained the highest standards not only of tuition but of personal research. They worked ceaselessly also to develop adult education movements, such as Ghana's People's Education Association (P.E.A.). Every resource was utilized—the accommodation and other facilities of the uni-versity colleges and colleges of arts, science and technology during vacations, and the offices, books and visual aid materials of organizations such as the British Council and the United States Information Service. Side by side with the extra-mural lecturers worked the community development, trade union and co-operative officers from the new branches of the Colonial Service who were given special encouragement under the Labour Government.

The emphasis on more good plain cloth in education was fully in accord with the views of African successor governments, notably the Ministers of Education, though all took pride in the African professors and students at Ibadan and Legon whose publications and post-graduate achievements in Britain and the United States won acclaim. *Investment in Education*, the report of the Ashby Commission on post-school certificate and higher education in

Nigeria completed on the eve of independence, is the most striking single survey of the total educational and manpower needs of a new African state. The United Nations specialized agencies have subsequently organized important conferences on African education at Addis Ababa, and they have promoted other inquiries, but the novel approach of the Ashby Commission and its estimates of needs in the largest West African state merit particular attention.

In response to the Nigerian Federal Minister of Education's request for an estimate of the nation's high-level manpower needs over the next twenty years, the Ashby Commission, composed of leading Nigerian and American as well as British scholars, chose to recommend a pattern of education to match Nigeria's aspirations, rather than restricting themselves to a much more modest programme which would simply represent an extension of former practice. They accepted that international aid on a very substantial scale would have to be forthcoming if their targets were to be reached. Their dominant assumption, which owed much to Professor F. Harbison of Princeton, was that Nigeria's urgent need of even modest economic development to meet the requirements of a population of about 50 millions in 1980* would necessitate an immediate dramatic change in educational organization and procedures. Of the two principal limiting factors on economic development, capital and high-level manpower, the latter was the more difficult to overcome, in that while money might be forthcoming for dams, power stations and factories, which can be built in a few years, it takes 10–15 years to train managers, administrators and engineers, and decades to prepare their teachers and professors.

The actual figures of the estimates are less important than their relative order of magnitude. But one or two may be given. In Nigeria in 1958 12,000 children entered secondary grammar schools as against the 30,000 who should have entered if by 1963–4 there were to be enough securing school certificates to go on to more advanced education. From the universities at least 2,000 graduates a year are required, as against the 300 in 1959–60 from Nigeria and the 700 or so returning from overseas. The shortfall in respect of non-graduates in the intermediate sector, that is those who can rise to responsible positions without a university education, was estimated to be even greater. Only some 1,500 men and women with two or three years' education beyond school certificate were being produced each year from Nigeria and abroad

* The disputed census of 1964 suggests a population of this order.

whereas 5,500 per annum were needed. The rapid expansion of "intermediate" education is therefore essential. In the senior and intermediate categories Nigeria possessed some 30,000 individuals (15,000 in each) at the time of the Ashby inquiry and it was estimated by Harbison that a total of 85,000 was to be aimed at over ten years (30,000 senior, 54,000 intermediate).

It was acknowledged by the commissioners, led by Sir Eric Ashby, Master of Clare College, Cambridge, and Dr. Kenneth Dike, Vice-Chancellor of Ibadan, that only a spectacular leap forward would assist self-governing Nigeria to reach the educational goals which have been outlined in the last paragraph. They were confident that outside nations would see that investment in Nigerian education was an "investment in her economic future and political stability" and it was with this in mind that they proposed for Nigeria an international Loan and Educational Aid Programme which would stimulate universities throughout the world, though chiefly in the United Kingdom and United States, to provide university places to train Nigerian teachers, and their governments to supply educational aid in the form of teachers and funds.

We cannot do more than give the above indications of the magnitude of Nigerian need. All West African countries—Ghana, Sierra Leone and the Gambia, Liberia and the French-speaking, the Portuguese and the Spanish—require external aid in the form of capital and assistance to improve their trained manpower resources. The lands of former French Equatorial Africa are educationally very backward in comparison with Senegal and the other states of what was French West Africa. Very few African professional men from these territories ever received medical or other professional education at the university institution at Dakar or the universities in France. Senegal, the Ivory Coast and other nearer countries were the principal beneficiaries of French higher education. Clearly it will take the decades envisaged by the Ashby Commission for all the West African states to reach the stage at which their overall economic and social development can be regarded by their several national leaders with some degree of satisfaction. There is always inertia in human action and only recently has it been possible, for example, to organize on the scale required the appeal for suitably qualified British teachers to go to Nigeria during the vacations to assist in intensive teacher-training courses.

Meanwhile in Nigeria new universities of the kind recommended by the Ashby Commission have been brought into being. The

University of Nigeria at Nsukka, one which commands the special interest of Dr. Azikiwe, seeks to harmonize, in the interests of Africa, the best elements in the educational traditions of the United States of America and of Great Britain. Shortly after Nsukka was established in 1960 the Universities of Lagos, Kano and Ife were instituted. There are also special administrative training colleges such as the important centre at Zaria in the Northern Region, now part of the University College. In keeping with national feeling there is a priority for African studies in the policies of many colleges and universities and it is to be expected that the history syllabus and other courses in schools, colleges and universities will become increasingly Africa-orientated.

There is no need to dwell on the importance of education if national and regional unity are to be advanced. As Professor Harbison and his colleagues have made clear, economic progress is essential for political stability—given the hopes and expectations of the many young West Africans who are acquainted with Western living standards. And, though tolerance is far from being a prerogative of the university graduate, properly educated men and women are those most likely to recognize the advantages of inter-regional co-operation and the long-term benefits of ignoring tribal or other ethnic differences. As for a specific British contribution it must be said that while it is obvious that large-scale international aid, preferably from the United States and the Commonwealth, is essential to provide help on the scale which has been indicated, there is a real place for the United Kingdom to continue its particular efforts in each of the former British West African countries. The quality of British education is prized by African leaders and the many established bonds between Nigerian and United Kingdom schools, colleges and universities should be preserved and expanded.

Inter-territorial co-operation in West Africa is perhaps more difficult for the newly independent territories recently administered by Britain than for those which were administered by France, because they are separated geographically one from the other. Yet too much has been and can be made of such physical separation. During the 1939–45 war there was the closest co-operation, even though the intervening lands were neutral or hostile and the waters of the Atlantic dark with the threat of submarine and surface attack. At that time, in the face of crisis, bonds between the British West African countries were drawn increasingly close, as they were between countries of the Commonwealth separated by whole oceans and continents. In Chapter 3 we outlined the development of this co-operation and mentioned the setting up of the West African War Council under a resident minister of Cabinet rank. In 1945 "War" was omitted from the title, and the Secretary of State for the Colonies, who presided at meetings in 1947 and 1948, assumed the chairmanship of the West African Council made up of the four Governors and a permanent secretariat. Under the auspices of the Council, heads of departments from the territories met from time to time to discuss questions of common concern. In 1951 the West African Inter-Territorial Conference replaced the Council, two representatives of ministerial or executive council rank coming from each territory for sessions which were held normally under the chairmanship of the Governor of Nigeria.

Until Ghana became independent in 1957 there was close interest in co-operation of all kinds apart from the common military command and the long-standing currency board which originated in 1912. A West African Court of Appeal, created in 1948, existed for a time. We have noted already that universities were established in each of the three larger territories, thus removing the need for negotiations over the single new West African university which once had been mooted. Interest in research was increasing rapidly, however, and the advantages of co-operation on grounds of cost, staff and comparative research material from different localities were obvious. Thus a West African Council for Medical Research was brought into being in 1954 with headquarters at Yaba, Nigeria, and research centres for different diseases in appropriate parts of Ghana and elsewhere. Cocoa, oil palm, maize and rice had each its own inter-territorial organization, with research institutes or principal stations in Ghana, Nigeria and Sierra Leone. Insect pests such as the timber-borer had a common organization to focus upon them. Building research was another important joint venture, an institute being established in 1952. The West African Institute for Social and Economic Research was also a product of the new age which held promise of a variety of fundamental inquiries, including comparative studies, and the pooling of scarce resources of men and women qualified in statistical and other social research techniques.

It was perhaps inevitable, though it is none the less regrettable, that considerations of politics and national prestige should supervene over research principles, especially in a zone where the maximum co-ordination of scientific effort is required if poverty, famine, illiteracy and disease are to be overcome with deliberate speed. Ghana's independence began a process of withdrawal from inter-territorial organizations. National research institutes were set up to replace the regional bodies but there was dislocation and in the background always a little too much of politics. West Africa was in no sense unusual in this; much the same disruptive influence of politics on science occurred in Central Africa when, before federa-tion, certain well-developed plans for scientific co-ordination, pre-pared under the aegis of the one-time Central African Council, were abandoned lest they should undermine the case for political unification. But by 1960 far-seeing young West Africans, alert to the emergency nature of the demand throughout the zone for in-creased food, crop and industrial production, and improved health and educational services, were urging the restoration and accelerated development of the machinery for inter-territorial co-operation. These men argue that the present challenge of peace are as urgent as those of war.

There is great good sense in the views of these young West African scholars and it is to be hoped that politicians, over-sensitive to the importance of their individual country being first or foremost, will increasingly encourage regional co-operation. The work to re-duce language and other barriers between French- and English-speaking territories must go on and be expanded, but it is absurdly unrealistic to talk of giving such efforts priority over strengthening the links between the English-speaking, and especially Common-wealth, countries. Such talk can be evasive of responsibility, rather than constructive, when there is a great uncompleted task to be accomplished by Britain and West Africa and by Commonwealth nations such as Canada who are in a position to give substantial help. Despite the recent actions of governments bent on demonstrating their independence, and the very different political approaches to the achievement of national unity, there is a striking similarity of institutions and outlook in Nigeria, Ghana, Sierra Leone and the Gambia, and many close personal bonds gained from the exchange of visits, and study, over generations and decades. The meeting of minds and tackling together of a few fundamental problems of West Africa could now inaugurate a new era of co-operation and progress more rewarding than any heated political discourse.

The Commonwealth supplies an obvious context for the West African countries to meet what Professor Busia has happily termed

K

"the challenge of responsible emancipation".* It is unfortunate that a cooling of relations affected Great Britain and West Africa in recent years, especially during the period when Nigeria and Ghana, though not Sierra Leone, reacted strongly against the political implications of Britain's application to join the European Economic Union. But even during the years of relative estrangement there were important Commonwealth conferences, educational and other, and an unhindered continuance of personal, academic and other contacts. The unofficial Commonwealth Conference in Lagos in 1961 may have owed too much of its inspiration and financial support to friendly Americans troubled by the obvious cooling of attitudes, but the conference itself did serve to rally many both in Britain and West Africa. The visit to Lagos in 1964 of the then Prime Minister of the United Kingdom, Sir Alec Douglas-Home, was a most welcome act indicative of a new and more constructive outlook on the Commonwealth in Africa.

Tensions and strains must mark British–West African relationships for generations ahead. From Nigeria, Ghana and Sierra Leone there will come repeated charges of "neo-colonialism". But there is nothing new in such charges. Similar statements were made by political leaders in the self-governing Canadian, Australian and New Zealand colonies in the nineteenth century. Canada, approaching in 1967 the centenary of its autonomy as a full federation, still produces leaders who object to certain forms of "neo-colonialism". What is new is to have such charges made by Africans, not to mention Asians. To many Britons, brought up in a tradition of empire and imperial responsibility, some of the African charges have been deeply disturbing in tone and content. They must, however, be accepted or borne, and treated perhaps like the strong egalitarian assertions of the Australian soldier in time of war. Equality of status and complete autonomy have been the hallmarks of Commonwealth Membership since 1926. They apply equally to Africa, and new accents of behaviour and criticism must be expected from each of the new Members, though they might be returned with equal warmth and vigour by a democratic Britain, recently freed from most colonial government responsibilities.

Hugh Gaitskell personified the Commonwealth ideals of British democratic socialism. His early death is a tragedy. Few British political leaders have had a clearer conception and a surer grasp of what is required to achieve the full promise of the new "multi-

* K. A. Busia, *The Challenge of Africa* (Praeger, New York 1962).

racial" Commonwealth. He was exceptional also in the depth of his understanding both of the problems facing African leaders in their advocacy of the Commonwealth and of their great potential value as new leaders of the Commonwealth. But there are others in his party and Conservatives and Liberals in Britain who share his views. They can be counted on to provide leadership on the vital questions facing Britain in connexion with the poorer, developing nations, not least the importance of assured, satisfactory prices and terms of trade for their commodities, in addition to educational aid and friendly, frank co-operation on questions of government and law.

Yet if the historic relationship between Britain and West Africa is to prosper there must emerge from West Africa political leaders of stature who will publicly proclaim, like Hugh Gaitskell, a belief and confidence in the future of the direct unilateral ties between Africa and Britain as well as in the wider Commonwealth. West Africa is at a very early stage of self-government in comparison with Canada, Australia and other nations. None of the countries has yet had ten years' experience of the independent conduct of international relations. Even India and Pakistan have barely exceeded that span. It is soon to look in West Africa for a Laurier or MacKenzie King,* a Curtin or Hughes, or a Nehru or Smuts. But the judges and doctors of West Africa have shown already over half a century and more that a similar reservoir of talent in constructive statesmanship exists and awaits its opportunity. Certainly nothing is likely to bring more heart and hope to the whole relationship between Britain and Africa than the rising to eminence in Commonwealth councils of a democratic leader from West Africa who is assured of wide support in his own country.

* Those who might think MacKenzie King an odd choice of example may care to read Nicholas Mansergh's *Survey of British Commonwealth Affairs*, Problems of War-time Co-operation and Post-war Change, 1939–52, p. 414.

6

BRITAIN AND EASTERN AFRICA

NO peoples of Africa are more varied, or more attractive in their variety, than those of the East-Central zone, nor is any part of the continent so physically interesting. The Great Rift Valley with its associated lakes, volcanic mountains and deep trenches supplies a certain geographical unity. The area remains rich in wild animal life which is now largely absent from West and Southern Africa. Sir Julian Huxley and Dr. L. S. B. Leakey of the Coryndon Museum, Nairobi, are foremost among Britons who have worked to conserve this wealth of nature and also the archaeological heritage. Others of Britain have done much during the past seventy years—forty-five in the case of Tanganyika —towards the exercise of responsible conservation, trusteeship and development. Isolated pockets of British settlers dot the zone alongside the more numerous immigrant peoples from India and Arabia. Most of what has been done by Britain will prove of lasting value to East-Central Africa; but whether it was done soon enough and in sufficient quantity to establish bridgeheads such as we have noted in Southern and West Africa is the question to which we must turn. Certainly there is no zone in which the uncompleted tasks of trusteeship are more numerous.

But before we consider the particular problems of the territories there is need to look at the overall composition and balance of the zone. For the reasons already stated Zambia (Northern Rhodesia) and Malawi (Nyasaland) have been grouped for the purpose of this essay with Uganda and Kenya, and Tanganyika and Zanzibar. Such a grouping, which treats the Zambesi as a southern border, is certainly in accord with contemporary African nationalist feeling. Though the Pan-African Freedom Movement for East, Central and South Africa (PAFMECSA) ranges farther south in its ultimate plans it acknowledges the reality of 1964, which saw Zambia and Malawi independent and hence all states to the north of the Zambesi autonomous.

Yet though the "freedom" element of the title be realized for PAFMECA, as distinct from PAFMECSA, the unity of the zone must for some time remain a matter of aspiration, not achievement. It could hardly be otherwise since only late in 1964 did two of the states become independent, while the others have known self-government for very few years at the most. Kenya became independent in December 1963. The overthrow of the Sultan of Zanzibar, the army mutinies in Tanganyika, Uganda and Kenya, and the various external threats which resulted in the rapid political unification of Tanganyika and Zanzibar, also indicate the unsettled nature of politics in the new states. But there are other reasons why unity will not easily be achieved. We must again examine the obstacles to national unity and development in the individual territories, because the longer-term total unity depends upon the strength of the constituent units; but it is specially necessary in the case of Eastern Africa to keep in mind some of the larger difficulties. The broad generalizations which may at least be attempted in the case of the British–West African and British–Southern African relationship cannot be offered for Britain and the six countries of East-Central Africa.

Political, cultural, economic and communications factors compel first attention in any consideration of the overall balance of the zone. We must take into account the possibility of a much more direct Ethiopian participation in the total entity, as well as the ties which exist between certain peoples of Zambia (Northern Rhodesia) and those of the Congo and Angola. There are traditional links also between some Africans of Malawi (Nyasaland) and some of Moçambique. The recent rapprochement between the Emperor Haile Selassie and Prime Minister Jomo Kenyatta of Kenya and the current rapid modernization of Ethiopia, coupled with the adoption of English as the second official language in place of French, may well result in changed centres of gravity in the north of the zone. Speculation as to tendencies in the southern sector are profitless until Dr. Kaunda is able to meet President Kasavubu, President Tshombe* and other leaders of the Congolese Republic on an equal footing, and with full power to bargain, but this influence on the south-western pole of the new axis cannot be overlooked.

Tanganyika's development and position in the future must obviously be of the greatest significance if the concept of Eastern Africa is to be fulfilled. If Tanganyika does not advance sufficiently

---

* President Tshombe has since become political head of the whole Congo (Leopoldville), and Dr Kaunda President of independent Zambia.

to serve as the centrepiece then it is easy to conceive the zone splitting into at least three portions: a northern comprising Uganda and Kenya; a southern made up of Zambia and Malawi; with a central portion made up of Tanganyika and Zanzibar, possibly together with Rwanda and Burundi. President Nyerere has supplied valuable leadership towards closer union in Eastern Africa, especially in that he has shown himself ready always to enter responsible negotiation with his neighbours, but his statesmanship must be backed by a strengthened economy. Tanganyika has the largest population ($9\frac{1}{2}$ million) of the six countries but it covers a vast area and is relatively poor. If it is to bear and balance the shifting weight of Uganda and Kenya against that of Zambia and Malawi, its own tensile strength must be adequate. Sisal, coffee, cotton and diamonds presently support the economy but production for both export and internal consumption must be increased.

The weight of the Zambian, or total Malawi–Zambian, economy is strikingly different in character from that of Kenya–Uganda. While the latter is primarily agricultural the former is substantially dependent upon mineral production. Uganda exported £$3\frac{1}{2}$ millions worth of copper in 1961 but its coffee and cotton exports were valued at £$30\frac{1}{2}$ millions. Kenya's economy is based on coffee, tea, sisal and other agricultural products, agriculture providing about 85 per cent of the national income. Though Malawi's economy also is overwhelmingly agricultural, the mainspring of the economy in the total Zambia–Malawi area is provided by copper and by the other minerals produced in Zambia. The tobacco, cotton, tung, maize and livestock output of the two territories is dwarfed in scale by copper, zinc, cobalt, lead and silver. Copper production in 1960 totalled over £121 millions.

In addition to their own significance the above facts and figures indicate one of the strong economic arguments which have been advanced for the early political unification of the countries of Eastern Africa—the need for the diversification of the total economy. The mineral wealth and industrial experience of Zambia could bring welcome strength and balance to the whole. But there is a formidable network of historical association to be loosened and many new pathways to be fashioned before this goal can be attained. In a zone where the precipitate catastrophe of the Tanganyika ground-nuts scheme is fresh in memory there may exist an undue tendency to caution which needs to be guarded against; but the task of altering established economic associations should never be minimized. There are strong historic economic links between Zambia, Malawi and South Africa which have drawn and still draw the Zambesi territories into the economic orbit of Southern Africa.

The mining industry, with all its technical expertise and special labour requirements, has over the past eighty years built up a complex of interdependent relationships between the peoples of Central and South Africa. The miners' frontier is a reality which embraces Africans and Europeans together. The capital, costly capital equipment and high-level manpower may stem from Europe, North America and the local European populations, but from the day of its foundation in Kimberley, in the early 1870's, the large-scale, modern mining industry of South-Central Africa has incorporated African workers. Each decade has seen African mineworkers advance in technical accomplishment and increase their working partnership with European miners and artisans. The descent of any mineshaft on the Copper Belt or the Witwatersrand, and the exploration of any stope or gallery brings home at once the strength of the human relationship, especially the sense of mutual trust and confidence in an environment where these qualities are essential and where peril and heroism, without regard for race or colour, are commonplace. Though other aspects of the experience may be criticized the comradeship of the mineshaft and rockface has long been talked about around village fires in Nyasaland, Barotseland and the other areas of Central Africa to which migrant African workers have returned.

Europeans and Africans alike, therefore, have been bound together in the service of the mining industry. We have indicated in the earlier chapters the legal and conventional barriers and the obstructive devices of trade unions which have preserved the higher incomes and status of the European workers and so increasingly aroused the resentment of African mineworkers and the officials of their organizations. We have also pointed to the social ill-effects of the migratory labour system, especially on African family and village life, agriculture and animal husbandry. Our object here is to direct attention to the broader economic implications of the mining relationship between Southern and Central Africa. Tens of thousands of Africans from Central Africa have earned, and continue to earn, their money wages on the mines in the south, and their families have long depended on their remittances for the payment of taxes, the purchase of bicycles and other consumer goods, and contributions to educational expenses. The relatively stable world price of gold has ensured regularity in labour recruitment and employment for and on the mines and in the associated manufacturing and other industries of South Africa.

Fluctuations in the world prices of copper and the other minerals of Zambia have, thus far, given less assured employment to both European and African mineworkers in Central Africa. Although they have enjoyed much better conditions of service the European mineworkers from the south have at times suffered also the disabilities of labour migration. During the early thirties, when there was a disastrous slump in the world demand for copper, thousands of Europeans were retrenched and there was a substantial exodus back to the south. There have been numerous other indications before and since of the reliance of Central Africa on the economic strength of South Africa. These facts of economics and primarily the importance of assured cash incomes to the peoples of Zambia and Malawi must be dwelt upon if there is to be realistic planning of future relationships within Eastern Africa and between Eastern and Southern Africa. In Kenya there is at present a mounting crisis of unemployment among Africans. The recession of the European planters' frontier is being accompanied by an expansion in African smallholdings but the former output of the European farms, which provided the greater part of the country's exports, has not yet been matched. The statutory requirement for employers to carry an extra quota of paid employees is affording only limited relief and can be counted but a temporary expedient.

Communications are of the greatest significance in the quest for regional unity. Though they are intimately related to economic considerations such as the location of mineral deposits and coastal outlets—and increasingly to local fuel resources of coal and electric power, refineries and factories—railways, roadways, airways and telecommunications in their alignment have all owed a good deal to politics, in particular to the historical colonial frontiers. The Kenya–Uganda railway runs inland from Mombasa through Nairobi to Kampala and on to the western frontier at Lake Edward. The German-built trunk railway across the middle of Tanganyika joins Dar-es-Salaam, the coastal capital, to Dodoma, Tabora and Kigoma, on Lake Tanganyika. Nyasaland's sole rail link joins Lake Nyasa to Beira, in Portuguese East Africa, and to the Rhodesia railway system. Zambia will continue to possess a long-established rail outlet through Katanga and Angola to the Atlantic, but her principal railway runs from the Copper Belt south across the Zambesi, at the Victoria Falls, to join the elaborate rail network of Southern Africa near the extensive Wankie coalfields of Southern Rhodesia.

There is no railway connexion across Tanganyika to join the northern and southern sectors of the zone. General Smuts' First World War railway from Voi to Arusha provides one link between Kenya and north-eastern Tanganyika; the Lake Victoria steamer service joins Kenya and Uganda lakeside termini to Mwanza and thence to Tabora and Dar-es-Salaam, but it is a circuitous and slow connexion. There is in prospect a new railway to join the present line between Lusaka and Ndola in Zambia to the relatively short "ground-nuts line" inland from the good port of Mtwara in the south-eastern corner of Tanganyika.* Other plans include a direct Lusaka–Dar-es-Salaam line. But the immensely long route which must cross much difficult country will prove very costly.† Any route by rail and sea between Lusaka and Dar-es-Salaam, or Lusaka and Nairobi by way of Mombasa, would be circuitous, like the present rail–sea route between Addis Ababa and Nairobi through Jibuti.

If transport economists should find against a direct axial railway between Lusaka and Nairobi and in favour of a motorway as the unifying trunk communication link of Eastern Africa, it will provide an equal challenge, and opportunity to the outside world to supply the necessary aid. A motorway or railway of the desired quality will require immense capital outlay. Equally important will be assistance with maintenance costs until the domestic economies have greatly strengthened themselves. The crumbling of the once impressive Italian autostrada between Mogadishu and Addis Ababa, Mussolini's *strada imperiale*, and comparable highways in the former Italian empire of north-east Africa, leave no doubt as to the rapid decay of even the best-engineered roads if maintenance is neglected, and the necessary maintenance is a costly recurrent item of expenditure beyond the financial capacity of the new African states. It is also an expenditure item difficult to justify in terms of any local budget, especially when vast unproductive areas have to be traversed as in the case of the tsetse-infested or arid portions of Eastern Africa, including the northern province of Kenya, which adjoins the highlands of Ethiopia.

In Ethiopia the United States, operating through the Imperial

---

* See J. D. Fage, *An Atlas of African History*, p. 58, Modern Economic Development: Central Africa; also p. 77 of *The Oxford Atlas*.

† The direct Lusaka–Dar-es-Salaam link is presently favoured.

Highway Authority, is constructing outwards from Addis Ababa an excellent radial network of trunk roads. In Tanganyika many young American engineer graduates of the Peace Corps are already assisting with the development of the roads essential for stimulating the national economy. But an imaginative venture, almost comparable in magnitude with the High Dam in Egypt, is required to give a unifying motorway system to Eastern Africa. It is perhaps a project the scale and cost of which might make it sufficiently worthy to be given a name such as the John F. Kennedy Memorial Highway in honour of a man who took a close, personal interest in the political and other advance of East-Central Africa.

Airways development merits a special word even though surface communications must provide the main basis for effective commercial and economic relations. Imperial Airways, South African Airways and Rhodesia and Nyasaland Airways (R.A.N.A.) pioneered the opening of the air routes in the 1930's. Efficient airfields, radio communications and meteorological offices were created. In the post-war period all services were greatly expanded for the large jet aircraft of the major international airlines, including B.O.A.C., successor of Imperial Airways. At Nairobi, Dar-es-Salaam, Livingstone and Salisbury, and at Entebbe, Lusaka and Blantyre, great sums were expended on new runways, airport facilities and air navigation equipment to make the airport fully international.

Internal air communications were also extended. Both East African Airways and Central African Airways have built up efficient local networks in association with B.O.A.C., in addition to operating certain through international services of their own to London. The "Africanization" of air-crews was accelerated recently, but something might be learned from the work of the American airline Trans-World Airways (T.W.A.), which has achieved excellent results in training Ethiopian pilots and radio officers for the Ethiopian Airlines. Although the rough local airfields of Ethiopia away from Addis Ababa and Diredawa will require substantial further investment, they are meanwhile being exploited with skill and provide valuable training.

Telecommunications in Eastern Africa do not present the problem of West Africa, where the interspersing of Francophone, Anglophone and other territories has led to situations where it is necessary, or easier, to get into touch with a neighbouring territory through links in Paris, London, and other former metropolitan centres rather than by any more direct local means. English, having long been the principal official language of all territories of Eastern Africa, has also facilitated the common reception of broadcasting, television and other services. Although Kiswahili is widely used as a lingua franca, increasingly in the parliament and Press of Tanganyika and to some degree in Kenya, English-language newspapers, journals and books continue to supply important media for communication by means of print. By some peoples, as in parts of Uganda, English is for local reasons of politics or prestige preferred to Swahili.

But though urgent attention must be given now to all aspects of communication between the territories if there is to be hope of greater regional unity within a reasonable time, it is necessary to remember that the overwhelming majority of peoples in Eastern Africa gaze from afar at the aeroplanes overhead and at the trains, lorries and motor-cars hurrying by. They are close-bound still to their clan and tribal lands, to their slow-moving flocks and herds of camels, cattle, sheep and goats, and operate within traditional ties of kinship. Increasing numbers are gaining some access to radio and television broadcasts but few have used a telephone and most, being illiterate, are unable to read newspapers. The improvement in the education, nutrition and health of such peoples is the principal challenge of contemporary Eastern Africa and there can be little prospect of durable unity within or between the countries until such fundamental obstacles to progress have been overcome. However, before we take up the question of the unity of the African peoples—an issue likely to prove of first importance in the independent Eastern Africa of the future—it is helpful to review the course of events in the several territories since 1945 and, in particular, to observe the ending of United Kingdom rule and, with that ending, the termination of the pre-eminence in local politics of the European and other non-African minorities.

Kenya and Northern Rhodesia demand prior consideration. Europeans, Asians and members of other non-African minorities who have served as the auxiliaries of British rule are to be found in each of the other territories, but there could be no question of their retaining positions of power or special influence in the "African states" of Uganda, Tanganyika and Nyasaland once Britain had abandoned control in the countries where Europeans were most numerous and where they, and their representatives in the legislative and executive councils, had long enjoyed special treatment as the co-trustees of the Imperial Government.

Of the two former "white men's countries" Kenya must be taken first. It is the country which has tested every assumption and hope of more recent colonial policy and practice, mainly that of the twentieth century, in contrast with the older policies and longer history of South and West Africa. It is also the country in which the decisive event of the post-war period took place: the outbreak of Mau Mau in 1952, with its continuation through the long years until 1958 or, as some would suggest, until December 1963, when the actual attainment of Kenya's independence brought the last of the "Freedom Fighters" from their forest hide-outs. Without Mau Mau the course of recent history could have been radically different. The twin targets of "multi-racial government" in East Africa and of "inter-racial partnership" in Central Africa would have been given much more hope of achievement.

The Watson Commission which examined the Gold Coast disturbances in 1948 sought their underlying as well as their more proximate causes. They were right to draw the attention of the Secretary of State to their views, and it is possible that only a much earlier awareness of profound Kikuyu discontent and a readiness to apply drastic remedies could have saved Kenya from its terrible troubles, of true Irish proportions. At the time, however, the Secretary of State and the United Kingdom Government were understandably satisfied that the political situation in the less developed dependencies of East and Central Africa was very different from that in West Africa, and that priority must be given to intensified economic and social development. The ground-nuts scheme into which so many millions were poured by the United Kingdom was but one venture in this direction. It was also an accepted opinion of the 1940's that development could be greatly assisted by closer regional co-ordination of services and production. It was such thinking which led to the institution of the East Africa High Commission in 1948 with its multi-racial Legislative Assembly containing European, Asian and African representatives from the constituent territories, and to the creation of the Central African Council.

African opinion, especially Kikuyu opinion, was alert to the trend of politics in West Africa as well as to the attainment of independence by India, Pakistan and Ceylon. The presence of men of Indian and Pakistani origin rejoicing in their midst could leave them in no ignorance of the Asian constitutional advances. Among many educated Africans, especially those who could perceive the rationale of the Labour Government's plans to co-ordinate the territorial economies of East and Central Africa in the interests of all-round advancement, there was a readiness to co-operate with Britain. Among others, however, including some of the more politically forceful, or embittered, there was a suspicion that greater regional co-ordination would necessitate continued European leadership and a substantial prolongation of colonial rule. This suspicion flamed into hostility after the general election in Britain in October 1951 saw the substitution of a Conservative administration for the Labour Government, which had been severely criticized at times by its opponents for its "liquidation" of the Indian empire and its over-readiness to make concessions to Asian and African nationalism. The manner in which the new Conservative ministers took up in 1951 and early 1952 the proposals for Central African federation which had been initiated by the Labour Government in 1950–1 also alarmed African leaders. To them it appeared that European ascendancy was to be extended and entrenched north of the Zambesi. In mid-1952 the Kikuyu and their allies struck. The Kenya emergency was declared, British forces were called in, and the prospects throughout East-Central Africa were transformed.

Before we recall the constitutional developments between 1952 and 1963, which reflect the British Government's desire to unite in amity the diverse peoples of Kenya, we should look briefly at some of the hopes and aspirations of those in Britain who had long been specially concerned with policy towards and in Kenya and East Africa. There is only limited utility in labels but it might be helpful to refer to the "Christian imperialist" group, of whom Dr. J. H. Oldham, Miss Margery Perham and Professor Roland Oliver represent successive generations, and to the "economic imperialists" who firmly upheld the importance of European settlement, investment and trade. The missionary societies and journals and church papers provided a domestic forum for the former; the Joint East African Board and the journal *East Africa and Rhodesia* for the latter. In their worst moments they might be tempted to think of one another as "maudlin moralists" or "Machiavellian materialists", but at their best they were ready enough to concede the necessity for both morals and economics. They did not have the field to themselves in the London world of influence, the applied anthropology committee of the Royal Anthropological Institute contained people of the calibre of Dr. Edwin Smith and Professors Radcliffe-Brown and Margaret Read, and there were others in education, government and international affairs who took a close and responsible interest in the affairs of East and Central Africa.

But the major battles over British policy were fought between the Christian and economic imperialists. Dr. Joseph Oldham was a foremost Christian campaigner. The key figure in British and international missionary organization, he was eternally vigilant and hard-hitting as is shown in his forthright criticisms of General Smuts's Oxford and other lectures of 1929, which were later published in one volume under the title *Africa and Some World Problems*. In addition to his own books* Oldham kept effective watch on the Colonial Office and maintained close liaison with its principal officers. He also served with distinction as a member of the Commission on Closer Union of the Dependencies in Eastern and Central Africa under the chairmanship of Sir Edward Hilton Young, later Lord Kennet. Every aspect of policy concerning African interests was mastered by Oldham, particular attention being devoted to the crucial question of land rights, which in Kenya was dealt with in 1933 by a commission led by Sir William Morris Carter, a judge from Tanganyika, who had in 1925 presided over the Southern Rhodesia Land Commission which provided the basis for that colony's Land Apportionment Act. The Kikuyu grievances over land in the Kenya highlands were a matter of special concern to international missionary circles where close consideration and study had been given to issues affecting Christianity and Kikuyu tribal rites.

The Kikuyu sense of suffering over past wrongs was never eradicated. A good insight into the thought and feeling of this most numerous and able tribe of Kenya is to be gained from reading Mr. Jomo Kenyatta's *Facing Mount Kenya*, first published in 1938, and from writings such as *Mau Mau and the Kikuyu* and *Defeating Mau Mau* by Dr. L. S. B. Leakey, himself a fluent Kikuyu linguist and an elder of the tribe. Though the Christian imperialist group in Britain fought for a maximum protection of Kikuyu and other African rights, and the economic imperialists for priority for more modern systems of land tenure and economic organization, both at times gaining concessions from successive colonial secretaries and

---

* *White and Black in Africa* (London, 1930) contains the criticisms of the Smuts lectures. See also Dr. Oldham's *Christianity and the Race Problem* (S.C.M. Press, 1924).

governors, these conflicts, which were never completely reconciled, had only marginal interest for a talented and determined people confident in their own destiny. Mr. Kenyatta, a student of social anthropology at London University in the 1930's, has been followed in his educational achievements by many other Kikuyu who have seized every opportunity for secondary and higher education at centres like the Alliance High School, Makerere University College in Uganda and, more recently, the Royal College, Nairobi.

The future of Kenya today rests very much in the hands of Mr. Kenyatta, his Kikuyu people and their friends and colleagues such as Mr. Mboya. On their ability to provide an acceptable basis of life for the non-Kikuyu, and the non-African, peoples of Kenya the unity of the nation must now depend. The exact course which they will follow is difficult to discern and it is impossible to know whether the elaborate "regional" constitution of 1963 will survive any longer than the provisions for regional devolution in Ghana's independence constitution of 1957. There is much to support the view of Mr. George Bennett as to why the many concessions to regionalism were made by Mr. Kenyatta and his Kenya African National Union (K.A.N.U.) to Mr. Ronald Ngala's Kenya African Democratic Union (K.A.D.U.) at the constitutional conference in London on the eve of independence: "K.A.N.U. was prepared to act thus since independence was its objective; after the rapid constitutional changes of the past years they had little respect for constitutions, believing that they could be destroyed as easily as they were made."*

Certainly Mr. Kenyatta and his Minister for Justice and Constitutional Affairs, Mr. Tom Mboya, who at Oxford and elsewhere has made a close study of political systems, incline very definitely to the view that the process of unification of Kenya's very diverse peoples can and should be forced, and that this is best done by a policy of central control.† Such a structure would not be dissimilar from that erected by the former British colonial administration in Kenya. But whether a system which depended upon the external régime of Westminster and Whitehall will be accepted as readily from a locally composed government in control in Nairobi is the question. It is one which we have considered already in the case of Ghana, where the peoples of the Northern Territories and Ashanti were as strongly opposed to a unitary constitution as the Somali, the

* *Kenya: A Political History. The colonial period.* (London 1963), p. 156.
† In November 1964 Kenya was proclaimed a one-party state.

Kalenjin, the Masai and other tribes and groups in Kenya, traditional competitors or enemies of the Kikuyu. In many cases the
tensions are deep-seated ones between pastoralists and agriculturists.

But whatever the course which Kenya's new rulers adopt in the
future they will be able to learn something from the efforts of the
British constitution makers of the 1950's: Mr. Oliver Lyttelton
(Lord Chandos), Mr. Lennox Boyd (Lord Boyd) and Sir Evelyn
Baring (Lord Howick) who, though they accepted the principle that
responsibility should still be exercised by Britain and representatives
of the Britons resident in Kenya, strove to make a successful reality
of multi-racial government. They built on the work of their post-
war predecessors, most notably Arthur Creech Jones, but under the
conditions of the emergency they were called upon to act more
urgently to bring together representatives of all the peoples of
Kenya in the executive, legislative and administrative branches. No
man gave more devoted, distinguished and courageous service than
Sir Evelyn Baring, who was called to the governorship of Kenya
after the gauntlet had been thrown down by the leaders of Mau
Mau. His wife, Lady Mary Baring, who on arrival in Nairobi at
once settled to the study of the difficult Kikuyu language and to
active welfare work among African women, deserves mention also,
both for her own attainments and as an example of the British
wives who have made important personal contributions to Britain
in Africa through the generations.

It was a remarkable feat for a governor whose reputed talents
lay in the economic and civil spheres, to prove so successful during
a prolonged period of insurrection and warfare. He was severely
criticized at times, not least for "overloading" the various branches
of government with too many ministers, parliamentarians and civil
servants. Yet never in the history of Kenya, or of East Africa, was
"multi-racialism" demonstrated more convincingly in the offices of
government than during the difficult, at times desperate, days of the
emergency. Additional portfolios, seats and desks may be question-
able on grounds of financial cost but, in times of grave crisis in a
multi-racial society, the benefits to be gained from securing a close
working partnership between all peoples—Africans, Asians and
Europeans—in the making and implementation of policy outweigh
any disadvantage. Material as well as moral gain results from reduction of ethnic tension. The "training" aspect of such multi-
racialism was of the utmost value.

During the time of the emergency there was concern for the extended application of multi-racialism outside Kenya as well. In Tanganyika the recommendations of Professor W. M. Mackenzie on franchise and representation were of particular importance. The commission of inquiry into the structure and conditions of service in the civil services of all East African countries, under the chairmanship of Sir David Lidbury,* placed a special emphasis on the need to remove or reduce all the racial and ethnic distinctions in recruitment, appointment and advancement, many of them the product of a long and complicated history in countries where differential practices had been welcomed at times in order to protect particular community interests. Outside government also the emergency years were remarkable for the rapidity with which entrenched patterns of social segregation were abandoned. The ministries of Kenya combed the statute book to weed out discriminatory laws and regulations; the public at large accepted, without fuss, "integration" in restaurants, theatres, sports clubs, cinemas and other places which formerly had been the preserve of one ethnic group, usually that of the Europeans.

Seldom have long-established social barriers gone down so quickly as in Kenya between 1953 and 1956. It is possible to attribute this phenomenon entirely to the shock of fear which was evoked by Mau Mau, but there was in the general response much to indicate that more worthy emotions were brought into play by the circumstances of the emergency. Shock there was certainly, and alarm for the future, but there was also a sharper recognition of the folly of ill-considered and out-of-date practices and unwarranted attitudes, together with a new appreciation of the necessity for active inter-racial co-operation. Those opposed to the evils of Mau Mau, Africans as well as Asians and Europeans, suffered together and together condemned acts of terrorism as they worked to preserve the essentials of community life.

There is little point in supplying details of the careful ethnic balance of the Executive Council and the Legislative Council which was worked out in the different constitutions introduced during the emergency. The membership of these bodies, together with the composition of new institutions such as the Council of State, a selected cross-section of senior statesmanlike members of the different communities, is to be found in the many books of

* Report of the Commission on the Civil Services of the East African Territories and the East Africa High Commission 1953-4.

L

reference, not least the Colonial Annual Reports, the annual Colonial Office Lists and the other official publications on the Commonwealth and dependencies. Somali, Arab, Hindu, Sikh, Masai, Kikuyu, planter, townsman—a place was devised for the representation of each interest and group. In these councils the "best man" principle was always permissible since politics were not paramount. Thus the famous A. B. Patel came to be an acknowledged key figure in Kenya's Executive Council until his eventual unshakeable decision to retire from the power and influence of his office to the contemplative religious life in India which was dictated by his Hindu conscience.

There is understandably today, in the first enthusiasm of independence, little readiness to analyse with detachment the reasons which underlay the particular provisions of the constitutions of the post-war era, nor the wisdom which governed the selection of particular individuals for important office; but Kenya's leaders of the future in times of strife might well profit from such reflection. There is place in a land of many cultural and racial groups for institutions such as a representative Council of State to protect communities against harmful discrimination; and place also for that generosity towards minorities which characterizes the best in Westminster and Whitehall, where the Scots, Welsh and Irish hold a not ungenerous proportion of principal offices among the native English.

On the personal, as distinct from the official side of life in colonial Kenya, Karen Blixen performed the great service of depicting with skill and sensitive accuracy the diverse peoples and scenes and life of Kenya during the peak moments of the British ascendancy. Her book *Out of Africa*, published in 1937, provides a valuable series of observations and sketches of the Somali as individuals and as representatives of their culture, and of the Masai, the Kikuyu and the Asians. The Europeans of Kenya are revealed with the same honesty and compassion. Danish aristocrat and British settler widow, she has been criticized recently by some of her fellow-countrymen, among whom she died a few months ago near Copenhagen, for writing from the standpoint of her personal and social background. But much of the criticism is as unfair as it is unhistorical. There may be forgiving irony in her brief sketch of her neighbour, the fashionable doctor turned planter, who asked to be excused from further calls to attend African servants because he had formerly "practised to the *élite* of Bournemouth", but it is wholly accurate in its evocation of one element in the settler population.

Karen Blixen's honesty led her to make plain that her Bournemouth neighbour had responded to her appeal and that it was his skill which saved the life both of her African servant in difficult child-birth and of her baby. Yet there were, and are, in Kenya the other British doctors who as government medical officers, private family practitioners and specialists, have through the decades borne impossible case-loads in remote rural clinics and dispensaries and in the large hospitals of the towns to relieve the sick and to promote the health of countless thousands of Africans. There were the working farmers too, British gentry and yeomen, and the Afrikaners of Eldoret. Karen Blixen's writings, like those of Elspeth Huxley, keep alive the Kenya of the colonial era.

Britons who served Kenya may serve again in the future, as many in fact are doing already; but it is the service of equals which they must bring, not that of the privileged. Mau Mau brought to Britain the full realization of her new position in Africa. Above all it emphasized with stark clarity the difference between earlier times, that is before India's independence in 1947, when she could summon to her aid the resources of the Indian empire, not least the Indian army, and the new era of the multi-racial Commonwealth, when a central support of her former power in Eastern Africa has been removed and replaced by independent India and Pakistan, alert to and critical of all aspects of colonialism. South Africa's resources also, in the age of *apartheid* after 1948, were beyond the call of Britain for aid in suppressing Mau Mau. The South African Air Force contribution was welcomed by the United Nations Force in Korea; but whereas it might have been possible for Britain to have accepted the help of Smuts, it was politically impossible in the new Commonwealth to seek aid from Malan and his associates. The military suppression of Mau Mau had to be borne by Britain alone, and most of the great cost of reconstruction and development. Appraisal of the experience of Mau Mau after 1958, and recognition of the strength of Kikuyu and African feeling, helped to lead Britain in 1960 to a decision in respect of African nationalism comparable to that of 1906 in respect of Afrikaner nationalism—political withdrawal and a transfer of power.

Northern Rhodesia's European population watched the course of the Mau Mau struggle with a deep sense of fellow-feeling for the "settlers". So also did the planters of Nyasaland. Sir Roy Welensky was assured of emotional receptions whenever he spoke in Kenya to audiences such as those at the agricultural shows, and his speeches were applauded at home in Northern Rhodesia. The Europeans of the northern territories of Central Africa were for several years, however, lulled by Federation into an expectation that the British ascendancy was to be maintained and that they would continue to serve as the privileged co-trustees of the Imperial Government. As they were led to conceive the position, it was their role and duty to supply leadership towards independent statehood, a process which, it was generally assumed, would require generations rather than decades or years. Such estimates were not excessive in comparison with contemporary forecasts for Tanganyika and Uganda.

The decision by the United Kingdom Government in 1952–3 to impose Federation on the unwilling Africans of Northern Rhodesia and Nyasaland had its psychological effect on almost all the European residents in the two territories, including those many settlers who had long accepted that they were living in "Colonial Office" protectorates which were destined to become "African states". Even convinced non-racialists among the Europeans, prominent in the inter-racial associations, explained to visitors that they were being obliged to readjust their outlook and behaviour to the new situation in which Europeans were cast in the explicit role of senior partners. Among several administrators of the colonial service, schooled in a tradition of the "paramountcy" of African interests, the abrupt termination of their assumptions and expectations had a traumatic effect, discernible in older and younger officers alike. Mr. Griff Jones's *Britain and Nyasaland** is an important book which analyses with scrupulous skill and care the story of the ten years of Federation through which he served Nyasaland, a decide which he sets against the wider political and historical background.

Attempts were made by certain senior European leaders to indicate to the Africans and Europeans, Asians and Coloureds, the scope and meaning of partnership. Sir Gilbert Rennie, Governor of Northern Rhodesia, who accepted the challenge of Federation and saw the benefits for all of intensified economic and social development, prepared at an early stage a comprehensive draft definition of partnership to serve as a basis for discussion. It is most unfortunate that his initiative was not at once followed up. Among European political leaders Sir John Moffat of Northern Rhodesia was also outstanding for his forthright presentation of the "Moffat

* London, 1964 (George Allen and Unwin).

Resolutions" to the Legislative Council in 1954. He made plain what partnership must mean if there was to be hope of inter-racial co-operation. In Nyasaland, and Southern Rhodesia also, there were Europeans who saw the importance of coming to grips at once with the urgent task of securing maximum African goodwill if the Federation was to have any hope.

The majority of Europeans, however, in characteristic human fashion, were content to accept the new fact of Federation and to adjust their lives accordingly. In this they resembled the Italians who at much the same time were offending Somalis in the Somalia to which they had returned by sanction of the United Nations, after the termination of the British military administration. Though the mandate was for a specific period of ten years the returning Italians spoke and acted as if the period was indefinite and their pre-war régime had been restored.

The Africans of Northern Rhodesia and Nyasaland may have lacked a leader like Mr. Jomo Kenyatta, and a people like the Kikuyu, but they nevertheless deeply resented the manner in which their views on Federation and their fears were seemingly ignored by the United Kingdom Government and by the local administrators whom they had learned to trust. The new attitudes of the Europeans about them, and the seeming abandonment of the concept of paramountcy by the Colonial Service officers who had previously been protective in approach, at first dismayed but then spurred Africans into new political organization and resolve.

Although John Chilembwe* had shown his spirit of independence in Nyasaland during the 1914–18 war, the Africans of Northern Rhodesia and Nyasaland were slow to organize effective political movements. Individuals from Central Africa, like Clements Kadalie, frequently played a leading part in trade unions and political bodies in South Africa alongside their friends from the Cape and Natal, but there was not the scope in their home societies for any major activity. Nyasaland from Sir Harry Johnston's time was a Crown protectorate in which missionaries and protective-minded administrators exercised the predominant influence, while Northern Rhodesia after 1924, when the Crown assumed responsibility from the British South Africa Company, increasingly placed an emphasis on the development of tribal government in accordance with the principles of "indirect administration". Chiefs and other

* See Shepperson, G. and Price, T., *Independent African* (Edinburgh University Press, 1960).

traditional authorities were thereby given fresh political importance.

When, in the last years of the 1939–45 war, attention was given to the development of African provincial councils and national representative bodies, it was natural for Britain to build a pyramidal structure based on the tribal authorities. In 1944 and 1945 African provincial councils were instituted in both Northern Rhodesia and Nyasaland, and in 1946 the African Representative Council in Northern Rhodesia and its counterpart, the African Protectorate Council in Nyasaland. In 1948 and 1949 the first Africans were appointed from these national consultative bodies to the respective Legislative Councils of Northern Rhodesia and Nyasaland. These dates serve to indicate how recently Africans were drawn into political participation at national level. It was, again, only under the post-war Labour Government that trade union officers were appointed to assist in the development of the African Mineworkers' Union, and other unions, although South African socialists had supported African labour organizations in the Copper Belt during the industrial troubles of the late 1930's and early 1940's.

Federation at once extended the horizons of all African political and organizational thought. The delegations to London to oppose federation, whether chiefs eager for audience of the Queen or African national congressmen and trade unionists eager to consult Michael Scott and Fenner Brockway, enlarged the scale of African discussion and activity. It confronted them directly with the significance of federation in a Pan-African, Commonwealth and world context and linked them inextricably with organizations based in London, New York and other international centres. After Federation was brought about in 1953, African leaders never lacked experienced outside consultants and advisers in Britain or the United States, most of whom were in active sympathy with African nationalism. In Northern Rhodesia and Nyasaland African organization strengthened in every direction—executive, administrative and financial; political propaganda and recruitment acquired a new sophistication. In Britain Dr. Hastings Kamuzu Banda, who for many years had engaged in family medical practice in London, provided Nyasaland with a representative intimately acquainted with British life and thought, while Africans who came from Northern Rhodesia to act on behalf of their organizations rapidly learned the metropolitan techniques of political pressure.

The year 1957, which marked Ghana's independence, was a critical year in the Britain–Central African relationship. The pro-

vision in the Federation (Constitution) Order in Council for review
of the constitution after from seven to nine years may only have
been inserted belatedly, but it provided nevertheless a constant
stimulus to statesmanship which, if it had evoked the right
response, might have saved the Federation. But politics, not statesmanship, prevailed. In place of a constructive response to the
pressures of Afro–Asian politics in the immediate aftermath of
Suez and Mau Mau there was in 1957 the agreement between the
United Kingdom and Federal governments which strengthened the
latters' position and control. The London Announcement of April
27, 1957, a joint declaration by the Secretary of State for Commonwealth Relations and the Prime Minister of the Federation,
enhanced the status of the Federal government in a number of
significant ways.

It was wholly understandable that Federal leaders, who were very
conscious of Sir Godfrey Huggins's (later Lord Malvern's) attendance at meetings of the Commonwealth Prime Ministers since
1937, should feel sensitive about Ghana having overtaken Rhodesia
in Commonwealth and international status, but little was to be
gained by hasty *ad hoc* modifications to the relationship between
Britain and the Federation. The Constitution Amendment Act of
1957 which changed the composition of the Federal Assembly was
also resisted by African leaders who were very conscious of the few
African voters on the federal electoral rolls, both general and
special. At August 31, 1959, for example, there were on the general
roll 64,622 Europeans from Southern Rhodesia, 18,851 from
Northern Rhodesia, and 2,171 from Nyasaland as against 1,211,
639 and 9 Africans respectively. Africans on the special roll
numbered 949 for Southern Rhodesia, 4,301 for Northern Rhodesia
and 23 for Nyasaland. True, more Africans could have been enrolled had there not been powerful pressure to boycott registration,
but that pressure itself called for understanding and remedial
action.

The copper recession before the Southern Rhodesia and Federal
elections of 1958, five years after the introduction of Federation,
played its part in heightening the anxiety of the electors, mostly
Europeans, including many new immigrants from the United
Kingdom. Unemployment and other difficulties led them to support
candidates who promised to give first attention to satisfying their
immediate needs. British immigrants, accustomed to national health
and educational services of the welfare state, were strongly critical

of Prime Minister Garfield Todd and of the outspoken non-racialism of Mr. Hardwicke Holderness and other leading members of the United Rhodesia Party in Southern Rhodesia, and there were comparable reactions among Europeans in Northern Rhodesia and Nyasaland. Mr. Todd's party, with its active African members, gained not a single seat in the territorial elections of July 1958. Such internal economic and political setbacks added greatly to the stresses of partnership and paved the way for riots and disturbances in all three territories of the Federation.

We cannot supply details of the disturbances of 1959, but they were almost as decisive in their effects in Central Africa as Mau Mau had proved in East Africa. The report of the Devlin Commission on the emergency in Nyasaland is a key document. It supplied facts and recommendations which could not be ignored. It was only open to Britain thereafter, through the Monckton Commission, which was appointed in July 1959 to conduct the review of the Federal constitution, to recommend giant strides towards partnership by means of substantial increases in African participation in federal and territorial government. When the Monckton recommendations, which ran counter to many of the assumptions underlying the 1957 London agreement between the United Kingdom and Sir Roy Welensky's ministry, were not accepted by the Europeans of Central Africa the fate of the Federation was sealed.* It is significant that though the Monckton Report, which was tabled in October 1960, was considered excessively liberal by most Europeans the opposite view was taken by most Africans. A considered statement of such critical African opinion is contained in the minority report of Mr. Manoah Wellington Chirwa and Mr. H. G. Habanyama. These commissioners differed from their colleagues on two matters of principle. They were unable to accept the continued existence of a Federation not based on consent and which, in their view, had not proved to be of benefit to the majority of the inhabitants and they considered that the Majority Report had failed to deal effectively with the all-important question of constitutional advance in the Territories.

Although the dissolution of the Federation did not take formal effect until December 31, 1963, little is gained from a recitation of the events of the last years. The senior British cabinet minister, Mr. R. A. Butler, who was given a special office in respect of Central Africa, presided with dignity and skill over the difficult conference

* Sir Roy's assessment is in *Welensky's 4000 Days*, (Collins, 1964).

at the Victoria Falls in June–July 1963 which set about the abandonment of an experiment which many had entered with high hope only a short decade previously. The secession of Nyasaland, agreed to in 1962, occasioned comparatively little trouble. The small, densely populated territory with its perennial deficit had been pushed into the Federation at least as much by the Imperial Government as it had been pulled in by the white leaders of Rhodesia, several of whom had been frankly reluctant to be saddled with the financial burden. Northern Rhodesia on the other hand presented a problem akin to that of Kenya at the time of the Lancaster House conference of 1960. A way had quickly to be found from a state of European ascendancy, in existence since the 1890's and reinforced in the 1950's, to an African-controlled government.

Northern Rhodesia's elaborate "multi-racial" constitutions introduced in 1959 and 1962 had much in common with those of contemporary Kenya. Whether their complicated arrangements for ensuring an ethnic balance in political representation provided the best machinery for moving towards African control of affairs may be questioned, but, as in the case of Kenya, there was undoubtedly a strong desire on the part of the governors and administrators to discover effective and peaceful means of preventing the suppression of the rights and interests of any community. Zambians of the future, like Kenyans, may find it rewarding to reflect on the practices or proposals of non-partisan British officials. Certainly the responsibility will be theirs now that Northern Rhodesia, under the name of Zambia, has become independent.*

Dr. Kenneth Kaunda, whose *Zambia Shall be Free* and the earlier *Black Government?*† reflect his responsible approach to the problems of independence, will shortly occupy a position which is as important as that of any other leader of independent Africa. His management of the internal affairs and external relations of the wealthiest single territory of Eastern Africa must obviously exert wide influence. But equally significant will be his handling of his political opponents and the fears of the several minorities. The African National Congress (A.N.C.) has lost to Dr. Kaunda's United National Independence Party (U.N.I.P.) in the crucial pre-independence struggle for power and it appears that Mr. Harry Nkumbula, who bore the early burdens of leading the African political struggle, must be content with leadership of the opposition.

* See *Postscript*.
† Written in association with the Rev. Colin Morris.

The Europeans, whose knowledge and skill are essential to the economic and social development of Zambia, and the Coloured and Asian minorities must likewise look to Dr. Kaunda for the protection of their persons and properties and the safeguarding of their cultural and community interests. It is to the credit of Dr. Kaunda that despite the lawlessness in the adjoining Congolese Republic he commands a wide personal confidence, including that of leading British settlers of the experience of Sir Stewart Gore-Browne.

The fact that there is a certain ethnic element in the African support for U.N.I.P. and the A.N.C. in Northern Rhodesia was not stressed in the foregoing paragraph but it is undoubtedly something which will require the closest attention when the first careless rapture of independence has run its course. There has been among U.N.I.P. officers the same, almost universal, colonial unwillingness to study seriously the long-term issues of national unity, such as policy in respect of official languages or the devolution of power to the provinces, lest such discussions defer independence. But it is desirable that sustained thought be given to such topics with a view to devising the best possible policies in the light of all available experience. Attention has been riveted on European–African relations during the past seven years, in which new statutory bodies concerned with the improvement of "race relations" have operated in Northern Rhodesia. But while substantial "tribes" such as the Bemba, Chewa, Tonga, Lunda, Luvale and Lozi, whose numbers exceed those of any non-African minority, are still conscious of their distinctiveness, it is very possible that Zambia in the future will be confronted with the problems of "tribalism" which have been examined in the past by Professor Clyde Mitchell and the late Professor Vincent Harlow.

In the new states of Eastern Africa which lie between the two former "white men's countries" problems of tribalism may also arise in the future. Malawi could find herself facing internal divisions of an ethnic kind though her record suggests that this might be unlikely. The Nyasaland battalions of the King's African Rifles were always noted for their lack of tribal consciousness, as were migrant Nyasa workers. In Tanganyika too the prospect of ethnic harmony is also comparatively good. Apart from the determination of President Nyerere to absorb into his single party—the Tanganyika African National Union (T.A.N.U.)—the energies of the Chagga and other proudly self-conscious peoples, his country has the advantage that it contains a great many African groupings of modest size rather than one or more predominant peoples like the Kikuyu in Kenya.

Uganda is perhaps more precariously placed than any of the other countries of Eastern Africa in terms of internal African unity, especially if we exclude the Somali problem of Kenya whose solution might best be found within a wider regional context. Of the 75,000 persons who make up the non-African population of Uganda—as against the $6\frac{1}{2}$ million Africans—over 63,000 are Indians, 6,000 Pakistanis and 3,000 Goans. There has in the past been serious conflict between Indians and Africans, stemming chiefly from economic differences. But each of the thirteen principal tribes into which the Government has classified the African population greatly exceeds the Indian population in number. The Baganda, totalling around a million and comprising approximately 17 per cent of the whole population, are the largest ethnic entity, but the Iteso, Basoga and Banyankole, who each constitute some 8–9 per cent of the total, are also numerous. There has at times been acute tension between the Baganda and Basoga, whose territories confront one another across the Nile below Lake Victoria, and it has not proved easy to secure co-operation even for much needed common economic development projects, such as those which have centred on the town of Jinja and the new industrial and commercial enterprises associated with the near-by Owen Falls dam and hydro-electric power station. Other neighbours of the Baganda, especially those proud of their own traditional rulers and sensitive to the historical growth of Baganda ascendancy, have experienced clashes with the people of the Kabaka. The Banyoro feel deep resentment at the fate of their "lost counties", and at the United Kingdom's failure to restore them before independence.*

The Baganda, entrenched behind their special agreements with the United Kingdom Government and located in the heart of Uganda around Kampala, the principal commercial city, Entebbe, the seat of the administration, and Makerere, adjoining Kampala, the site of the University, have always presented the most difficult problem to those concerned to devise a constitution for the whole country. It required a decade and more of intensive negotiation, sometimes a major clash of wills—as when the Kabaka was banished to Britain for the period December 1953–October 1955— before a formula was prepared. A federal-type system of

* The independent government of Uganda has acted recently to restore the "lost counties".

government was agreed upon and Buganda was thereby assured of a substantial measure of autonomy. Whether the special position of the Baganda will be respected in the future is impossible to predict; but in the short period since Uganda became independent in October 1962 wisdom has characterized the treatment of the Kabaka and his kingdom by the Prime Minister, Mr. Milton Obote, of the Lango people from the Northern Province. True, Mr. Obote's Uganda People's Congress needed to add, by means of coalition, the 21 seats of the Kabaka Yekka Party to his own 37 in order to form a government, with the Democratic Party (24 seats) in opposition, but it is nevertheless important that he did install the Kabaka as first president of the whole of Uganda when a republican constitution was introduced in October 1963. It was as if Dr. Nkrumah had decided to appoint the Asantehene as a Ghanahene, or constitutional monarch, in the manner in which the sultans of Malaya have been incorporated into the modern political system. In the years ahead there will be need for many comparable acts if harmony is to obtain and if the several traditional rulers and peoples are to become fully reconciled to working together in the interests of a united Uganda.

Many have argued in recent years that the best hope of reducing inter-tribal and other ethnic friction in Eastern Africa lies in much larger political associations, preferably one which embraces not only all the present members but others, such as the Sudan, Ethiopia, Somalia and those countries in the south and west which were mentioned earlier in this chapter. Only within an association of this kind, the argument holds, is it likely that the fears and hostilities which at present exist between immediate neighbours and competitors are likely to be overcome. Again, only by merging into a greater political society will people abandon their present reluctance to surrender any part of their "national" land, a potent source of national pride or prestige, if simply through its representation on a map. In a larger association, it is felt, the rights of minorities will be shown greater respect. There is force in this argument and the goal of a wider unity is obviously one which merits sympathy and support.

Yet, as in the case of West Africa, it would seem better for regional unification to proceed on the basis of the existing foundation than to be impelled from the outset towards a more ambitious objective. The Prime Minister of Uganda, with the backing of Ghana's President, has thus far provided the major obstacle to the closer political unification of the East African territories. He has assumed a more militant posture in respect of some of the major issues on which Pan-Africanism was, and is, agreed—the need for breaking up the Rhodesia–Nyasaland Federation and the need for strong action against *apartheid* in South Africa. The recent fusion of Zanzibar and Tanganyika, following the army mutinies which affected Uganda as well as the other countries of East Africa, may now encourage Uganda towards unity with Kenya and Tanganyika–Zanzibar (or Tanzania). Uganda's inhibitions over closer union are due in part to internal difficulties, but there is in part also a traditional sense of resentment about the priority of attention given to Kenya. It may not have been a tactful act on the part of those responsible for the Uganda Colonial Annual Report for 1956 to remind Ugandans of Labouchere's criticism of Uganda as a *damnosa hereditas* and the Uganda railway as a "gigantic folly" which "goes nowhere", even though their purpose was to highlight the westward extension of the railway.

Tanganyika also has had frequent occasion to question Kenya's presumption, especially Nairobi's repeated assumption of the role of regional capital. It was perhaps natural, given the fact that Tanganyika was only entrusted to the United Kingdom in 1919–20, that the northern, and central, territory and its principal city should have acquired seniority, but Tanganyika's and Uganda's British governors as well as their African leaders have not always viewed the arrangement with pleasure. A new Brasilia-type capital might ease such feeling. If Eastern Africa is enlarged to incorporate Zambia and Malawi it could well be deemed a necessity.

But wherever the headquarters of a more unified East Africa might be located and whatever the form of political constitution it must be emphasized that a network of most valuable common services has been built already by Britain, in company with East Africa's leaders, during the past fifty years. The conquest of Tanganyika made closer association possible and the whole process was given impetus by the Hilton Young Commission. Its 1929 report* placed major emphasis on the need for careful, comparative study, especially within the region, and the closest inter-territorial co-operation. The Governors' conferences of the 1930's, and the further experience of co-operation in war-time between 1939 and 1945, led naturally to the East Africa High Commission in 1948.

The achievements of the East Africa High Commission were impressive in their quality, extent and variety. It is important for

* *On the Closer Union of the Dependencies of East and Central Africa.*

the whole of the zone, and for the wider Africa, that in December 1961 the High Commission was replaced by the East African Common Services Organization, still with headquarters in Nairobi, to administer the inter-territorial services. The United Kingdom Government withdrew completely from the new organization, leaving it to the local administrations and their successors to carry forward the work. Ministers and other representatives from each constituent territory are together responsible for the formulation of policy. From a long list it is possible to select only a few services but the mention of the Desert Locust Survey and the Trypanosomiasis Research Organization, in addition to the more familiar railways, harbours, telecommunications, veterinary, medical, agricultural, meteorological and other services, reminds one of some of the specific challenges of the whole zone. Only discussions in their laboratories, or encounters in remote places with officers of the Desert Locust or other departments, bring home the full meaning of the nature and importance of their work. It would be tragic if national politics were to bring any disruption to such fundamental services.

The extent of the social and economic needs of Eastern Africa need not be laboured. They were documented in detail in the report of the *East Africa Royal Commission 1953–55*, which included, in a chapter entitled "The Basic Poverty of East Africa", facts such as a comparison of the net cash product per head in selected African countries. From about £100 per head in South Africa the figure ranged to £47 in the Rhodesias, £34 in Ghana, about £16 in Uganda and £14 in Kenya. The economists on the Commission were realistic in their appraisal but they were in no sense pessimistic. To them the overall East African economy resembled that of South Africa some forty years previously, that is before the inter-war advance in manufacturing industry in the Union. Whether the total resources of the zone would permit a comparable rate of industrial and agricultural development could not be forecast with any accuracy, but the commissioners in their survey pin-pointed the major initial obstacles to be overcome and made many valuable recommendations as to how this conquest might be accomplished.

The implications of some of the recommendations of the Commission were far-reaching. Their advocacy of inter-territorial economic and administrative involvement in large-scale projects such as that of a Lake Victoria Basin Development Authority inevitably aroused suggestions of closer political union between Uganda, Kenya and Tanganyika. We have referred already to the emphatic resistance of the Africans of East Africa to any initiative towards federation on the part of the United Kingdom Government which had brought about the recent Central African Federation. Even a hint in this direction from a visiting Secretary of State in Nairobi provoked an explosive reaction. But, whether or not the present Common Services Organization will in the future evolve into an African-sponsored federation, the Royal Commission was right to emphasize the advantages of the closest inter-territorial co-operation in tackling some of the more fundamental economic and social obstacles which are to be found in each country.

The lack of trained manpower and the urgent need for education is made very plain in the report. Only one chapter could be devoted primarily to the subject, and the technicalities of providing universities and advanced colleges were left to the Inter-University Council for Higher Education Overseas. But even the barest figures of the primary, secondary and technical schools led the commissioners to speak strongly on the inadequacy of facilities and the high rates of wastage. One comparison shows that whereas in England and Wales in 1953 some 550,000 children had continued to the fourth class of primary education from an original entry of 584,000, only 104,000 children in East Africa were still at primary school four years after 1949, when 255,000 of them had entered. The Lidbury Commission on the Civil Services of the East African Territories and the East Africa High Commission in 1953–4, which conducted its inquiries at the same time as the Royal Commission, were concerned to discover the likelihood of increased local recruitment. It is not surprising from the figures which follow that they were forced to conclude that "the East African territories are not yet in sight of being able to staff their public services entirely from their own resources". School Certificate passes in the four countries of East Africa in 1953 together amounted to a total of 1,219; the number of Higher School Certificates which were gained was 53. Of the 420 African boys who gained the School Certificate, 186 did so in Uganda, 139 in Kenya, 94 in Tanganyika and 1 in Zanzibar. Only 14 African girls—all from the three mainland territories—received the School Certificate. No Africans appear to have passed the Higher School Certificate in 1953: the list shows only 23 European girls, 21 European boys and 9 Asian boys.

The last ten years have witnessed determined efforts by Mr. Tom Mboya, President Nyerere and other African leaders to accelerate the education and training of their people. The United Kingdom has co-operated, and each year has seen significant advances. In addition to the more usual courses of study Africans from East Africa have entered Sandhurst and other military, and police, colleges. The Africanization of the commissioned ranks of the armed forces and the police only began very belatedly, as was made clear during the recent mutinies, but the urgent need of trained officers is now generally acknowledged by Britain, the United States and the Commonwealth countries of West Africa in a position to offer some help.

The "investment in education" philosophy which inspired the Ashby Commission in its approach to Nigeria's economic and social needs has extended also to Eastern Africa. New schools, teacher-training and technical colleges have been built and new universities established. Makerere, the pioneer university college in Uganda, was followed by the transformation into a university college of the Royal College in Nairobi, and Dar-es-Salaam has now its own promising university college. These three university colleges were incorporated recently as constituent colleges of the University of East Africa. The Kivukoni Adult Education College near Dar-es-Salaam deserves mention as a special venture which seeks in its own way to meet certain of the trained manpower needs of an independent state by preparing trade unionists and community workers for more informed leadership.

There is little to be gained from listing too many figures, significant though each might be and vitally so to each of the countries concerned. It may be of interest, however, to indicate something of the position in regard to higher education. There were, in 1960, 399 students from Kenya studying at Makerere in Uganda, 201 at the Royal College in Nairobi and 1,158 Kenya students taking courses of higher education in the United Kingdom. The majority of the latter were Asian and European, only 126 being African. Uganda supplied 279, mostly African men and women, of Makerere's 912 students, and there were 509 Uganda students overseas, of whom 334 were African. The United Kingdom received the majority of the overseas students from Kenya and Uganda, though India and the United States also took significant numbers. Tanganyika's position has been somewhat behind Kenya and Uganda in respect of higher education, but determined efforts are being made to increase the few hundreds who have been able each year to make use of the facilities at Makerere and Nairobi and those available overseas in the United Kingdom, the United States and India.

In Central Africa the educational need of Africans is also most urgent. Singularly few Africans have had the opportunity of secondary education and very few have been able to qualify for university entrance. There was in both Northern Rhodesia and Nyasaland a substantial increase in secondary enrolments during the 1950's, but in 1958 there were still only 1,890 secondary pupils in the former and 1,189 in the latter territory as compared with Southern Rhodesia, where the number of Africans in secondary schools was about equal to that of both northern territories together. The sixth-form position has been much the same. The Munali School, near Lusaka, is a remarkably good school, but it has had for too long to try alone to meet the whole of the advanced secondary education requirements of Africans in Northern Rhodesia. Dedza, in Nyasaland, developed its sixth-form work very much later. Against this background it is not surprising to discover that up to June 1959 a total of 35 Northern Rhodesia Africans, 34 men and one woman, had completed courses of higher education. Twenty had secured degrees in arts, eleven in science, and one had graduated in each of engineering, fine art, domestic science and law. At that time a further 26 were reading for degrees. Nyasaland statistics reveal, at June 1959, a total of 28 who had graduated from universities or comparable institutions since 1891, with 14 enrolled as undergraduates in 1959.

The South African schools, colleges and universities which have traditionally played an important part in providing education for Africans from Nyasaland and Northern Rhodesia continue, or continued until very recently, to draw their quotas from the two northern territories. Fort Hare, the Durban Medical School and other centres still receive students from north of the Zambesi. But with the establishment of the University College of Rhodesia and Nyasaland in Salisbury, Southern Rhodesia, men and women from the north turned more to the nearer university, though some were obliged to go to Makerere in order to pursue particular studies not available in Salisbury. Bristol University and other British universities have in recent years taken more Northern Rhodesian and Nyasaland Africans but the number is still desperately low. Every possible university place must be seized, and it is for this reason that the politics which have recently affected the Salisbury University College are to be regretted. Salisbury must continue to serve its neighbours even though new universities are being established in Malawi and Zambia (where the copper-mining companies are not only giving generous support to the university project but are also engaged in supplying new higher technical education facilities for the Africans of Zambia).

Although astringent when viewed from the standpoint of the needs of an independent modern state, the educational and economic facts and figures given above are not meant to support an indictment of neglect against the former British colonial administration or to imply the superiority of a cash over a subsistence economy, or of Western education over traditional ideas and methods of instruction. But because more modern economic and educational institutions aid the efficiency of larger-scale organization, and are at the same time actively sought by the leaders of independent Africa, such indices of preparedness for full self-government do possess a certain importance. The Makerere Medical School has made substantial contributions but there is a serious shortage of medical practitioners throughout Eastern Africa and a critical situation would arise if there were to be a precipitate withdrawal of British and other "expatriate" doctors. An even graver crisis could occur in the administration of justice, as the recent report of Lord Justice Denning on legal education in East Africa made clear. Lord Kilmuir established important personal links with courts in East Africa during his tenure of the Lord Chancellorship, but for long-term value such liaison requires to be underpinned by a strong body of African barristers and solicitors. The new law school at Dar-es-Salaam will in course of time do much to supply this deficiency, but time and energetic effort are required.

The problems of rapid and harmonious modernization which are common to all the territories of Eastern Africa extend also to Ethiopia. The cultural riches of this ancient kingdom and empire— the stele at Axum, the rock-hewn churches of Lalibela, and the illuminated Amharic manuscripts—are an important heritage of the whole eastern side of the continent, fully equal to the Benin bronzes and artefacts of West Africa; but Ethiopia's present intensive development must be continued apace if she is to serve as a headquarters worthy both of a large zone and of independent Africa as a whole. The adoption of English as an official language and the strengthening of relations with the United States of America as well as Britain have placed Ethiopia in a good position to work closely with her neighbours on matters of more local concern, in addition to the links which emerge from her general role as the base of United Nations' Economic Commission for Africa and other specialized international agencies.

But whether or not they are linked with Ethiopia or are included with other East African territories which have been mooted for possible inclusion in a wider confederation, those countries upon which we have been concentrating in this chapter have had thrust upon them already some challenging responsibilities, which both threaten them and hold the promise of developing their individual and collective maturity.

Somali irredentism is an issue which affects the whole of North-Eastern Africa as well as the new state of Kenya. It is an issue which must continue to arouse special distress in the United Kingdom, in view of its historical friendship with Ethiopia, Somalia, and Kenya, until some workable solution is agreed by them. All parties are resolutely uncompromising at present and each enlists aid in the dispute from outside the continent. The best opportunity for a more rational adjustment of frontiers which could have gone far to satisfy the deep-felt desire for "Greater Somalia" occurred during the early years of the British military administration, after Mussolini's fascists had been cleared from the whole of North-East Africa in 1941. It is understandable that war-time preoccupations distracted Cabinet attention, but it is regrettable that determined action was not taken subsequently to draw the parties into realistic dialogue and decision before the transfer of power was imminent and before considerations of prestige became paramount. Britain's cession of Jubaland to Somalia after the 1914–18 war was a notable contribution to the economy of a country poorly endowed with natural resources and Britain's ready support for the recent fusion of the Somaliland Protectorate into Somalia is also to be commended. But the last-minute attention given to the Somali question in the Northern Frontier Province of Kenya could accomplish little and two ill-prepared countries have inherited a serious threat to their peace and security.

Apart from the Somali question there has been constant challenge to supply shelter and aid to the thousands of refugees who have fled from the Sudan and Rwanda into Uganda and Tanganyika. Sophisticated political refugees have escaped from South Africa to Tanganyika and recently Northern Rhodesia (Zambia) has been called upon to accommodate less educated men and women fleeing northwards from *apartheid*. The prolonged tragedy of the Congo has confronted each African leader of Eastern Africa with a major threat as well as an example of the supreme value of law and order within a united country. The Zanzibar *coup d'état* and the attempts from within as well as from outside East Africa to exploit the revolutionary situation have also supplied severe tests to the five principal African leaders and their ministerial colleagues.

It is greatly to the credit of the Commonwealth countries of Eastern Africa that they have responded so ably to the threatening situations which have arisen. Their balance and their determination not to lapse into arbitrary counter-action promise to confound the predictions of those who have forecast at best a century and a half of Latin American revolution and counter-revolution, at worst chaos and barbarism. The police of the territories have displayed a particularly valuable discipline and poise which reflect credit on themselves and their tutors. The soldiers, too, have remained loyal and disciplined despite the appalling example of the Congo and the disaffection of some of their comrades in each territory who not only saw, but for a time successfully exploited, the naked power which weapons, equipment and organization can confer on lawless military men.

It would be wrong to give undue emphasis to one state when all are important, and wrong to single out one political leader, when co-operation between all on a basis of frank equality in council is essential. But for the reasons emphasized in the early part of this chapter Tanganyika does occupy a central and key position. Her political stability and effective leadership is therefore of supreme importance if there is to be hope of wider regional unity and a constructive example for the Congolese Republic and other African neighbours. Fortunately these two necessities have obtained since Tanganyika became independent in December 1961, even though both have been either threatened or questioned. Recurrent doubts about the political stability of the country have arisen from reports of serious division within the cabinet. Dissension soon after independence was attributed to trade union endeavours to wield directly the power of the workers. There were rumours of differences in the executive and party at the time of the Moshi conference when international communism was represented in strength. More recently, the military mutiny which followed the dispatch of Tanganyika policemen to Zanzibar aroused rumours of disloyalty at the highest level and of the planned overthrow of President Nyerere, as he had come to be styled when Tanganyika's republican constitution was introduced in December 1962.

The conjectures and assertions of political commentators are often well founded, and it would be wrong as well as possibly misleading to dismiss out of hand all reports to the effect that President

Nyerere is not secure in office. Yet there may well be danger that those who refer to such insecurity, and those who couple with it allegations of personal weakness on the part of the President, are failing to perceive undemonstrative strength because of their expectations of flamboyant display. President Nyerere possesses the capacity for firm decision as well as the gift of quiet determination, and he has the inner confidence of a man of genuine modesty who is convinced of the rightness of his cause. He has distinguished qualities of intellect as well as character. He was impressive, not weak, when within two months of independence he handed over the premiership to a colleague for a year while he set about improving the organization of his party, the Tanganyika Africa National Union, T.A.N.U. His capacity for judging the time for withdrawal appears to be as successful in terms of avoiding civil strife as is his flair for recognizing swift action. The dispatch of a well-trained police contingent to Zanzibar and the rapid negotiation of the Tanganyika–Zanzibar Union were highly responsible actions. Whether these actions can withstand the threat of serious Communist penetration remains to be seen.*

We could multiply the instances of personal leadership on the part of Tanganyika's President, not least in preserving the whole structure of the East African inter-territorial services which Britain had built up since the 1920's, but he would himself insist that leadership within his partner-nations is in every way as essential as it is within his own Tanganyika. He has also emphasized repeatedly the importance of a close continuing partnership in development between the relatively ill-prepared countries of Eastern Africa and Britain and other nations in a position to help. Certain of the social and economic needs of Eastern Africa have been indicated, and we must in the next chapter consider some of the more general aspects of the hasty transfer of power and its consequences. But no matter how formidable the needs and problems of Eastern Africa, the zone is presently blessed with many leaders and followers who value co-operation with Britain and the West, and many young people who welcome the opportunities afforded by membership of the Commonwealth as well as the United Nations. If there is appropriate response from Britain the assumptions and hopes of those who looked to Eastern Africa to show that the "dual mandate" could be made an enduring reality can be fulfilled.

* See *Postscript*.

7

BRITAIN AND INDEPENDENT AFRICA: PARTNERSHIP—THE UNCOMPLETED TASK

THE rightness of representative self-government, the central principle of British colonial policy since Lord Durham reported on the affairs of British North America in 1839, has made itself apparent on every one of the many occasions in recent years that a newly independent African state has taken its place on the world stage. John Stuart Mill, a few years before the passing of the British North America Act of 1867, which launched the federal Dominion of Canada into full statehood, wrote that "there is no difficulty in showing that the ideally best form of government is that in which the sovereignty, or supreme controlling power, in the last resort is vested in the entire aggregate of the community."* The attitude towards independent Africa of Britons who share his view on the "ideally best polity"—and they are the large majority—must therefore be one of sympathetic welcome and congratulation.

Yet when we recall that the great liberal philosopher was also a realist, who insisted that representative self-government required suitable circumstances to make it "practicable and eligible", it is appropriate to suggest that not only is each of the independent states of Africa today facing a challenge of internal democracy but that, viewed against the perspective of centuries, the continent as a whole has seldom been more vulnerable.

Africa's selfhood was imperilled during the generations of the slave-trade, when her peoples were plundered by Europe, Arabia and South Asia. More recently, materialism and other alien philosophies have eroded wide areas of African traditional morality. The damage inflicted by outside influences has to some degree been mitigated by those who bore to Africa and shared with Africans the values and ethical practices which lie at the core of their civilizations: Christian, Islamic, Hindu or Judaic. Their gifts of science and technology also have contributed substantially towards restoring a balance between loss and gain.

So far as Western civilization is concerned, the supremacy of the

* *Representative Government* (1861), Chapter 3.

West during the past five centuries has led to the establishment of bases and bridgeheads in each of the separate lands of Africa. Everywhere there is to be found architecture, artefacts, languages and institutions of European origin. Despite urgent desires to "Africanize" the continent, elements of European culture remain prominent, sometimes starkly so, at this peak moment of the Western imperial recession. Independent Africa has not incorporated, nor is she yet wholly in a condition to incorporate, all such elements effectively into her own Africo–European syntheses. New nations must be united, new states strengthened, the arts and sciences of large-scale modern government, and of economic and social development, must be mastered. Until this is done and all the latent resources of Africa are fully mobilized a vacuum of power will exist, a vacuum tempting to giant nations confident in their ideology and with vast reserves of manpower on which to draw.

The challenge of choice to Britain and the West concerning Africa can be posed in alarmist terms. The past half-century has seen many references to the "Yellow Peril", to "Asian hordes", the threats of Communism, whether Leninist, Trotskyist, Stalinist, or the rival communisms of contemporary Russia and China. The inappropriate use of such terms by politicians in Africa and by colonial administrators has aroused scepticism as to the reality of the danger of communist subversion or the penetration into Africa of new imperialisms. With a recent, often painful, memory of the abuse of political terms many leaders of the newly independent states have understandably clutched at "non-alignment" as the only satisfactory working first principle for the conduct of foreign affairs. They ask for patience from the Western rulers who have transferred power to them and from the non-colonial powers of Europe and North America while they take time to assess the intentions of the non-Western nations from whom a long era of colonialism has kept them separate.

Yet Africa's leaders already have certain facts of which to take stock, not least the tremendous problems of population pressure facing Eastern régimes. The unused potential of Africa, agricultural and industrial, has impressed many high-level Asian observers, who have referred in the frankest terms to the greater beneficial use which Asian cultivators and workers would make of the available lands and materials. Where Africa's relatively poor agriculture has thus far had little appeal to the better-circumstanced European and North American producer, it has been viewed with different

eyes from the hard-pressed East. The mineral resources which have
had greater appeal to the West might also be more attractive to
Eastern countries, and likewise the general manufacturing potential
of Africa. Certainly several Asian visitors to Africa have expressed
a wholly unsentimental impatience with what they regard as an
African want of industry and thrift, and they have made plain their
view that Asians would make more efficient use of the resources.
Such visitors from the East, like many from the West, have seldom
grasped the reality of an African philosophy which includes contentment with a modest livelihood. Increasingly Africans have been
urged to adopt a more militant, materialist ideology. "African
socialism" may succeed in harmonizing African traditional thought
with modern demands, but the concept is still in process of refine-
ment and is meanwhile in competition with Communist ideology.

At the moment of Africa's vulnerability, Great Britain, the pre-
eminent imperial power in Africa during the past two centuries,
has stood uncertain. Though the several countries of ex-British
colonial Africa supply the most extensive, and some of the most
strategically exploitable, areas for rivals and enemies of the West,
Britain has felt unable to act constructively save in association with
allies who can share the cost and burden of fulfilling the objective
of bringing each former African ward, together with the rest of
independent Africa, to a more "viable" or confident self-government.

It is important to consider why Britain left uncompleted so many
of the tasks of trusteeship which she had undertaken before 1945,
and which she redefined and amplified during and after the war.
The Colonial Development and Welfare Acts give clearest expression to the spirit and intentions of the period. In Chapter 6 on
Eastern Africa a special significance was attached to Mau Mau as
leading to a wide-ranging reassessment of Britain's position. Certainly Mau Mau serves well to direct attention to Britain's crisis of
resources in Africa and the wider world.

Open party political controversy over Mau Mau in Britain turned
chiefly on issues such as the large number of convicted terrorists
who were executed, the high proportion of Mau Mau killed to
wounded among battle casualties, the treatment of "hard core"
prisoners at Hola and other camps, and the harsh behaviour of
individual military officers. Such detailed concern on the part of
public representatives and the attendant full publicity were the
normal concomitants of overseas engagements in which the United

Kingdom was directly involved. But at a deeper level there was an assessment of the meaning of Mau Mau in terms of the future government of Kenya, and of the wider colonial empire in Africa. There were those who argued that the Kikuyu were a special case and the members of Mau Mau only a small proportion who should not be allowed to determine the fate of a whole embryo nation, or of British Africa, by causing a premature abandonment of the colonial mission, even though several who expressed this view conceded that Mau Mau cohesion and strength had proved greater between 1952 and 1958 than they would have predicted.

Those responsible for Britain's policy in Kenya and Africa were obliged to take account of a world context and of many besides the purely military or strategic matters, not least the economic and social implications of colonial responsibility in a new age of universal welfare and development. Campaigns in Korea and Malaya had stretched the military resources of Britain who, since 1945, had been burdened with inescapable defence commitments in Western Europe on a scale which she had not known before. And scarcely was Mau Mau contained in Kenya when the Suez campaign revealed the difficulties for a national army which was integrated into a Western alliance completing a large-scale independent operation without the full backing of its partners.

As to the new "revolution of rising expectations" in Africa requiring accelerated economic and social development, Britain had been obliged recently to consider the skilfully presented demands of Malta for full integration into the social security system of the United Kingdom and comparable claims for assistance from the British West Indies. Although each was presented as a special case there were more general implications which could not be ignored by a metropolitan government responsible, and responsive, to an internal electorate. Mau Mau served to reveal the vast extent of the educational, health and other investment required to achieve the desired constructive rehabilitation of Kenya and the advancement of East Africa as a whole. The resources required for this task were plainly beyond the capacity of Britain alone to supply and each of the wealthier members of the Western alliance, notably the United States and West Germany, had to be looked to for a substantial sharing of the burden.

Given the continuance of United States policy whereby, in the "containment of communism" strategy, European colonial rule was accepted as the best means of ensuring stability in Africa, United

Kingdom administration might well have been supported as the best agency for achieving the accelerated development required to prepare the British African territories adequately for effective self-government or independence. Surveys conducted even so late as 1958 revealed the poor state of preparation, especially in terms of trained manpower, of each of the non-self-governing territories of Africa, none being less ready than the lands of Eastern Africa. Given the handful of qualified African administrators, lawyers, doctors and other professional men in these territories in 1958 and the very few African pupils completing even secondary education, senior British administrators and educationists estimated that a minimum period of from ten to fifteen years was required for training and experience in office, if there was to be any confident expectation of future stability.

Despite the readiness of certain Governors and their senior officers to state in private, if pressed a minimum period for intensive preparation for self-government, and an optimum period also—though this was less relevant to the immediate political climate—there was a general British unwillingness to accept any suggested time-table. This was true of Tanganyika, a British Trust Territory under the United Nations, no less than of the colonies or protectorates of East and Central Africa. The stubborn official British refusal to discuss a time-table is the more strange since a ten-year limit was placed on the Italian resumption of trusteeship for Somalia in 1950. Though the Italians behaved in the first years as if they believed that the period would be extended indefinitely, it was subsequently made clear that the United Nations would insist on adherence to 1960 as the date of independence, a development which led the Italian administration to anticipate the final date and advance the day of independence, in an understandable endeavour to transfer power with the maximum of goodwill. The value of the set span of years in the case of Somalia was that it led to the intelligent mobilization of all conceivable international as well as Italian aid and the training of key police, army, administrative and social welfare officers for the responsibilities which would inevitably be theirs after a defined period.

The Somalia time-table did, in the event, and as was predicted, influence the British Government to accelerate beyond reason the advance of the Somaliland Protectorate to full independence so that the British territory might merge with its ex-Italian neighbour to form a greater Somalia. In terms of even rudimentary preparation the "Somalization" of key posts proceeded at a ridiculously rapid pace, involving overnight promotions of men with little or no serious training for senior legislative, administrative and judicial work. Only the ethnic homogeneity of the population, the presence of a few well-trained practical leaders who had proved good pupils of the British Military Administration, and the self-confident "flair" of the Somalis—with the devoted help of Somaliphil Britons—averted disaster.

In the case of the larger and more heterogeneous territories under British administration, it was estimated in 1958 that an optimum period of from 25 to 30 years' intensive training would prepare them for reasonably efficient and stable modern administration, an estimate in broad correspondence with that made in 1956 for the Belgian Congo by Professor van Bilsen. Although van Bilsen was subsequently criticized by Belgian authority for opposing the precipitate transfer of complete power to an ill-prepared Congo in 1960, he was in 1956 attacked by senior Belgians for allowing only thirty years for the process of preparation. Analysed purely in terms of the length of school and university education, professional training and experience required for a sufficient body of men from whom, for example, judges to compare with their fellows in Europe might be selected, thirty years was by no means excessive, given the fact that scarcely a handful of Africans from East Africa were receiving legal education in 1958. On grounds of practical international politics the period before independence had to be much shorter, but whether it need ever have been the totally inadequate one or two years which eventuated is open to doubt.

After 1956, however, the United States in particular of the Western Allies became increasingly impatient, and eminent American spokesmen, both official and unofficial, urged Britain and the other European colonial powers to hasten the advance of Africa to independence. The motives for the change in United States' outlook were varied. The traditional sense of domestic anti-colonialism was always in the background, a compound of the recollections of the War of Independence and the Monroe Doctrine influencing in a real if generalized manner even sophisticated diplomats of the United States Foreign Service. There was also a frank feeling that continued imperial rule by European nations was out of place in the new world of United States supremacy, and that African recognition of America's topmost position was affected by the continuance of European administration. Cold War strategy added its effect : it was believed that goodwill towards the West on the part of African leaders, all aspiring to full self-government after Ghana's rapid constitutional advances, could best be gained by early concession of independence rather than resistant tardiness. It was pointed out to American analysts that India's maturity in government owed much to the patient determination which had been forced on the Congress, but arguments based on the importance of organization, administration and trained manpower were subordinated to those of political psychology. Argument held that such preparation and training must follow, not precede, independence.

African leaders in the British territories were for their part never so naïve as to press blindly for immediate independence. Though they could not make public pronouncements suggesting to their followers any readiness to mark time, and though they were not prepared to accept anything like so long a delay as Indian leaders had done, they indicated plainly in private that they were ready to postpone independence for some years at least, provided that they received assurance that money, materials and personnel would be forthcoming in more generous quantities from the metropolitan power to assist in the tasks of preparation. Even the radical and emotional Patrice Lumumba made plain his readiness to accept a delay of up to five years. All save Sekou Touré in France's *Afrique noire* demonstrated openly the same awareness of a need for a continuing partnership with the metropole. Though material considerations might have been uppermost other elements are associated always with the material. African leaders in Britain's territories were educated and Western-oriented men fully alive to the educational and economic needs of their countries. Certainly they could not reject offers of early independence when their public demands were accepted publicly at face value, any more than, say, Natal's leaders had been able to do in 1893 when self-government was thrust upon them. It must always be regretted that definite time-tables backed by financial and other commitments were not openly assessed before the frank inspection of the world. When accepted by responsible African leaders and agreed by the United States and the "non-colonial" powers of the Western world, such time-tables could have achieved much and could have withstood the strongest criticisms of politically hostile and self-interested powers.

As it happened vast areas of vagueness were left in the negotiations preceding independence and there was minimal understanding and co-operation between the Western nations most directly concerned—Belgium, France, the United States and Britain. Although every whit as concerned as the others, Portugal must be excluded if only because her ancient mystique of a closed *imperium* rendered dialogue difficult. It would, however, be harsh and inaccurate to say of British territories in Africa that, acquired absent-mindedly, they were allowed absent-mindedly to drift into a world where unsentimental and calculating forces of new and powerful imperialisms competed for their material and ideological domination.

In the rapidly changing circumstances of the world there were no clear-cut courses to be pursued by a nation with wide-ranging international commitments and responsibilities. For an empirically minded people whose homeland is dependent on world trade there were few practical guarantees, or examples based on sufficient evidence, to warrant absolute decisions. Clearly the fulfilment of the uncompleted tasks of the trusteeship era necessitated reliable partners among the well-endowed and reasonably well-developed nations. Britain was required to take stock of her several international associations. Each of these principal associations must be examined in turn with special reference to the British–African relationship.

Pride of place must be given to Britain, Europe and Africa because the United Kingdom's most emphatic recent decision in foreign policy, and one undertaken with the strongest backing of the United States of America, was her application to be permitted to unite, under the Treaty of Rome, with France, West Germany, Italy, Belgium, the Netherlands and Luxembourg. Pan-Europeanism, like Pan-Africanism, has a specially powerful appeal to United States citizens, nurtured in a tradition of Pan-Americanism, and the Anglo–American relationship would have suffered had Britain not made a determined effort to enter the European union.

Although a first emphasis was placed on the economic arguments, brilliantly marshalled by Mr. Heath, it was acknowledged that the political significance of Britain's entry into the European Common Market would be at least as great as the economic. The Treaty of Rome provided for a wide range of political developments of fundamental importance, not least the immediate concession of freedom of movement within the union for all citizens and workers of the contracting countries. While Britain's membership of the European Free Trade Area of the seven represented no more than participation in a local regional association, to be seen on a par with several similar commercial arrangements, the European Economic Union required much more binding commitments involving in a deeper way questions of sovereignty, nationality and citizenship.

There was division of opinion in Britain over the proposed entry into the European Common Market, but what was perhaps of greatest import was the undoubted readiness of a majority of Britons, of all political parties, to take a decisive step in a direction opposite to that of British overseas policy throughout the long period of Western imperialism. Singularly few took seriously the arguments of the liberal-imperialist school who saw in the end of empire the logical and hopeful commencement of a new era of Commonwealth. Many more were disenchanted by the manner in which colonialism was seen to be drawing to a close; they were affected not least by the strident hostility towards the colonial powers of certain nationalist leaders. Surrounded by European neighbours who were experiencing similar reactions, it is not surprising that a pervading sense of a need to assert metropolitan independence was accompanied in Britain by a readiness to associate with others who had had similar experiences of decolonization.

The common subjection of European nations to a heavy volume and wide variety of criticism, including criticism from the United States of America, for five centuries of colonialism supplied a political bond of real importance to representatives of European countries meeting in conference or informally. Together, many of them believed, a united Europe could hold her own against the world, including the United States, the Soviet Union and China. For those conscious of a responsibility to the wider world it seemed that the combined economic and other resources of Europe would permit greater contributions to overseas aid.

It is impossible to say whether a union contracted within such a climate of ideas would have prospered after Britain's accession. The veto of President de Gaulle was not only decisive in preventing Britain's admission but served also to remind Britons of the continuing potency of the idea of nation on the European mainland. De Gaulle might be widely assailed as wholly unrepresentative of the new spirit of Europe, but his rejection of Britain not only succeeded in rebuffing an actively sought-for alliance but compelled recollection of a wealth of similar acts by different national leaders of Europe during the twentieth century, not to mention comparable incidents, conflicts and wars during earlier generations.

It is perhaps worth observing that France's rejection, through

Charles de Gaulle, of a Britain which had been morally unassailable at the time of France's deepest humiliation brought some solace to wounded French pride. It also helped other members of what has been called Europe's "league of the defeated"—though many senior Germans, Dutchmen and other "Europeans" were undeniably grieved by the exclusion of Britain. This psychological levelling of Britain in the eyes of mainlanders may well prove of long-term value in helping Britain's eventual acceptance into closer European association.

Stillborn, nevertheless, were the hopes of those in Britain who had looked to the European Economic Union as an immediate instrument for increasing economic aid to Africa. How strong was this group it is impossible to say, for many who were given to throwing in a reference to overseas aid as an extra argument were plainly obsessed by the vision of an economically powerful Europe which would be largely self-sufficient *vis-à-vis* other continents and inter-continental groupings. Also on the negative side were those in France who, while they wished to continue generous aid to the French-speaking territories in Africa and Madagascar, were reluctant to add a large number of needy ex-British African countries to the dependencies for whom the six Common Market countries had together been persuaded by France to accept a collective obligation. It would be unjust nevertheless to overlook the sincerity of the European unionists in Britain who believed that the closer economic and political integration of Western Europe would result in substantially greater surpluses for direct overseas grants and larger, more efficient factories and markets to stimulate international trade, notably trade with the economically underdeveloped lands of Africa, Asia and Latin America. Men of this outlook have given substantial support to the Organization for European Economic Co-operation and to its successor, now strengthened by American and Canadian accession to membership, the Organization for Economic Co-operation and Development (O.E.C.D.).

The Organization for Economic Co-operation and Development perhaps provides the best transition to consideration of Britain's second area of major international alliance, that of the North Atlantic Community. Although O.E.C.D. thus far has given priority to economically underdeveloped countries in Europe, notably Greece and Turkey, for whose benefit special consortia have been established, the Organization has a lively awareness of underdeveloped countries lying farther afield. Substantial work has been done on the co-ordination of overseas aid by officers of the O.E.C.D. working under the direction of a Scandinavian secretary-general. De Gaulle might deny to Britain membership of a narrower union in which France had a decisive voice but he could not exclude her from older European associations. Still less could he reduce Britain's active participation in that trans-Atlantic co-operation which, from the beginning of Marshall aid, has been responsible for Europe's post-war recovery.

Although Britain will continue always to accept her close bonds with Europe it must be acknowledged that to many in the United Kingdom, as to many also in Eire, the concept of trans-Atlantic alliance, as embodied for example in the North Atlantic Treaty Organization, has more powerful appeal than any purely European political and economic association. Voluntary societies such as the Atlantic Treaty Association and the English-Speaking Union work actively on behalf of the Atlantic idea and seek to extend activities far beyond those of defence.

The appeal to Britons of adding North America to any European alliance has many obvious reasons. The English language, spoken by fifty million in the British Isles, receives more than a fourfold increment when the United States and Canada are added. The whole web of Anglo-Saxon political and legal institutions and traditions is likewise strengthened. Most significant, perhaps, given the experience of two world wars, is the fact that the most powerful arsenal of democracy is incorporated into an Americo–European entity by means of North Atlantic treaties.

Beyond the Atlantic the American alliance is also welcomed. Although many in Britain were offended by the exclusion of Britain from the Anzus (Australia, New Zealand and United States) pact, there is widespread readiness to admit that the conception of Atlantic community must be extended to embrace Australia and New Zealand. Some spokesmen for this extension have emphasized the desirability of such wider union on frankly racial grounds, being advocates for the protection of "white interests"; but the majority have canvassed support primarily in terms of the need to strengthen Western cultural achievement, notably democracy and the rule of law. The Pacific outposts of the West have a vital role to play in demonstrating the work of democratic institutions and values and in serving as centres of education and other aid.

The common use of the English language has provided an in-centive for "Anglo-Saxon" co-operation, notably Anglo-American, in Africa, in much the same manner as French has acted as a argument for the various advocates of specifically Franco–African or Latin–African associations. Despite the endeavours of organizations such as C.C.T.A. (Commission for Technical Co-operation in Africa South of the Sahara), the language barrier between the French- and English-speaking areas of Africa continues to remain high. Estimates of the numbers of English- and French-speakers on the continent vary greatly, but the principal fact to be noticed is the division which exists between the many millions who use one or other of the European languages as a lingua franca, or "vehicular language", for the communication of ideas of modern science, technology, art and commerce.

Faced with the desperate urgency of Africa's need for technical aid from outside, it seems inevitable that the greatest volume of assistance and co-operation between African and Western countries will flow within established language channels. Bilingualism in French and English is very desirable, especially at higher levels and in frontier situations. Current endeavours to expand the mastery of both languages must be supported. But Africans who already have had to become bilingual by adding a European language to their own traditional tongue can be helped most rapidly and effectively through the European language in their possession. This can of course be seen also in cases where Italian, Portuguese, Dutch, Spanish or German has been learned by Africans, but English and French affect by far the greatest numbers. The influence of language is made obvious by the co-operation between French-speaking scholars and students in Africa, France, Belgium and the French-medium universities of Canada. It is also reflected through the long-established links which exist between French Catholic and French Protestant missionary societies and African churches, schools and hospitals.

A fact which must be emphasized, disturbing though it is to France and to admirers of the French language, is the growing preference for English in Africa. Within the foreseeable future every possible French school and college and other centre will be required to work at fullest capacity to assist in meeting Africa's educational needs. France, officially, is already alert and active and determined to maintain the widest usage of the French language. But circumstances of the modern world, notably the division between political East and West, which emphasizes the importance of the Russian and Chinese languages and the desirability of learning one or other of them, has led to English acquiring pre-eminence as the language medium of the West.

Had the United States chosen to be multi-lingual and not to have adopted English as the sole official tongue of the Union the position could well have been otherwise. But the presence of 200 million English-speakers, in addition to America's vast material resources, has been decisive in tilting the balance towards English in Africa. Ethiopia, despite close historical and economic ties with France, has in recent years substituted English for French, as the European language of the empire, Amharic remaining the other official medium. This notable accession to English, and the continued use of English in Liberia, has greatly reinforced its position in a continent where generations of British administration and English-medium education have given the language extensive expression, albeit sometimes in forms not immediately recognizable to Western users.

The flow of American Peace Corps and Crossroads volunteers to independent Africa in numbers greatly exceeding those from similar organizations in the United Kingdom highlights in one form the contemporary importance of the Anglo-American alliance. Such co-operation at youthful, junior levels serves to crown the economic, political, military, educational and medical activities in which both the United States and Britain have engaged and combined for several generations. Early in the nineteenth century American missionary, educational, health and welfare centres were already strongly established in British colonies alongside commercial and industrial concerns. It is essential that such Anglo–American co-operation in Africa should continue and expand as rapidly as possible side by side with the fullest preservation of British and European co-operation in the continent. One must question, in this context, the views of certain global strategists who would assign a more substantial role to the United States in independent Africa in exchange for an increased British priority in Latin America, so that "neo-colonial" misgivings in both continents might the better be mitigated. Such superficial expedients produce little or no profit, save perhaps in the shortest term for commercial companies and the like. Both Britain and the United States have deep roots in Africa and Latin America, and all constructive associations of the past and present require to be nourished and extended, not terminated or abandoned in the pursuit of doubtful ephemeral advantage.

Increasing co-operation, either British–European or Anglo–American, in respect of Africa should not be allowed to minimize or damage either the Commonwealth of Nations or the United Nations. These associations comprise the remaining two major alliances of which Britain is a member. The dichotomy in British attitudes towards the United Kingdom's "colonies of settlement", or "Dominions", on the one hand, and her "colonies of administration", or "exploitation", on the other has had an unfortunate effect on the whole approach to both the new "multi-racial" Commonwealth of Nations and the multi-racial United Nations. There has been an unmistakable tendency within both organizations for "ethnic associates" to side defensively with one another rather than to display greater trust in people of different racial and cultural origin. Africans, Arabs, Asians and Latin Americans have demonstrated this characteristic and it has accentuated an entrenched reaction among North Atlantic nationalities. We have made evident already why this tendency is not difficult to understand, given the weight of "social-Darwinist" history among the latter and the volume of criticism of the "imperial West" among the former, but it is none the less unfortunate.

The Commonwealth must be taken first of the "multi-racial" associations. Great Britain is the founder and the principal member, and it is difficult, though perhaps not impossible, to conceive the association continuing without Great Britain's membership. In respect of Africa, Britain has perhaps revealed most clearly her indecision as to the future of the multi-racial Commonwealth. This indecision springs primarily from a dualism in past African policy which has never been faced with sufficient frankness. Until the eleventh hour of empire the association once known as "Great Britain and the Dominions", or "The Anglo-Saxon Commonwealth", continued to enjoy a special relationship and most intercourse of a consciously Commonwealth kind took place within it.

It must be repeated that, given the circumstances of history, it is wholly natural that there was such intensive Anglo-Saxon or European intercourse through organizations such as the Commonwealth Parliamentary Association, the Royal Empire (now Royal Commonwealth) Society, and various sporting bodies such as those responsible for the "Empire Games", cricket, rugby and the like. The particular history of the British colonies of settlement in South Africa also explains why the Union of South Africa and Southern Rhodesia were included as members of the inner association and why Southern Africans and East Africans, of both British and Dutch descent, were recruited alongside Australians, New Zealanders, Canadians and Britons for service in Britain's colonies of administration throughout Africa and the wider empire. The imperial contribution of men like Rhodes and Smuts, Schlesinger and Oppenheimer also explains why men of European origin in Africa have traditionally been accorded a substantial place in British universities, and centres concerned with Commonwealth and international affairs.

But though the special treatment of such South, Central and East Africans is historically understandable, the extreme inertia which has characterized the separation between the "white" and "nonwhite" parts of the Commonwealth must be criticized. The tardiness in recognizing opportunities for fruitful co-operation was never shown more strikingly in recent times than in 1959, when the Monckton Commission was appointed to review the constitution of the now defunct Federation of Rhodesia and Nyasaland, the preamble of which had emphasized the objective of inter-racial partnership. The suggestion that wider Commonwealth resources be drawn upon was accepted by the United Kingdom Government to the extent that a Canadian and an Australian were appointed as members under Lord Monckton. But there was no apparent response to the suggestion that eminent Africans and Asians from outside Central Africa should be added. A senior Indian or Pakistani civil servant and a West African judge could have made particularly beneficial contributions. All too little evidence has been shown in African policy of a readiness to mobilize or to draw upon all the available resources of the multi-racial Commonwealth which has been in being since 1947. On the many occasions when Britain has been faced with difficult problems more of the imaginative realism which was so evident during the last war might have been displayed. Individual ability was then used on a best-man basis without regard for country of origin.

Lack of imagination has been stressed rather than a Machiavellian determination to "divide and rule" because it would appear to be the more potent cause of the widespread failure to mobilize available ability in the service of Commonwealth Africa. It would be inaccurate to dismiss all charges of divide and rule tendencies, and very misleading also to deny the play of party politics, notably the general practice among cabinet ministers and politicians of ignoring inconvenient evidence or of by-passing individuals whose advice might not be in accord with current party aspirations. But all political viewpoints of the United Kingdom, conservative, socialist, liberal and neutral, are shared by individuals and groups in Africa and Asia. They share also the metropolitan concern for competent organization and the preservation of high standards in the conduct of the public services. The presence on appropriate commissions or boards of Africans and Asians would have helped to remove or minimize the ethnic, racial or cultural suspicion which has regrettably undermined the effectiveness of many valuable recommendations.

Outside Africa, Commonwealth citizens of appropriate qualification might have been recruited from countries which have had experience of the problems of plural or multi-racial societies. Ceylonese and Malayan constitutional experience has much that is instructive for Africa. Caribbean and Mediterranean history— British Guiana and the defunct Federation of the West Indies, or Cyprus and Malta—can teach not only citizens of their own particular territories. Within Africa, South African history from 1497 offers a rich record both of heartening success and dismal failure.

Some administrators and scholars have perceived the value of comparative study. Milner, faced with the task of devising workable constitutions for the colonies and territories of Southern Africa after 1902, urged that some help be sought from Colonial Office files stuffed with precedent. Bryce, an eminent contemporary of Milner, drew on a very wide framework, including both South America and the United States of America, in his approach to British overseas policy. Later examples are Professor Sir Reginald Coupland, Beit Professor at Oxford, Professor Sir Fred Clarke* and Professor W. M. MacMillan, whose *Warning from the West Indies: A Tract for the Empire*, published in 1936, shows how a background of detailed research in Africa enabled him at once to identify and to illuminate certain fundamental problems elsewhere. Professor Sir Keith Hancock's surveys of *British Commonwealth Affairs* and other writings demonstrate the same gifts from an Australian background.

Yet though these examples serve to bring home the value of comparison and co-operation, such men and women have been exceptional. Seemingly few of those in positions of power and influence have incorporated within one perspective the comparable

* See his *Quebec and South Africa. A Study in Cultural Adjustment* (O.U.P. 1924).

problems of the Dominions and the colonies of administration. Rather has there been a distinct compartmentalism which is discernible in University and Church as well as State.

Thus in university organization the substitution of "Commonwealth" for "Colonial" studies has sometimes brought little change in emphasis. The traditional dichotomy between the study of the "old Dominions" and "the colonies" has been perpetuated even though "new states" and "underdeveloped" territories from outside the Commonwealth may have been added to supply academic ballast. The effect has been to continue traditional separation. Australian, Canadian and New Zealand students have been kept away from active involvement in discussion of territories recently under British colonial administration. Such students, by virtue of their origin and tradition, are readily absorbed into British life, and so participate with the majority of Britons in courses of study which touch little upon peoples of non-Western culture and tradition. African studies have had their own most unfortunate divisions until the last few years.*

The Church is little different in its organization. The Christian church has possessed its own distinctive compartments which have served to divide believers. The traditional division between "metropolitan" and "missionary" is understandable, and there is no need to dwell upon the important role of specially trained Christian evangelists in the process of Western expansion overseas. But a profound inertia has retarded the modification of traditional ecclesiastical organization in order to bring it into line with modern requirements and, above all, to attune the Church to African cultural needs and aspirations. The principles of authority and celibacy of the clergy appear to have assisted Roman Catholicism in certain areas to act more independently of restrictive opinion, in promoting African priests and in advancing oversea provinces more rapidly from missionary status in the hierarchy. Where African clergy have been sympathetic to traditional cultural traits, specially useful bridges have been built. But even within the Church of Rome there has been extreme caution. Westernized Asian and

---

* Only in 1963 was a multi-disciplinary African Studies Association of the United Kingdom instituted. The Oxford University Africa Society first came into being in 1955 to bring together members of the separate regional societies. In formal academic organization an inter-faculty liaison committee in African studies has still to be created at Oxford, although such committees have now been set up for Russian and Middle East studies.

African clergy of all denominations have frequently taken refuge in excessive Westernism.

In church debates the missionary clergy and their supporters rightly remind their audience of the continuing importance of evangelical work in overseas areas and the special need for financial and other assistance to African, Asian and Amerindian peoples. They also emphasize the need to preserve separate churches wherever the use of different languages is necessary to preach the gospel and otherwise to minister to pastoral requirements. The substance of criticism here as in the university context is not directed so much towards separate organization within the church, which is historically explicable, but rather towards the slow tempo of adjustment to meet changing situations. Many African university graduates, including Catholic graduates, have expressed strong resentment after being assigned automatically, without thought, to a missionary priest or chaplain when they have been in pursuit of information on questions of advanced theology rather than pastoral guidance as members of a particular ethnos or community.

In the realm of Government the inertia of organizational separation has been at least as apparent as in the worlds of Church and University. There have been ministerial and official critics of barriers between "Foreign Office", "Commonwealth Relations Office" and "Colonial Office", but for the most part the divisions have been accepted. The general view among individuals who gave any thought to the matter, and they are fewer than might be supposed, since most citizens are preoccupied with domestic issues within the purview of the home departments, is that since the overseas world had to be divided for convenient treatment, "foreign", "Commonwealth" and "colonial" ministries and secretariats supplied sufficient answer. And, as in the cases of university and church, the historical logic of the arrangement is not easy to assail. What must be questioned once more is the continued failure to respond effectively to changing world circumstances. Where a keen sense of the dynamic was essential, satisfaction with the static too frequently has been allowed to prevail. Organizational upheavals are disliked always by those in senior office or in the middle rank of a set career, and civil servants are at least as prone as others to resist changes in their bureaucratic structures.

Internal changes within one department evoke resistances enough but when, as in the case of the three overseas departments of state, there were substantial differences in pride, behaviour and outlook, the obstacles to re-organization have been both more apparent and more serious. The Foreign Office has taken pride in professional diplomacy, in detached analysis, in "realistic", unsentimental appraisal of countries and situations. The Colonial Office has placed contrasting emphasis on "responsibility", trusteeship, involvement, tutelage. The Commonwealth Office has tended to be forced into a somewhat savourless neutralism which cannot be described simply in terms of a position intermediate between the other two. It has been rather a buffer department which has had to absorb as best it could the strains and uncertainties of constantly altering relation-ships within a highly dynamic international association possessing ill-defined objectives and a varied, turbulent membership. Now, as a result of the recent belated and reluctant rearrangements com-pelled by the rapid dwindling in the number of dependent terri-tories under the aegis of the Colonial Office, a hasty conglomerate has been contrived of the "Commonwealth and Colonial Office" alongside a politically neutral "Department of Technical Co-operation".* In order to deal belatedly with outstanding Central African questions, an *ad hoc* Central African Office was created.

A word on the barriers between colonial powers as well as inter-departmental barriers is appropriate here. There have been many criticisms of the failure of Western nations with specific overseas responsibilities to engage sufficiently in frank discussion of common colonial problems in Africa, Asia and elsewhere. That such criticism is warranted must be acknowledged by anyone who has participated in attempts to secure a more effective sharing of knowledge and experience based on different or varying principles of policy and practice in differing environments. Every credit is due to those few in government, and in voluntary organizations such as the Interna-tional Institute for Different Civilizations (formerly the Interna-tional Colonial Institute) and the Atlantic Treaty Association. Such organizations have attempted, usually with the co-operation of universities, to bring together responsible officers from Belgium, France, Italy, Portugal, the Netherlands, the United States and Britain to discuss common problems. But it seems regrettably true that the processes of "decolonization" were attended by as great and competitive a scramble on the part of each nation to "get out" of Africa as there was to "get in" during the last quarter of the nineteenth century. The Congo disaster has served to highlight the Belgian failure to heed the experience and advice of her Western

* See Postscript note on new Ministry of Overseas Development.

associates, but no metropolitan country has shown any real readiness to listen to others or to act in concert with them, even though co-ordinated disengagement and mutually agreed transfers of power would have better served the interests both of the West and of Africa.

Yet critics of the barriers of "nation" which have divided the colonial powers must be the first to acknowledge the reality of departmental—and comparable—walls within each of their own countries. Such internal barriers have very frequently proved as powerful as those between countries. In fact, to the commonplace observation that scientists and artists are international in outlook there might be added the reminder of the genuine freemasonry which has existed between individual metropolitan officers responsible for overseas government and development. Both in the field and at home such men and women have shown a genuine spirit of colleagueship. It seems the more regrettable therefore that in respect of British African responsibilities the pattern of United Kingdom departmental organization should have been one of separate compartments and of competition rather than of co-operation. It is the custom to dismiss such division in humorous terms and, in particular, to cite treasury control as the over-riding incentive for the competition which is acknowledged to exist. But the truth is that separation and competition in domestic departments have had serious consequences abroad. Otherwise admirable traditions of individualism and of amateurism have helped to prevent the active sharing of relevant knowledge and experience, and foolish pride has been allowed to damage relations between colleagues engaged in overseas service.

Africa has experienced metropolitan compartmentalism to the full. The Foreign Office and the Sudan Service, the India Office and Indian Civil Service, the Colonial Office and Service, the Dominions and Commonwealth Relations Offices, the Central Africa Office, are state departments which have each exercised substantial responsibilities for separate portions of the continent. The armed services, Navy, Army and Air Force, likewise have had their distinctive associations. One of the commonest explanations for the traditional lack of inter-service liaison is to be found in the answer from serving officers that they have had more than enough to do within their own immediate service or territory; also that the Treasury has shown little inclination to subsidize the exchange of visits, for observation or for conferences, especially in a continent so large as Africa. The

Nile Valley, the Gulf of Aden, West Africa, East Africa, Central Africa, the High Commission Territories of South Africa, South Africa: each sector or region was more than sufficient in itself to require a lifetime for its comprehensive understanding. Such were the arguments at best when eyes could be lifted from the workaday demands of an active career. Yet, as visiting commissioners saw clearly enough from time to time, great gain flowed from visits of liaison and comparative study. No territory or people was so isolated, nor its problems so peculiar, that something of general interest and overall value might not be learned from it.

Central Africa, as has been suggested before, provides perhaps the clearest recent example of a failure to bridge sufficiently the traditional gulfs in governmental organization. The Zambesi was a frontier both in Whitehall and in Africa. Profound mutual ignorance divided civil servants in London and administrative officers in Central Africa. Since 1923 the paths of organization had diverged increasingly between the "Colonial Office" territories of Northern Rhodesia and Nyasaland and the "Dominions Office" territory of Southern Rhodesia. The Limpopo also supplied too great a divide between neighbouring countries, part of the same Commonwealth. The instructive details of the lessons of South Africa were a closed book to almost all in Whitehall and in the Central African territories; while the remoter lands of West Africa were scarcely encompassed in comparative thought. Desperately, and during its days of dissolution, the Central Africa Office referred to above was created in London to deal with the affairs of the Federation and of the two Rhodesias and Nyasaland. But the mobilization of all available resources, British, Commonwealth, Colonial and Foreign, was required in the early 1950's, the years of decision, not in the 1960's, the years of dissolution. This was pointed out plainly at the time, chiefly by the few students of recent African history and international affairs in the universities of Britain and the Commonwealth; but politicians and career administrators were on the whole not only unheedful, but determined that particular personal convictions should prevail.

It is impossible to assess in any detail the damage wrought by particular political and constitutional acts. And, as we have remarked before, the student who is critical of enactments such as the South Africa Act of 1909 or the Federation of Rhodesia and Nyasaland Order in Council of 1953, sometimes to the point of tracing many subsequent major ills to them, must be prepared always to weight the evidence against his point of view and to take note of the undoubted gains. But there can be little doubt that the granting of majority powers to the minority of whites resident in the Central African territories in 1953, in the face of virtually unanimous African opposition, was a most grievous blow to the prospects of inter-racial partnership in Africa and throughout the new, self-consciously multi-racial Commonwealth which was launched effectively in 1947, when India and Pakistan became full members. Had there been any substantial initiative after 1953 to reveal a readiness to work towards internal partnership as rapidly as possible and to draw on the resources of the wider Commonwealth, including at least a quota of co-operation from the independent Asian and African member nations, the situation might have been saved, though even that must be doubtful, given the vehemence of the African protest against the imposition of federation. But only during the death throes of the Federation, and as a device to try to prevent a hasty declaration of independence by the Rhodesia Front Government in Southern Rhodesia, was the principle of consulting the multi-racial Commonwealth invoked by the United Kingdom Government.

Yet, if Britain's insistence on the need to consult the wider Commonwealth over the case of Southern Rhodesia may be taken as a precedent, as the initiation of an important new general procedure, it could prove of great long-term benefit. What has been lacking in the Commonwealth since 1947 is a readiness to define the principles and methods which are required to give coherence and assure consistency and continuity. Given British ways of thinking and behaving, in government as in every other sphere, it is wholly understandable that an experimental period should have been allowed, albeit sometimes unconsciously, to test empirically the reality of the multi-racial Commonwealth before seeking to define any principles which might be held to govern relationships. But no association can continue indefinitely without damage unless there is some agreed consensus, some framework to ensure "expectability", to use a valuable word of Sir Ernest Barker's.

The "Anglo-Saxon Commonwealth" of Great Britain and the Dominions possessed the Statute of Westminster, 1931, as well as important preparatory declarations such as that of the Imperial Conference of 1926, which emphasized the principles of Dominion autonomy and equality in allegiance to the Crown. And it is directly relevant to the argument for new, comprehensive definitions for the

Commonwealth to acknowledge that the primary pressures for the declaration and enactment of the 1925–31 principles came from the non-English elements of the Commonwealth—the Irish, the French-Canadians and the Afrikaners. "European" by "race", they were more conscious of certain important differences in their "cultural" heritage which they wished to preserve within the overall context of Commonwealth unity.

If this lesson from earlier Commonwealth experience had been understood more widely, especially the priority of "cultural" or "national" feelings over the purely "racial" or "colour" factors, there would have been better preparation for the emergence of the so-called "multi-racial" Commonwealth between 1947 and 1957–64. The Irish of the Twenty-Six Counties, the Quebecois, the Afrikaner nationalists made plain early enough that preference for the widest and frankest consultation as well as for the principle of republicanism which was insisted upon later by India, Ghana and Nigeria in more recent times. In numerous ways also these earlier "colonial nationalisms" served as valuable portents of the adjustments which would have to be considered or made if the association were to take the strain of the complete transformation from empire to commonwealth. As it happened, few frank discussions took place and no clear signposts were erected and South African governments, for example, were allowed for far too many years to believe that *apartheid* could be compatible with Commonwealth membership. Other member nations also in recent years have received wholly contradictory indications of British and other attitudes towards their suppression of the independence and freedom of their judiciaries, political parties, the Press, the universities, religious organizations and individuals.

An exceptional opportunity to give leadership towards the explicit clarification of a concept fundamental to the new Commonwealth was lost when the United Kingdom, between 1951 and 1953, rejected the repeated suggestion that the objective of "partnership" should be defined in the case of British Central Africa. The related suggestion that African, Asian and other member nations be associated with the formulation of an acceptable definition therefore fell away. The use of the word "partnership" in the preamble to the constitution of a new political association within the Commonwealth, especially one located between *apartheid*-governed South Africa and Mau Mau-stricken Kenya, offered a major challenge to the intellectual resources and combined experience of all members, not least the new members facing problems comparable to those of the Rhodesias and Nyasaland.

But definitions were held to be "un-British" and more apposite to "foreign" international associations like the United Nations. No great depth of thought accompanied such vague dismissal, but it possessed sufficient plausibility to ensure acceptance among well-placed politicians and journalists. In one sense, namely that of evading trouble, the avoidance of definition may be counted to have proved beneficial to the Commonwealth, since it was left to the United Nations both to venture upon definitions and to handle the several subsequent international conflicts, including sharp controversy between Commonwealth countries. Thus India's recurrent charges against South Africa from 1946 over the treatment of the Indian–South African minority, and associated questions, were fought out in the forum of the United Nations, not the Commonwealth of Nations. The issue of the South-West African mandate, and more recently that of Southern Rhodesia, have likewise been given first prominence within the world association, not the more intimate body of the Commonwealth. Certainly the existence of the Charter of the United Nations, more of a constitution than anything available to the Commonwealth, and detailed statements such as the Universal Declaration of Human Rights and the Declarations on Race have prompted and facilitated world debate and action. Only if the avoidance of debate in pursuit of the lowest common denominator of cohesion is thought preferable will the continuing absence of defined procedures and principles in the Commonwealth be understandable.

Such debate and action have point and purpose, stimulus and challenge, which in the long run are likely to prove beneficial to the United Nations Organization and to mankind. The first short decades of United Nations' existence have certainly witnessed sustained attacks against the Western nations and European peoples; but increasingly there have been signs of a readiness to apply more widely, including within the Afro–Asian world, tests hitherto applied exclusively to the conduct of Western powers. This trend is likely to gather momentum as more and more states and peoples gain experience and sophistication through increased participation in regional and international assemblies.

The Indo–Chinese conflict, the Indonesian–Malaysian confrontation, the cleavages between the "Casablanca" and "Monrovia" groupings in Africa are but early manifestations of encounters which have provoked reflection and dialogue of the kind required if headway is to be made towards the eradication of double standards and towards better world organization and production. The shirking of definition and open argument which is possible, perhaps even desirable, within a country like Britain is scarcely helpful in the international context, given the diversity of peoples and interests which exists throughout the world. Only delusion at high levels encourages facile optimism such as that which governed the British advocates of appeasement in the thirties, or that which so misled those who naïvely believed in de Gaulle's readiness either to accept, or to be manœuvred into accepting, British entry into the Common Market in 1963.

The Commonwealth is a microcosm of the United Nations, and the principles and methods devised for the world organization, many of them by British thinkers, are applicable also to the more restricted association. Self-deception over this matter has perhaps been encouraged by the excessive and superficial use of terms such as "family", "club" and the like to describe the Commonwealth. Unnecessarily extravagant claims have been made also about the importance of the Crown as a result of the acceptance by all members of the Queen's headship of the Commonwealth. Proper emphasis must be given to important unifying elements, notably a person and symbol of the quality and distinction of the Queen and Crown, but they are not served by the misleading glossing over of significant differences in attitude between peoples of the different realms and republics which now compose the Commonwealth. African citizens of the Commonwealth, like Asians, French-Canadians, Afrikaners and Irish before them, have been embarrassed or irritated by the repeated assumption that they must feel precisely the same personal and national loyalties as are felt by natives of the United Kingdom of Great Britain and Northern Ireland. Greater emphasis on considered principle, less on blind allegiance, would have helped.

Thus, if the Commonwealth is to survive and to fulfil its potential as one principal means of bridging the continents and sharing between peoples important values and institutions of universal merit, then a greater readiness to be explicit about the definition of objectives and procedures seems essential. There need be a minimum of sanction or penalty and a "family" readiness to lean wholeheartedly towards assisting those in difficulty or default to return to the paths of open democracy and justice if and when they deviate from them. But the attainment of worthy ends is scarcely likely unless those ends are specified in plain language, and acceptable methods of proceeding towards them are made equally clear.

The new states of Commonwealth Africa have made evident their own desire for a declaration of Commonwealth principles or objectives. Time and again in every university of British origin in independent Africa, and elsewhere at unofficial conferences, attacks have been made on unsatisfactory vaguenesses in Commonwealth relations. Frequently the attacks have come from those who have in fact exploited vagueness to their own ends, but most critics have shown a readiness to face the fact that definition can be a two-edged weapon and that principles, whether of law or custom, must possess that generality of incidence which alone can make for equity and acceptability. In other words, thoughtful Africans concerned for their countries' future are eager to reject double standards. Many insist that mature nationhood and worthy political systems can come only from the application to their own leaders, political parties, courts and other institutions of the criteria of conduct which they formerly expected and demanded from Western administrations during the colonial era.

In the Organization of African Unity, formed in 1963, member nations of the Commonwealth are prominent and it is through them that important values and institutions which stem from Britain, and have been absorbed into an Africo–British synthesis, can best be transmitted to the African continent as a whole. Several distinguished civil servants from the Sudan, Ghana and Nigeria have demonstrated already in Pan–African contexts not only their personal quality but the general merit inherent in the British system of civil service training and conduct. The same is true of policemen and soldiers, especially where the depth of training and experience has been sufficient to result in the firm acceptance by the individual of particular values and practices of police and military behaviour, above all a sense of personal responsibility and a trust in one's fellows which encourages the taking of initiative when necessary.

In parliamentary-type debate, as at councils of the Organization for African Unity or general meetings of the United Nations Economic Commission for Africa, ministerial and other representatives from Commonwealth African countries have likewise shown certain distinctive and desirable qualities, such as practicality, economy and responsibility, which again reflect an important conjoint, Africo–British tradition. At more junior level, as at Pan-African student conferences, assumptions about orderly procedure, relevance, rules of debate, have manifested themselves to the general benefit. African judges, magistrates and prosecutors from Commonwealth Africa have enjoyed regrettably limited opportunities outside their own countries to reveal their important distinctive qualities, but independent Pan–Africa already has had cause in several areas to remark and admire the independence and integrity of individual judicial officers, and the soundness of the principles by which they consciously regulate their behaviour and that of their courts.

No cultural chauvinism is advocated for Commonwealth African countries in their relations with independent Africa. The merits of other Eurafrican syntheses are recognized and welcomed. But no serious student with experience of comparative field study should undervalue the particular merits of Africo–British qualities nor blind himself to Africa's urgent need for more men and women like them, and for the wider adoption throughout Africa of the codes or norms by which they operate. Since the rejection of Britain by the Common Market there has been evidence of a readiness even on the part of hitherto unsympathetic Britons to give greater priority to the strengthening of Commonwealth links and established British–African associations. But, to be effective, very much more must be attempted and performed. Through the bridgeheads available to Britain in Commonwealth African states, and in countries still linked closely with the United Kingdom—for example the Sudan and South Africa—Britain can continue to offer her special "gifts". If accepted, there can be confident expectation of mutual reward both in the long term and the short term, though the proper emphasis should perhaps be on generations rather than decades, on decades rather than years.

The publication of the Plowden report necessitates the insertion of a brief additional comment at this point. If acted upon vigorously and in the right spirit it could mark a significant turning point. In the course of an able analysis the need is recognized to achieve the optimum mobilization of Britain's resources of knowledge and experience in the service of more effective overseas policy. The importance of removing or reducing domestic departmental barriers is stressed, especially those between the Foreign and Commonwealth Offices. A single diplomatic service is recommended with interchangeable representation. It is proposed, however, for the immediate future at any rate, to continue with a Commonwealth as well as a Foreign Minister, the view being taken that there is a sufficiently distinctive relationship with Commonwealth countries to warrant two Ministries. It was also believed that overseas Commonwealth sentiment would prefer the preservation in London of a special minister. Whether this last assumption is correct is difficult to determine until there are sufficient considered reactions from members of the Commonwealth, though there is a view that rather than a single special Commonwealth Ministry in London there should be direct and closer relations between ministers and civil servants in every department of state—finance, education, defence, agriculture and fisheries—and their opposite members in New Delhi, Canberra, Wellington, Montreal, Lagos and the other capitals.

The important thing is that the Plowden report, wholly correct in its essential diagnosis, should not be allowed to deepen division and to damage both foreign and Commonwealth policy. The danger was made manifest by a letter in *The Times* of 2 March 1964 from Lord Gladwyn, prominent in the *Britain in Europe* movement, who after an unexceptional general comment on the Plowden report proceeded to draw a false distinction between Commonwealth and other countries by positing, in emotional words, a choice for Britain between "France" and "Zanzibar". If the debate is to be conducted in such terms by experienced ex-ambassadors there can be little hope of achieving the necessary domestic re-organization and inter-departmental co-operation in the interests of Britain.

Each of Britain's international associations—European, trans-Atlantic, Commonwealth and United Nations—are complementary. By accident of recent history, the Commonwealth and trans-Atlantic alliances have involved Britain in deepening comradeship of a specially intimate kind. The cemeteries in the care of the Commonwealth War Graves Commission in France and North and East Africa, and countless other corners of the world, including United Nations cemeteries in Korea and those everywhere over which fly the flags of the United States and Britain, provide but one simple proof of this inescapable fact as well as perennial reminders of basic values held in common. As Professor Hugh Trevor-Roper has reminded us, national history cannot be repudiated save with

o

moral damage.* Zanzibar, East Africa, and other parts of the Commonwealth may at times be politically and economically inconvenient, but some recognition of historical responsibility by Britain is imperative.

There is fortunately no need for Britain either to seek to abandon responsibility or to repudiate her imperial past. There are no inherent incompatibilities between Britain's four principal international associations and her long-term goal of a politically united mankind, the overall objective stated by Sir Julian Huxley and other British thinkers who have devoted much of themselves to the creation and strengthening of the United Nations. Whether Britain might most effectively promote international peace and security by strengthening European regionalism, or assisting African unity or development, or by extending North Atlantic co-operation is impossible to determine; also such activities are consistent with United Nations purposes as laid down in the Charter. So also is active support for the Commonwealth, which we have described already as a microcosm of the United Nations and which might properly be seen also as it prototype or nucleus since so many of the ideals and principles expressed in the Charter, in the Universal Declaration of Human Rights, in Trusteeship Agreements, and in the constitutions of the several United Nations regional economic development associations, and other agencies, owe much to British thought and practice.

Yet while it is both right and necessary to remind ourselves of British contributions to the United Nations, the fourth of Britain's major international associations, it would be disingenuous to pretend to any substantial warmth for the political aspects of the United Nations on the part of Britain. The genius of individual Britons has given depth to its philosophy of world unity, and the ability and character of others have added quality to a wide range of specialized operations. In education, food and agriculture, world health, irrigation, refugee and rehabilitation work, the checking of slavery and forced labour, British men and women have won praise. Their intellectual distinction, sense of responsibility and determined achievement have repeatedly given the lie to those who have alleged that only the less competent and unwanted of the United Kingdom have opted for international service. For the practical organization

* The point was made with reference to the holding of a war crimes trial by the West German Federal Government, but it has general applicability.

of aid in times of disaster or of task forces in emergencies British individuals have earned high reputations. In the lobbies and corridors beyond the chamber of the Security Council and the hall of the General Assembly the official, political representatives of Britain are also held in regard for practical wisdom, straight dealing and a genuine liberalism. There is nevertheless not only an overall attitude of cool correctness on the part of the United Kingdom towards the United Nations, but an undeniable ambivalence in the United Nations' attitude towards Britain.

The reasons for Britain's difficulties with the United Nations are not difficult to discover. Put simply Britain is a "have" nation of long standing with so deep a history of complicated relationships as a "great power" throughout the world that she has accumulated substantial entries on both sides of her national accounts—moral, social, economic and political. Nor have the negative entries lacked British initiation. Frequently the force and detail of weighty criticisms have derived from British originators possessing easy access to official and other evidence and to all the means of open inquiry and exposure available in a free society. Voluntary associations such as the Movement for Colonial Freedom have had indefatigable members of Parliament, like Mr. Fenner Brockway,* to press remorselessly for detailed answers to parliamentary questions. Newspapers, books and journals have accumulated and presented strong criticisms, and the radio and television programmes have permitted the expression of strong condemnations of the Government and of national policy. University teachers and research workers likewise have enjoyed substantial freedom of inquiry and criticism; their colleagues in the churches also. Britons overseas have insisted upon comparable freedom. In the earliest days of the Cape Colony editors Fairbairn and Pringle withstood an autocratic governor hostile to Press freedom; in more recent time individuals like the late J. D. Rheinallt Jones, Director of the South African Institute of Race Relations, have produced voluminous documentation, all of "decimal-point accuracy", on the condition of the African, Coloured and Indian populations of South Africa.

Such evidence has been seized upon and used to maximum effect by "have not" nations and underprivileged peoples in a United Nations which is most to be distinguished from the League of Nations by the majority representation which it provides for what Trygve Lie called the "rising non-European nations of the world".

* Now Lord Brockway.

Understandably there have been few ethical misgivings about launching strong attacks based on evidence supplied by self-critical nations themselves, or by groups from within them. Rather has there been delight at the nature and quality of the evidence provided. The day may arrive when other nations choose to emulate the British example of allowing substantial freedom to those who attack their own official overseas policy, or the treatment of minority groups or underprivileged peoples within their own countries, but the time is not yet.

Given the fact that "anti-colonialism" is the contemporary rallying cry for the overwhelming majority of members of the United Nations, it is not surprising that Britain has been a butt of criticism since 1946. In Africa criticism has focused on Britain's exercise of international trusteeship in respect of Tanganyika, British Togoland and the British Cameroons; the character of her administration of her non-self-governing territories; Britain's reluctance to join in attacks on South Africa over *apartheid*, South-West Africa and the Union's treatment of her Indian minority; and, more recently, her refusal to admit that internal events in Southern Rhodesia offer a threat to international peace and security. To each charge under these heads Britain has a reasoned answer. In many instances her record is good and has won praise, as from certain impartial visiting missions to the Trust Territories.

In the field of direct international politics, as distinct from more administrative or historic responsibilities, Suez and the Congo stand out as major African actions involving Britain which have punctuated the first twenty years of United Nations existence. The first proved disastrous to Britain's position in the Middle East. It also damaged her relations with the United States, with many members of the Commonwealth, and with the United Nations. Relations with France, principal ally in the Suez venture, were also adversely affected by the halting of operations. France for her part thereafter abstained from the United Nations' Congo operation by refusing to contribute to either expenses or forces. In other ways she sought with Gallic logic to reduce to a minimum her obligations to a world organization whose principles and methods seemed incapable of achieving the declared ends of international peace, security and justice in a manner consonant with French interpretations. Britain's more pragmatic leaders adopted no such clear-cut position after Suez and the United Kingdom in due course accepted her measure of responsibility for assisting the United Nations in the attempts to repair the Congo breakdown. Whether, in the eyes of the world, Britain emerged with credit from the Congo, is doubtful. Commonwealth African policemen and soldiers from Nigeria and Ghana, together with British officers, won praise for their good discipline and competence. Individual representatives also earned good reputations. But as is perhaps made most clear in Dr. Conor Cruise O'Brien's *To Katanga and Back*, there were doubts as to the United Kingdom Government's single-minded support for United Nations policy, notably in respect of the forceful subjugation of President Tshombe's régime to the authority of the central government in Leopoldville.

We said above that Britain has answers to criticisms of her administration of Trust Territories and to other charges. She also has a case to present over Suez and the Congo. Lord Avon's memoirs and other documents which have been published recently assist understanding of Suez. The more recent Congo operation is also being presented in clearer perspective.* It is not to be expected, however, that the majority of the members of the United Nations in their present mood will accept the British official versions. Still less is the majority likely to prove responsive to *tu quoque* replies to charges, no matter how well justified or appropriate they might be. As in the case of the multi-racial Commonwealth it must be accepted that double standards do exist and that the stronger criticism is likely to be the lot of the United Kingdom for years ahead.

More important, however, is the development throughout the United Kingdom of a progressively more constructive attitude towards the United Nations. This is essential for world peace. It is equally necessary if Britain's uncompleted task in Africa is to be discharged more satisfactorily. The United Nations may not have the highest priority in Britain's conception of associations or alliances but it must be fostered alongside each of the others. European continental *apartheid* is impossible, the isolation of wider "white" ethnic associations equally so. Conceptions of Pan-European solidarity may be necessary to reassure certain elements who are anxiously aware of the minority position in the world of "Europeans" or "Caucasians" or "whites". And it is a fact to be taken into account that people who think defensively in that way appear to be either increasing in number or strengthening in organization and publication, in North America and Europe today,

* A contemporary account by a non-partisan American journalist Mr. Smith Hempstone, *Katanga Report* (London, 1962), merits special commendation.

side by side with "Black Muslim" and other militant "anti-white" racial societies. Through the Commonwealth of Nations and other historic links Britain is provided with abundant bridges to other races and cultures overseas, almost all of whom share with her national memories of mutual trust and confidence in circumstances both adverse and propitious. The partially built Commonwealth must be completed and strengthened over future decades. It cannot, however, be an end in itself but must serve rather as one of the surest means of advance to an eventual stronger world unity.

Neither the improvement of Britain's relations with the United Nations nor the reform of the organization itself will be achieved easily or in short term. Yet both must be attempted without respite at official and unofficial levels. Internally, within Britain, efforts must continue to reduce damaging separations between voluntary bodies such as the United Nations Associations and the various Commonwealth Societies. The latter can be offensively nationalistic or jingoistic, the former perversely blind to the reality and value of the Commonwealth. But comparatively little often needs to be done by way of leadership and education to bring home to those inclined to support the one at the expense of the other that what they hold in common far outweighs any difference.

At official level Britain must not seek to improve relations with the majority of the United Nations at the expense of important principles. Responsible membership requires a readiness to be unpopular and to take issue with the most materially powerful nations over fundamental questions. The defence of constitutionalism even on behalf of deservedly unpopular governments is an important act of maturity. So also is the insistence that major powers meet their financial obligations or suffer the penalty prescribed for defaulters. Little of worth can be achieved by an organization if members are allowed either to exploit their majority position at the expense of proper procedure, or to use their might to exert power without responsibility or a sense of financial obligation.

If the United Nations can succeed in strengthening itself in the ways which have been indicated it can have a substantial beneficial influence in Africa. A constructive administrative achievement can be claimed already for the Trusteeship division. Its work in preparing Italian Somaliland for self-government as well as its supervision of British and French Trust Territories has on balance proved satisfactory. The Economic Commission for Africa with headquarters in Addis Ababa has also demonstrated its worth and potential. Social as well as economic development has figured prominently in the plans of the principal officials, among whom there have been notable Sudanese and Ghanaian graduates from Oxford. In addition to valuable economic surveys of the continent conferences on education have been held. Health and community development also have received priority. Through technical co-operation in support of endeavours under the auspices of the United Nations Britain and other Western nations can make some of their most effective contributions to Africa.

On the political issues troubling independent Africa, notably the obstacles to national unity in all the states and the difficulties of regional unity, the United Nations might over time give effective and durable aid. It is difficult even for an analyst sympathetic to the United Nations to be enthusiastic about operations in the Congo. The imperfections are too obvious, though the simple yet funda-mental gain of keeping the naked cold war away from Central Africa may be seen to dwarf all defects when the events of 1960–64 are reviewed in perspective. In neighbouring Rwanda and Burundi the political aspects of the United Nations appear to have supervened over the administrative, in that the trusteeship organiza-tion proved largely helpless when it became necessary to safeguard the lives and property of tens of thousands of Africans. Fears of charges of "neo-colonialism" prevented Belgium and other Western helpers from intervening to assist with the maintenance of law and order and the administration of justice by trained officers.

The events in the three Belgian successor states highlight in extreme form some of the political problems which might persist for generations in independent Africa. In the case of ex-British Africa we have suggested that a continuing close, though not ex-clusive, co-operation with Britain and other non-African Common-wealth countries might be specially helpful in contributing towards the eventual resolution of constitutional and minority problems. The many and varied Commonwealth countries offer a peculiarly rich record of experience ranging in time from the uniting of Eng-land, Wales, Scotland and Northern Ireland to the contemporary difficulties of Cyprus, Malaysia and Ceylon. Knowledge of such experience could be brought also to the United Nations and there fused with other national and international experience of success and failure. But only through the deliberate shedding of prejudices, stereotypes or set positions will members of the United Nations be able to contribute constructively towards moral and practical solutions of the problems of disunity which afflict Africa and much of the world.

In the cases of the Congo and Rwanda and Burundi many of the worst impulses were brought into play by the states who were most directly involved, including several of the newly independent African states. Ghana's insistence on a Lumumbist-type centralism was unhelpful, Belgo–Rhodesian support for an independent Katanga under Tshombe equally so. The concomitant polarization of positions among and within other nations, not least Britain, over Congo and Rwanda and Burundi issues served to extend the damage. In addition to the distressing fact that tens of thousands of innocent men, women and children suffered death, famine and other disaster, the fundamental problems of the afflicted countries and peoples were hopelessly obscured by emotion and dogmatism. Only the acceptance of facts, whether inconvenient or not, and their rational appraisal are likely to assist the African states to cope with their minority and other problems. Studies such as Maquet's *The Premise of Inequality*, an analysis of the Tutsi in Rwanda and their traditional relations with the Hutu, must be read with academic objectivity, not swept impatiently aside, and so also must works like *Congo Tribes and Parties* by Mary Douglas and David Biebuyck, which revealed the strength of tribal feeling in the Congo and showed its effect on voting behaviour.

No single policy conclusion can emerge from the study of such books, any more than from the important writings of Colin Legum on *The Congo Disaster*, and Patrice Lumumba, which also merit the closest attention. But *a priori* positions, national or personal, must be abandoned if ways towards unity are to be found by the African states. A readiness to consider awkward issues such as the position of minorities in the Ethiopian empire or the Sudan must be expressed in a detached, analytical manner if the United Nations is to serve its long-term purpose. Many subject or minority peoples on the eve of independence in Africa protested that local imperialism was as abhorrent, sometimes more hateful, than imperial rule from overseas. Their voices were inconvenient in the world-context of anti-colonialism and decolonization, but their continued pleadings must be given serious hearing in a largely decolonized world if the United Nations is to fulfil an important political role in the African continent. Britons who have fought fearlessly and consistently for the freedom of colonial peoples are best placed morally to give a lead to the United Nations in this direction.

Michael Scott, defender of the subject Indian minority in South Africa, critic of independent India's treatment of the Nagas, is an outstanding example. The issues are too important to allow false posturing: side by side with emphatic condemnations of *apartheid* in South Africa must go criticisms of oppression, discrimination and compulsory separation elsewhere. As with the Commonwealth of Nations so with the United Nations; though Britain must be prepared for a long era of double standards, she must at the same time be prepared always to point the way towards that ultimate single standard which alone can reflect the full and equal dignity of all mankind.

In conclusion we repeat that it is in partnership with other nations that Britain must work if she is to fulfil the tasks in Africa begun during the imperial past. This necessity is being driven home poignantly by immediately contemporary events. The death of Pandit Nehru has followed closely on the triumphant visit of Mr. Khrushchev to President Nasser's Egypt in order to open the great Russian High Dam project on the Nile, a river whose hydrology and rational use has derived most from British research and the British presence during the past three generations. The Soviet Union has now made powerful entry into a zone from which it was ever a first principle of British diplomacy to keep Russia away. Mr. Nehru's death, and the attendance at his funeral of Lord Mountbatten, last Viceroy of undivided India, first Governor-General of the Dominion of India, has evoked memories of the recent past, when the Indian army was at Britain's call throughout the Indian Ocean, the Red Sea and the Persian Gulf.

The homage to Mr. Nehru on British television, radio and in the Press has referred frequently to Mahatma Gandhi, and such references have recalled the South Africa of Smuts, with whom Nehru as well as Gandhi had so many encounters and exchanges. Only a few hours before the announcement of Mr. Nehru's death the television, radio and newspapers were focused on Sir Roy Welensky, visiting London in an aura of pathos on the occasion of the publication of his book denouncing Mr. Macmillan and the dissolution of the Federation of Rhodesia and Nyasaland. Reports of Sir Milton Margai's death in Sierra Leone seemed also in their way to mark the end of an epoch of Britain in West Africa.

The poignancy of such reflections should stimulate realistic appraisal by people in Britain of relations with Africa, but none of these recent events warrants pessimism or despair. Mr. Nehru's preservation of national unity and democracy in India for seventeen years is a constructive achievement which must be supported and everything done to strengthen British–Indian ties. Africa will benefit from such a development, not least through an increase in African–Indian trade, scholarships and other aid. We need not itemize the type of continuing co-operation and help which might best be supplied by Britain to West, Southern and Eastern Africa. Strong British bridgeheads exist in each zone and can be developed with mutual African–British benefit. And even in Egypt there is no need for defeatist pessimism. Apart from important if unpublicized facts such as the employment of the fleet of extra-powerful Rolls-Royce trucks which alone made it possible for the time schedule of the High Dam to be adhered to, the contribution of the Soviet Union to large-scale aid projects is to be welcomed in terms of a more equitable sharing of the burden of material assistance to underdeveloped countries. The Soviet leader's pronouncement in Egypt that "Arabism is not enough" might also have its long-term beneficial effects in reducing the sharpness of nationalism throughout the continent, even though it offers an urgent challenge to the West to intensify efforts to substitute for communism its own more valid universalist ethic.

That universal ethic, fundamental to the life and peace of Africa, has been threatened and tested in the upsurge of African, Afrikaner and Arab nationalism since 1945. New men, bent on sweeping away the past, have come to replace the older leaders. Yet there was good as well as evil in the past and it is important for Africa and the world that the good is preserved. It is to the newer generation of leaders, who will succeed the present ethnocentric nationalists and nostalgic imperialists, that we must look to achieve the necessary syntheses of the best of African and other thought and tradition so that the urgent tasks of social and economic development can be completed. John F. Kennedy's assassination tragically removed from the world a younger leader who more than any other bridged the generations and, as a child of the idealism of the 1939–45 war, including its powerful non-racist idealism, offered a new and more hopeful prospect to the world.

During President Kennedy's leadership it seemed that Britain was to be relieved finally by the United States of the role of moral top-weight in the handicap steeplechase of ceaseless international competition. To many in Britain who believed that their country had been asked for too long, like the gallant horse Mill

House, to make extravagant concessions to all fellow-runners the prospect of relief was not unwelcome. But President Kennedy's sudden death, like that of Hugh Gaitskell, drove home in tragic fashion the democratic truth of the danger of over-reliance on one leader, even one nation, in the conduct of world affairs and in the fulfilment of international responsibilities. Partnership, with its shared risks and rewards, supplies the essence of democracy, partnership between nations as well as between groups of individuals within each nation. Every possible person must be involved in some conscious way in the processes of partnership if the harsh and forbidding inequalities of the modern world are to be removed and international peace and security are to be assured.

It was John Stuart Mill once more who observed that "the worth of a State in the long run is the worth of the individuals composing it". In the context of British–African relationships there are daily reminders of the accuracy of this truism. In Britain there are individuals on every hand who possess an affection and respect for the African men and women whom they have come to know through the numerous contacts which the opportunities of their lifetimes, both long and short, have afforded them.* Up and down Britain there are those who, whether or not they have lived in Africa, welcome to their homes, common-rooms, laboratories and workshops African friends and colleagues. A meal and musical recital in a simple and gracious North Oxford home count as much as a Guildhall banquet. In their voluntary associations British men and women from all backgrounds devote long hours of hard work to vital unofficial aid to Africa.

Africans bring much of value to Britain—music, poetry and art, and not least a zest and optimism and a deep sense of the vital rhythm and warmth of human relations. The mutual trust and confidence between individuals on which international relations ultimately rest makes it essential to keep in view the African contribution to Britain. Yet from the standpoint of England it is fitting to end by recalling the rich variety of the individuals who continue to serve in Africa now that the proconsuls have withdrawn. There are talented ambassadors and able directors of British

* Colleagues in African studies in West Germany have directed attention to the importance of such contacts. There are, significantly, still a few older German-speaking Africans from the former German colonies who visit Germany, but the interruption of relations between 1918 and 1948 has left it to the West German Federal Republic to develop links anew.

Council agencies and an impressive array of university teachers and international civil servants performing important work in the capitals of Africa. But alone in a remote government hospital in poverty-stricken Northern Ghana will be found a nursing sister from County Durham serving with skilled matter-of-fact compassion African children stricken with diseases of malnutrition. Matron, theatre-sister, sister-tutor and friend, she performs tasks more demanding and varied in scope than were ever conceived in her large training hospital at home. She, and a young Englishman running single-handed a refugee camp in Uganda, are other less obvious representatives of the United Kingdom. As Pandit Nehru said, of the Commonwealth, it is such relationships in the aggregate which bring to an embittered world "their touch of healing".

POSTSCRIPT

A POSTSCRIPT is added because many events of great concern to Britain and Africa have occurred since the above essay was completed in May 1964, on the eve of my departure to Africa, where I remained until January 1965.

In the United Kingdom a Labour government, elected by the narrowest of majorities, replaced in October the successive Conservative administrations which had ruled for thirteen years. The general election was marked by the unmistakable entry of race and colour issues into domestic political debate. The Commonwealth Immigrants Act occasioned considerable general discussion, the most notable instance of recent "coloured" immigrants affecting the vote was seen in the Smethwick (Birmingham) constituency where the established member, the Right Hon. Patrick Gordon Walker, Labour's Foreign Secretary designate, was defeated. The result, long foreseen as a possibility by those in touch with the Midlands, came as a shock to many inside and outside Britain, especially to those who had regarded Mr. Walker as an enlightened moderate rather than a radical during his distinguished service as Secretary of State for Commonwealth Relations in the Labour Administration which held office before October 1951.

Labour's leadership nevertheless attempted to impose an immediate new liberal stamp on overseas policy by means of several imaginative acts. A ministry of Overseas Development was instituted with the Minister, Mrs. Barbara Castle, being given a seat in the Cabinet, a status unique in the world. Lord Caradon (Sir Hugh Foot) who had earlier resigned his post at the United Nations in protest against Conservative policy over Southern Rhodesia was appointed head of the British delegation to U.N. The creation of a Commonwealth Consultative Council was announced, the intention being to ensure more effective dialogue and co-operation between Member nations. In public pronouncements both the new Prime Minister, Mr. Harold Wilson, and his Commonwealth Minister, Mr. Bottomley, bluntly condemned any possible unilateral declaration of independence by Southern Rhodesia's ruling party, the Rhodesia Front, led by Mr. Ian Smith. During their initial "hundred days" they were also more outspoken than Sir Alec Douglas-Home on other African matters such as the supply of armaments to South Africa.

More time, however, is required to see whether major changes are in fact likely to be made by the Labour Government in Britain's African policies and in her established relationships with the continent. There seemed, for a brief period, to be the possibility of a major rupture between Britain and South Africa when it was suggested that a contract for sixteen Buccaneer military aircraft, ordered by South Africa at a cost of £20 million during the Conservative administration, might be cancelled unilaterally by Mr. Wilson. Dr. Verwoerd, in reply, referred at once to South Africa's possible revocation of the Simonstown agreement under which Britain operates her major naval base in the South Atlantic. It was subsequently declared that the sixteen aircraft were to be delivered, together with all the necessary spare parts which will be required in the future, though no further military equipment is apparently to be supplied by the present Labour Government to the existing South African régime. The latter have since been reported to have had many favourable responses from elsewhere to preliminary inquiries about alternative sources of arms. Debate has meanwhile been joined over the whole question of overseas sales of arms by Britain, and of the value and utility of Simonstown and other bases.

The Labour Government has none the less continued to make full use of Britain's overseas bases and to honour all international commitments, especially her obligations to the United States and other N.A.T.O. allies, even though several of her actions have been strongly criticized by certain African and Asian countries, and have been at variance with much popular left-wing sentiment in Britain. The most notable controversy within the African context arose from the permission which was granted for the use of the British island of Ascension as a staging post for the American and Belgian aircraft and paratroops taking part in the Stanleyville and North-Eastern Congo operation to rescue Belgian, American and British missionaries and other hostages held by the forces in rebellion against the Leopoldville government. In addition to the widespread Communist condemnation of such British and Western "imperialism"—including hostile demonstrations against British embassies in Communist countries of both Russian and Chinese persuasion—the majority of independent African States rallied strongly in support of the Communist attacks on Britain and her allies for their having undertaken the Congo rescue operation. This fierce African criticism was specially disconcerting to supporters of Lord Caradon and Mr. Adlai Stevenson, both of whom had to withstand a powerful combined Communist-African assault at the United Nations.

The vigorous defence of their countries' rescue operation by these two enlightened representatives of Britain and the United States served to highlight the intractable nature of the Congo issue, the extent of the world ideological division over African questions, and the depth of feeling which can be aroused among Africans by Western intervention of any kind in the affairs of the continent.

President Moise Tshombe's leadership of the central Leopoldville government has served to heighten tension, though many of his African critics have been compelled, like those in Western Europe and North America, to acknowledge that he appears to provide the only present hope of restoring orderly government and constructive development in a devastated country from which the United Nations has withdrawn politically and militarily. President Tshombe's effective non-racial pragmatism and his courage in travelling to Cairo and Nairobi to confront his critics in the Organization for African Unity (O.A.U.) have won him grudging admiration even from those who once clamoured for his complete overthrow and for the total subjugation of Katanga. The attempt to humiliate him in Cairo misfired and, if anything, won sympathy for him from fellow Africans sensitive to Arab endeavours to control the O.A.U. President Tshombe's business acumen has also stood out in relief against a background of past Congolese economic inefficiency and the near-bankruptcy to which the United Nations has been brought through the refusal of the U.S.S.R. and the other nations to pay their dues, notably those for the immensely costly Congo operation.

The present plight of the North-Eastern Congo, especially the ruthless mass killings which have characterized the continuing civil war, has led several observers to consider the desirability of a partition which would recognize separate Leopoldville and Stanleyville régimes. Such recognition, however, could mark the consolidation of the "cold war" in the heart of Africa and it is for this reason opposed by those who still hope to see truly independent African governments assert their full control in the Congo (Brazzaville), in Burundi and Tanzania.

It must be noted that nothing in Africa during the past year has been more disturbing than the intrusion of a more powerful Communist imperialist factor across the middle of the continent. East Germany has secured a foothold for Russian-type communism in Zanzibar but the influence of the representatives of the Chinese Peoples' Republic has been more potent. In both Zanzibar and Burundi, as well as north of the Congo river, in Congo (Brazzaville), Communist Chinese leaders have established centres from which their revolutionary ideas are spread and put into practice among the rural populations to whom they assign ideological priority. One of the more tragic aspects of the rebel campaign has been the systematic killing of Congolese who possess any background of Western education.

A foremost question which has arisen during the past year concerns the ability of President Nyerere to preserve control in Tanganyika and to exert beneficial influence in Zanzibar. Those close to him are confident that his authority is not threatened and that his senior subordinates in Tanganyika remain wholly loyal. They point also to the skill with which he has won the confidence and support of Vice-President Karume and to his sensitive handling of Zanzibar, the very much smaller component of the new union. Pessimists, on the other hand, give greater weight to the strength of the Communists and to the success of anti-Western, notably anti-American propaganda. President Nyerere's comparison between the Stanleyville rescue operation conducted by American aircraft, and Pearl Harbor, aroused keen and widespread resentment among leaders and citizens of the United States. The alleged "American plot", and the strong rumours of imminent American invasion into Tanzania, also worsened relations which culminated in the recent mutual expulsion of diplomatic representatives. If Tanzania should opt for the political East, or be drawn into its control, there can be little hope of a unified and strong democratic Eastern Africa of the kind indicated in Chapter VI. But the issue is far from decided and powerful Western and British influences remain operative. Not least among recent events has been the vigorous reconsideration of the Zambia–Tanganyika rail link, the construction of which is now thought likely to begin in the near future. Substantial Western financial and technical aid is confidently anticipated for this major "prestige project" which might rival the Nile High Dam in international political significance.

Communist Chinese efforts to gain greater influence in Kenya have thus far been thwarted and President Kenyatta's government has remained firmly in control despite economic difficulties. President Kaunda's government in Zambia has also shown promise of stability. Dr. Kaunda was subject to some criticism earlier in the year for the alleged severity with which his armed forces put down the Lumpa religious sect, fanatical followers of Alice Lenshina, but the problem was no simple one and he wisely welcomed the co-operation of Church leaders who gave effective assistance in the tasks of pacification. After Zambia's independence in October 1964 —marred to some degree by the shadow of events in Malawi— President Kaunda was able to fly overseas on an extended mission to Western countries. He, with his experienced Vice-President Kamanga, and his able Cabinet, including the vigorous and perceptive Mr. John Mwanakatwe, Minister of Education, have initiated far-seeing development plans, among which one of the more notable is the institution of the new University of Zambia which is to be a major instrument in overcoming the country's deficiency in trained African manpower.

Malawi's unity and political stability were regrettably short-lived. After independence in July a major division occurred between Dr. Banda and his leading fellow-Ministers. The precipitating cause was reputed to be a difference of opinion over the acceptance of an offer of substantial aid from Communist China. Ministerial advocates of "non-alignment" opted for the aid but Dr. Banda was emphatically opposed to its acceptance. He drove his senior colleagues from office, into hiding or exile, and has since sought to buttress his authority by new and restrictive legislative and administrative measures.

In Southern Rhodesia the advance of Malawi and Zambia to complete self-government was keenly felt by Mr. Ian Smith's Rhodesian Front Government, and by many citizens and voters who had not previously reacted strongly to constitutional issues. A wave of bitterness swept the country when Mr. Smith was denied the place at the Commonwealth Prime Ministers' conference, which had been open to all his predecessors at the invitation of successive United Kingdom governments since before the 1939–45 war. In addition to the tensions which arose between Europeans of divergent political view the Africans also were deeply divided between the rival Zimbabwe African National Union led by the Rev. Ndabaningi Sithole and Mr. Joshua Nkomo's Peoples' Caretaker Council. The phrase "civil war", used by an English academic observer to describe the relations between the rival African groups is an illuminating exaggeration between the rival African groups is an illuminating exaggeration of the nature and extent of internecine acts of violence.

Reaction against violence within the country, and fear lest the continuing subversion, chaos and bloodshed in the Congo and other parts of middle Africa should spread and take hold in Southern Rhodesia has led the Europeans of the country to close their ranks with a new determination to preserve law and order, even though the methods chosen might arouse protest from lawyers schooled in liberal Western traditions. The killing of Dr. Paul Carlson, the American medical missionary, and of many other hostages held by rebel Congolese in Stanleyville led to noticeable public revulsion in Rhodesia and to a distinct hardening of European attitudes during the month of December. The issue of *Time* magazine of December 4th, 1964, dealing with the murder of Dr. Carlson and the other hostages, which indicated comparable reactions among many in the United States, was prominently on display and sale in Rhodesia. Despite widespread distaste for the extremes of Afrikaner-nationalism and *apartheid* in South Africa and for aspects of Salazar authoritarianism in Moçambique and Angola, most white Rhodesians—and some Africans, Coloureds and Asians—state that they have felt compelled to look to the régimes of Drs. Verwoerd and Salazar for defensive alliances until there is clearer indication from the newly independent African States of an ability to preserve law and order and to promote orderly economic and social development.

Southern Rhodesia's importance as a frontier state between the old and the new Africa, a position occupied also by Zambia, gives special significance to her immediate policy. The substantial defeat of Sir Roy Welensky and Mr. Sidney Sawyer in recent Salisbury by-elections leaves no room to doubt the strong electoral support now enjoyed by Mr. Ian Smith, a position made yet clearer by the result of the referendum of November 5th, which endorsed the pursuit of independence on the basis of the new Southern Rhodesian constitution, negotiated in 1961 by Mr. Duncan Sandys, Sir Edgar Whitehead and other United Kingdom and Rhodesian leaders. A general election which is expected to give Mr. Smith a two-thirds majority in parliament is imminent. How any such result will be rumours and speculations abound, including confident predictions of an early unilateral declaration of independence and a substantial reduction of effective African parliamentary representation. The interpreted by Mr. Smith cannot be known at present, though of civic power and responsibility is also forecast. In so far as Africans are accorded positions of influence the emphasis is expected to be increasingly upon Chiefs and other conservative traditional authorities.

The threat of the disruption of the important federation of Nigeria was real enough in December 1964 when the first post-independence general election was held, but statesmanship prevailed among Nigeria's foremost leaders, and unity was preserved despite passionate charges of corrupt practice, and threats of drastic action by senior holders of Federal office. Dangers of disunity certainly remain but the comparisons which many made between the Congo and Nigeria seem wholly out of place given the quality of Nigerian civil servants, and the other professional guardians of the stability of the state.

Finally, South Africa and Ghana remain as disquieting challenges to the spirit of optimism which I allowed to govern my appraisal of Africa's future, and of the British–African relationships. In the *Introduction* I remarked that the case for pessimism is appallingly easy to make. This observation, made in respect of the whole of the continent, can be applied with special force to Ghana and South Africa, on which most limelight has been focused. Yet even in the face of further distressing events in both countries during the past year, and the evidence of deep unrest which is provided by trials for major political offences, sentences of death, the prolonged detention of former Ministers and Members of Parliament, harsh prison conditions and the like, my recent experience of Africa has renewed rather than extinguished my hope for the future of Ghana and South Africa, provided constructive external co-operation is maximized.

South Africa's economy continues to make dramatic advances, and policies of "job-reservation" on grounds of race and ethnic group have been proved impracticable by the need for the effective mobilization of all available industrial and commercial manpower. Church leaders such as those of the newly founded Christian Institute of South Africa have shown impressive courage and leadership despite harsh attack from narrow nationalism. The liberal Universities also have continued to demonstrate resilient courage and faith.

Though Ghana's once healthy economy is presently reported to be in a state of near-bankruptcy, experts agree that there is a deep-seated economic buoyancy which could be built upon by an abandonment of damaging doctrinaire ideology and a return to policies of pragmatic co-operation with those countries and agencies which have proved their willingness to engage in mutually beneficial practices of trade and aid. Ghanaians certainly have the ability to overcome their present difficulties, and to demonstrate convincingly at home the depth and reality of the wisdom and competence which so many of their fellow countrymen now demonstrate in the service of the United Nations, and other organizations, outside Ghana.

Facile optimism is always out of place. But given confidence in the West, and especially realistic and determined co-operation by Britain, Africa's gifts, both human and material, can contribute to the world in the manner which was foreseen in the past by Lugard and the other pioneers who proclaimed the principles of the "dual mandate".

April 1965

INDEX